A LIFE ON THE OPEN ROAD

James Mateer

To Joyce
With Best Wishes
James Mateer

Published by
EDYPLUS PUBLICATIONS
50 Groomsport Road, Bangor, Co. Down BT20 5NE

Typeset by december publications
Printed by The Universities Press

ISBN 0 9527487 0 3

To My Wife Edith With Love

Author's Note

Apart from some members of the family, all names are fictitious. And because this is a recollection of early boyhood I may not have remembered exactly where and when certain incidents occurred.

Contents

How it Was

Gypsies have caravans.
Tinkers have tents.
But the playactors had to
win hearts and fire the
imagination in order to find
shelter in the hungry thirties.

1

A Life on the Open Road

The lorry revved, rattled, backfired and sent clouds of black oily smoke round the legs of the village postman. The driver stuck his head out of the cab, grinned, shouted "Mornin' Davy", and remarked to the attractive young blonde with the two-year-old child on her lap who was pressed close to his side, "I'm afraid the old lady's not firing very well this morning."

The young woman laughed and came back with, "I thought she fired rather well."

They both laughed and instinctively turned their heads in the direction of the fourth occupant, a middle-aged lady squeezed tight against the other door who, in response, raised her eyebrows, smiled graciously and with that perfect diction and calculated delivery that was common to all actresses of her age and experience, offered her own opinion.

"I thought," she turned her head slowly, "though of course this is only my considered opinion, that the old lady gave a rather *splendid* performance." They all laughed, the bright-eyed little girl on her mother's lap joining in.

"Right!" The driver let out the clutch, accelerated, and the vehicle leapt forward to the accompaniment of yells, thumps and hammerings from the back of the lorry. "The boys in the back," the driver leaned across the young woman and had a quick look through the small window behind her head, "seem to be enjoying themselves alright."

"Are they still *there*?" she asked in mock disbelief.

"Oh aye, the tailboard will stop them falling off."

More laughter as the passengers on the back, a young man, a middle-aged man and a small boy of five, climbed back under the canopy formed by the cargo of scenery, props, luggage and all the worldly goods the little band possessed, and made themselves comfortable on their improvised seats. The lorry charged down the main street, the few villagers, patrons and old friends by now, who were about, or at their front doors, waving and bidding the travellers "Safe journey and come back soon".

"We will!" And we did. The village of Kesh on the shores of Lough Erne in the lush county of Fermanagh would welcome us on two more occasions. Occasions I for one was not likely to forget.

Pettigoe was the next small town "blue pencilled" on my father's ancient map (a treasured possession) of Northern Ireland and the Irish Free State. And the first inkling the inhabitants of the lonely farmlands, labourers' cottages and that small border town had that our company was looking in their direction, had come a few days earlier when a solitary stranger in a shabby grey overcoat but wearing a collar and tie, an ancient but impressive broad-brimmed hat, and smoking a pipe, suddenly appeared on the landscape and cycled slowly and sedately down the main street. Father always managed an air of quiet dignity when riding a bicycle. He sat very upright (of course bicycles were made like that in those days) even when he had a headwind to contend with, and what with his hat, pipe, and the slow methodical manner of his peddling, he exuded an air of great confidence and even contentment.

Although there was an occasion once when, on reaching the crest of a small hill that led down to one particular village, he took his pipe out of his mouth, put it in his overcoat pocket, straightened his hat, pushed off and freewheeled regally down the main street totally unaware of impending doom until an old fellow who had lumbered to his front door, not to see if anything exciting was happening because it never did, but in order to get a breath of fresh air, suddenly caught sight of him and stared and stared as though my father was some kind of freak. Father bid him a cheerful "Good-day" as he cycled past. The old fellow didn't reply, he merely opened his mouth, raised his right arm and ran out into the street pointing to a thin column of grey smoke that was streaming out from behind the cyclist and cried out, "Excuse me! Excuse me! *Yer on fire!*"

The large hole burnt by the smouldering pipe was patched by my mother who at that time must have been the worst seamstress in Ireland. Or if I do her an injustice and she was just trying to stop father from wearing the overcoat when the weather didn't warrant it, then she reasoned as ineffectually as she sewed. Not that inefficiency or anything else for that matter ever held mother back. Indeed she even went on once and pointed out that not only was the article of clothing unnecessary but it was none too clean. In response to which, instead of kicking some inanimate object across the landscape as was often his custom when he felt personally attacked, father graciously brought down the curtain by declaring, "My dear lady, it is not the clothes, it's the man that's wearing them that counts."

On entering Pettigoe the first thing the solitary stranger, actor/manager, scene-painter/ public-relations officer had done was head for the local pub or rather *one* of the local pubs, because no decent Irish town would make do with only one public house. And by the time he had finished a couple of glasses of stout (and as a connoisseur he maintained that not only was stout a food, it was the only real drink there was) he'd done a fair bit of canvassing and collected all the information he needed to know. That there was a small hall on the other side of the river, and of course the border, for as those familiar with Pettigoe will know, the town lies right across the demarcation line with the smaller part resting in County Fermanagh in Northern Ireland, and the rest in County Tirchonaill (that's how father's map designated Co. Donegal) in the Irish Free State. That there was nothing going on in the hall at the moment as far as the publican knew. That the caretaker, who was employed by the council, was working up behind the Customs Office on the Northern Ireland side. And that there was a woman who lived on the Free State side who had been known to take in people in the past.

Father located the caretaker, bargained over the price of the hall, booked it, walked the full length of the town distributing bills (we never called them posters) to several shops and of course the post office, had another glass of stout and gleaned another piece of information that was music to his soul.

"Aye, and of course, what wi' the cattle business …" Father's informant didn't smile, but a definite glint came into his eye as he mentioned the subject.

"Ah yes, of course, the *cattle* business."

"Aye, what wi' the cattle business and the like, there's a few folks in the town and a wee bit of money around at times."

Our ambassador, cycling up the middle of the road, returned to the village of Kesh in a cheerful mood, leaving the citizens of Pettigoe in general, and a small group of the publican's patrons in particular, reading aloud what was boldly printed on the three foot long by one foot wide, bright yellow bill that was displayed in the publican's window.

THE BROADWAY PLAYERS

present

March 13th for SIX nights in the Memorial Hall
(or it might have been an Orange Hall, I can't remember now)

Monday … The Mormon Peril – A tale of the white slave traffic
"Oh, that'll be a good one, Eamon."

Tuesday … The Man who won the Irish Sweep
"And that'll be worth seeing as well."

Wednesday … Darby and Joan – The tragedy of old age
"Ah, that'll be one for the wife."

Thursday ... Ten Nights in a Bar Room
"And that'll be one for yerself, Davy."

Friday ... Sweeney Todd – the demon barber of Fleet Street
"Oh God, Eamon, we can't miss that one."

Saturday ... Cattle Smuggling on the Border – The latest Irish play introducing smuggling songs and recitations.
"Och, who would think of such a thing, Eamon!"

Also, Variety and Farce, featuring
WEE JIM – Ireland's Greatest Young Comedian

Doors open 7.30 Commence 8.00
Admission 1/3, 9d, 6d

Children's Matinee at 2.30 on Saturday. FREE toys & gifts.
Admission 4d and 3d

Everything was arranged. We gave our final performance in Kesh to a packed house on the Saturday night, pulled down the scenery, packed up the props and the costumes, had supper (our main, indeed our only substantial meal of the day) went to bed and slept, apart from me and my little sister, till lunch time on Sunday. The rest of the day we had to ourselves.

We had done good business in Kesh. Along the border seemed to be one of the few areas left in the early thirties where people could afford to pay for their entertainment ... *and culture.* For what we offered was more than entertainment, which is why in one town we caused a "near riot", and on a second occasion were under siege in our hall for the night.

Most of the time we stuck to the northern side of the border because in the South conditions were poorer and the population was even more thinly spread out. Though father still managed to tick off on the southern side, Castleblayney, Monaghan, Belturbet, Ballinamore, and just a wee bit back across the green line he even put a cross against the village of Crossmaglen! Why the cross and not a line, I wonder? Did we not play there? And why outside the village? Was the hall some distance away, maybe at the crossroads? I'll never know.

Anyhow, on the Northern side and also on the north and south shores of Upper and Lower Lough Erne his pencil marks lay thick and blue and I was there and able to confirm that they were not just names on a map. We played at Lisnaskea, Lisbella, Letterbreen, Derrygonelly, Maguires Bridge, Enniskillen, Ballinamallard, Ballyshannon, Bundoran and Belleek. And of course *now* we were all looking forward to Pettigoe. Even I, who as a child loathed leaving any place where I'd settled in and made friends, was excited. Though it wasn't the prospect of good takings I have to admit, it was the thought of the *cattle business* that intrigued me.

2

Foxes have Holes

Though it wasn't a long journey to Pettigoe we had all had more than enough of being shaken, gassed by the driver's fags and thrown all over the place when the lorry stopped short at a narrow stone bridge that would have taken us over the border into the Free State, backed up a little way alongside the river and then came to a halt at the front of a long, low, wooden building – our hall. The driver switched off the engine and everybody got out, sighed, stamped, brushed down and generally rearranged themselves.

"Here ye are ladies ... safe an' sound."

"Well, safe maybe ..." grandma bent over and hobbled a few steps, acting of course, "... but *sound!*"

"There are parts of me," mother reached round and placed a hand as low down on her hip as she decently could, adding, "that will never be the same again."

There was more talk, laughter and good-natured bantering, so quietly I detached myself from the group, walked on a dozen paces or so and stood looking down at the river.

The air was warm, the sun was bright, and the world was very peaceful. A wonderful sense of relief and well-being began to rise up in me and as it did so the powerful, pungent smell of some weed that was growing in profusion at the side of the river slowly crept into my consciousness. A smell that haunts me to this day. For reasons that are completely beyond me I associate it with some meaningful, or series of meaningful experiences that I can no longer remember. It took me years, wandering the countryside in search of wild plants, a hobby that grew out of yet another profession, to track down the plant responsible for the smell. And when I did, working first through English and then Irish floras in the belief that it must have been a rare plant, perhaps confined to that area and nowhere else, I suddenly realised that the simple solution was that there were *two* plants, the one I had seen and associated with the odour, and another nearby, probably cowparsley or hogweed, which hadn't attracted my attention. It was the hogweed that gave off the smell, a smell that still stirs in me the positive feeling, the tantalising idea, that way back in the beginning, the darkness, something happened, something of considerable importance, but I can never remember what it was.

"*Jim!*" Just when I had decided the grownups would go on talking forever and it would he interesting to scramble down to the water's edge and explore underneath the stone bridge, mother called, then beckoned. "We're going into the village." I rejoined her and grandma (mother's mother). "So we'll leave you," mother smiled at the driver and took hold of Eileen's hand, "and the rest of the company to do the hard work."

"That's the idea."

The rest of the company, of course, consisted of father and grandad. Originally there had been a cast of eight, now we were four and a half. And in time my grandparents would leave and go back to England, Uncle Joe (father's younger and only brother) would return from his adventures in Canada, and to my great delight travel with us for a while, and then he too would leave to take up a job that gave him a steady income (steady by our standards) as a Kleeneze salesman in the city of Belfast where he was born. And that would leave father, mother, and because Eileen was too young to work, me.

"Right! Let's get this into the hall." Father gave the order and immediately grandad, already inside the building depositing the small attaché case which contained his personal belongings, and the long brown, well-worn leather overcoat he never went without, came charging out of the doorway, head down, arms at the ready (he'd been a wrestler in his own father's barnstorming company in his youth) and laid hands on the tailboard of the lorry. Father was the boss of the company, there was never any doubt about that. He was in charge, his word was law, and it wasn't only the Depression (a term I never heard used in Ireland to describe a condition that was as natural as the going down of the sun), nor the ravages of that newfangled craze "The Moving Pictures" that had forced him and mother out of bigger and better companies across the water. Father didn't like being bossed. He would not take orders. He did things his way and his way was always right. I don't think I ever heard him admit to a mistake or say that he was sorry. If something went wrong then either the cause lay "way out there" in some preordained, premeditated, probably Tory inspired machination, or the person to blame was standing right in front of him at the time. A company of his own where he was actor, manager, writer, producer was the only solution.

So the men were left to unload the lorry, settle up with the driver, and before our opening performance that evening convert the small, dreary, dead little hall with its dirty windows and heaps of chairs (some broken) and backless forms piled up on the low platform that would have to serve as a stage, into something more promising, exciting, *alive* … A THEATRE! While the women and children headed for yet another strange town, and strange people (for grandma was English and although mother had married an Irishman she herself was an Anglo-Scot), in search of food and a couple of families who would, before the end of the day, take in six complete strangers, two of them under five, and provide them with a bed (two beds at least) and a home for the week.

"Mam, you try this lady ... let's see ... I wrote it down ... Mrs Maguire. The driver says she lives next door to a butcher's shop. She's a widow, doesn't take lodgers as a rule but he thinks if you mention his name you might talk her into it. He and her husband worked together once. That might do for you and dad."

"Very good, I'll see what I can do with Mrs Maguire. How long has she been a widow, did he say?"

"Oh, I don't know, long enough. I'll go along with this pair and try the other lady the driver mentioned, Mrs Mitchell. She's had children of her own though they're all grown up and away. And she's taken in the odd commercial traveller in the past, so she might be willing."

"Where does your Mrs Mitchell live?"

"Right down at the end of the street near a sweet shop."

"And the one I'm going to, is she a catholic?"

"Oh, I expect so, everybody on this side of the border would be catholic."

"Not that it matters but it's always useful to know. I'll head for Mrs Maguire. That must be the butcher's shop across the street, unless there's two of them."

"Oh and mam, in case my lady's not interested would you ask your lady if she could suggest someone else who doesn't mind children?"

"I'll do that. See you later. Good hunting!" Grandma started across the street while mother walked on, little Eileen by her side complaining bitterly.

"I'm hungry."

"I'm hungry too." Mother took a firmer grip on my little sister's hand. "And if you don't behave and we don't get a place to stay tonight you'll be hungrier still." Then she turned on me. "And you stop dragging your feet."

"I'm not dragging your feet." I hated these excursions. I was five and didn't want to go with the women, I wanted to work in the hall with the men. But of course digs had to be found and in the proceedings we all had a part to play. So I picked up my feet, came alongside my mother and we continued down the long main street. Irish villages always had long main streets, that is if they didn't have long *wide* main streets.

Grandma, having located the house she was looking for, knocked on the door which opened almost immediately, nobody even looking out of the window first to see who it was.

"Oh, good morning." One of grandma's gracious smiles beamed at the lady standing in the hallway.

"Good morning." The response was cordial but slightly puzzled.

"Are you Mrs Maguire?"

"I am."

"Then I've come to the right house and the right lady first time. Our lorry driver who just brought us over from Kesh, Sam ... Sam ... Oh dear, I've forgotten his second name."

"Sam Mullen?"

"The very man, Sam Mullen ... I've a terrible head for names. Yes, Sam gave me your name, said you were old acquaintances, and he'd been a very good friend of your husband."

"Oh yes, Sam and my husband worked together at the building for years."

"Your late husband I should have said, because I believe you lost your dear partner fairly recently?"

"Yes, two years go," Mrs Maguire said solemnly, "this very week."

"Oh, I'm very sorry to hear that."

"Thank you."

"Two years can seem a long time, but where the loss of a loved one is concerned it means nothing. Time can never erase ... you can never forget."

"You cannot."

"I still have my own soul mate, thank God, but I know how you must feel because a long time ago I lost a little girl who was only ten, and two years before that my only boy who was barely fifteen."

"Oh dear God! What happened?"

"The little girl died of diphtheria and the boy of rheumatic fever."

"That's terrible, terrible. And was that all the family?"

"No, I have one girl left and she's married to an Irish man and has two children, a boy and a girl, two lovely children. And at this very moment they are at the bottom of the street calling on a Mrs Mitchell ... but what a terrible gas bag I am. Here I am telling you my troubles, dragging you away from your work ..."

"Oh, that's alright, that's alright."

"And I haven't even told you my name or why I knocked on your door. So I'll start again. My name's Mrs Wynn and I'm here in Pettigoe with my husband and son-in-law who are over the bridge at the little hall unloading the lorry ..."

"Ah!" Everything was suddenly clear to Mrs Maguire. "You've come with the playactors!"

"Yes. My husband, daughter, son-in-law, even my little grandson, we're all members of The Broadway Players and we will be presenting drama and variety in Pettigoe all this week. And that's why we are looking for lodgings."

"Oh well, I don't usually take people in."

"I know, Sam said that, but he thought in this case you might just make an exception. It would only be for my husband and myself, for the week. We would only need a small room, and a bed of course, and we are both very quiet."

"Oh, I'm sure you are."

"We don't get drunk or break up the furniture, or anything like that."

"Of course not."

"People sometimes get very strange ideas about actors, but really our lives are simplicity itself, we just eat, sleep and work like everybody else. And if we do have any spare time I sew, make costumes or new clothes for the children, and my husband reads or goes out for a walk. We need very little attention and we would clean the room and leave it tidy. So what do you think, Mrs Maguire?"

"Well, I have a spare room of course, it's not been much used since my own family grew up and went away."

"And of course, though we are not millionaires we would pay a reasonable rent, in advance if you like."

"Oh no, I wouldn't want that."

"And as far as eating is concerned, well, whatever arrangements suit you will suit us. We can cook our own if you'd let us use your kitchen. Or if you like, as our landlady in Kesh said – we had wonderful lodgings there — 'Oh, you just put your potatoes in my pot and we'll all eat together'. I suppose the only small problem is that we eat our main meal of the day after the show, and that can be a little late for working people."

"Oh, that wouldn't matter, I'm quite late going to bed myself sometimes if I have a neighbour in. There's no need to get up early now that Patrick's gone."

"So what do you think?"

"Well ... Would you like to come into the house for a minute or two and have a cup of tea and we can talk about it?"

"Mrs Maguire, there is nothing in the whole wide world I would like better at this moment than a nice cup of tea."

"Come in then. And mind that bucket, I was just about to give the hall a bit of a wash."

"And I've stopped you, and the water will be stone cold."

"Oh, I can soon get some more hot water. Into the kitchen."

"Thank you."

"And I'll just shut the front door again for there's a bit of a breeze blowing up the street this morning. Normally I leave it open."

"Ah, Irish doors are always open to friends and strangers alike I have found."

"Of course you're an English woman."

"From the Black Country, Staffordshire. I was born and raised near a town called Walsall."

"And how long have you been over here in Ireland?"

The conversation went on for another half hour and by the time grandmother came back out into the street to look for us she had obtained lodgings for herself and grandad.

*

Further down the street, however, the operation didn't look as though it would be quite as simple, or satisfactory. We were just passing the sweet shop when a man came out opening a packet of cigarettes and mother spoke to him.

"Excuse me, but can you tell me where Mrs Mitchell lives?"

"Up there," he pointed back the way we had come. "She's just come out to her door."

"Oh yes, thank you very much."

The man got on his bicycle and rode off while the three of us stood silently and with some concern, regarding the small, grey-haired lady wearing a long apron and a very severe expression, who had just come out to her doorstep and was looking in our direction.

"Oh dear," mother said quietly. "Mrs Mitchell looks rather formidable."

"She looks *fierce*!" I was more positive.

"Something must have upset her, or somebody, or maybe she's like that all the time. Well, we'll have to give her a try, that's the only name I've got."

"Should I go along first and ask her for a drink of water?"

"Ah yes, that would be a good idea."

"Then I could see what she's like."

"And we could hang on here and see how you fare."

"I'll go."

"Just a minute." Mother patted my fringe into place. "Now be polite."

"Of course," I said scornfully. I was well aware by this time that politeness and respectability were essential in winning the approval of grownups, particularly landladies. Landlords were different, they just didn't want you running around the place making a noise.

"And pull up your socks."

"They are up."

"And straighten your tie."

"You're choking me."

"And remember, don't put your hands in your pockets when you're talking to the lady."

"I never do."

"Off you go then. You can give us a nod, though not when she's looking. We'll wait here." Mother set little Eileen down on the footpath and turned her attention to the sweet shop window. An action you might have thought foolish considering the two year old had already declared she was hungry. But Eileen, like myself, already knew that there was no point in asking for things that couldn't be afforded, especially from her mother.

So she just stood and looked into the shop window while I walked back to where the angry lady, it was even more obvious as I got nearer, glared up the street and then down. When I drew level I stopped, looked her full in the face, smiled and asked very politely,

"Excuse me, but do you think you could let me have a glass of water please?"

There was a slight, though it didn't seem slight to me, terrifying pause, and then …

"Certainly." The woman smiled. The fierce expression evaporated and she actually smiled. She wasn't an old witch. I think she was just short-sighted. Everything was going to be alright. "Just wait there a minute."

"That's very kind of you." She disappeared into the house and immediately I turned in the direction of my mother who was watching and vigorously nodded my head. Mother nodded back. The lady returned with a large mug, not of water, but of *milk.*

"There you are, that'll do you more good than water."

"Oh, thank you very much indeed." I took the mug carefully from her hands. "I'm very thirsty and I couldn't see a pump anywhere in the street."

"Oh, there's one further up, but milk's better for a growing boy."

"It certainly is." I drank heartily but not noisily, and when I was about halfway through and had come up for air the lady continued.

"You're a stranger in the town then?"

"Yes, we've just come over from Kesh this morning with my father and his theatrical company."

"Ah, you're with the playactors!"

"Yes. I'm with my grandma, grandad and my mother and little sister." I turned in the direction of the sweet shop. "Look, this is my mother and my little sister coming along now."

The lady looked, mother smiled, picked Eileen up in her arms and advanced towards us.

"This lady has very kindly given me some milk." I brought the two parties together.

"Milk! Oh, that's very kind of you indeed."

"Not at all. Your wee boy is very polite and that's not a thing you come across every day."

"Oh well, I do my best to teach them good manners and they're really very good, the pair of them. Though they have their little turns at times."

"Don't they all."

Mother looked down at me and then leaned towards the lady confidentially. "I wouldn't want them to get swollen heads."

"Of course not."

"Jim is the quiet, thoughtful one." Mother put an arm round my shoulder. "He's his mammy's boy, aren't you?" I forced a sickly smile. I had never had any choice in the matter. Eileen was daddy's little girl, the apple of his eye, so automatically, to even things up, I became mammy's little boy.

"And Eileen's her daddy's little girl. Say good morning to the lady." Eileen turned her head in the direction of the lady and politely, if without much warmth, did as she was told.

"And that's a very nice wee girl as well." The lady stretched out a hand and chucked my sister under the chin, an action that brought a definite scowl to the nice wee girl's face.

"Well, they're not too bad really, the pair of them." Mother set Eileen back on her feet. "But has my son told you who we are?"

"Oh yes, you're the playactors."

"That's right. We've just come over from Kesh … Oh, and such lovely audiences and such generous people … we're going back there again as soon as we can. We only arrived about half an hour ago and, as a matter of fact I was on my way to see you."

"To see *me*?"

"Yes. Aren't you Mrs Mitchell?"

"That's right."

"The man who brought us over, our lorry driver, Sam Mullen …'

"Och, Sam Mullen!"

"Everybody seems to know Sam."

"Oh, he's a bit of a head case."

"Yes, well, Sam gave me your name and suggested I should call on you. You see we're looking for lodgings and he said you used to take in commercial travellers."

"Oh, I did the odd time, but they were always men on their own. I never took in any children or families."

"No, he said that, but he thought in our case you might just stretch a point. It would only be for the week and all we need is a room and bed for my husband and me, and maybe a couch or something for the little boy. Eileen has her own cot. We can cook for ourselves, or share the cooking, and we would keep the place clean, and the children would be very quiet, and we'd keep out of your way. We'd be no trouble."

"Oh, I'm sure you wouldn't, and I have a big spare bedroom and a single bed that my own children used."

"I'm sure we could agree on a reasonable rent – we'll pay in advance if you like."

"Oh no, you're very respectable people I can see that. And I wouldn't mind taking you in. Children round the house would be no hardship to me, I'd like it. But I'd have to have a word with my husband first."

"Of course, of course. Husbands always have to be taken into account. Not that they ever do any of the work or suffer any of the inconveniences."

Mrs Mitchell laughed out loud. "You're right there."

"As long as they get their grub and their smokes and the whole house is as silent as the grave when they want to read their paper or have a sleep … But your husband may not be like mine."

"Course he is, they're all the same."

"So do you think you could have a word with Mr Mitchell?"

"I could."

"I suppose he's out at work at the moment?"

"He is, but he comes home for his dinner, and just as it happens he's coming up behind you at this very minute."

Our three heads swung round in unison and focused on the tall, lean, weather-beaten man in working clothes and a cloth cap who had stopped short of our little gathering.

"This is himself."

"Mr Mitchell," mother greeted the latest obstacle likely to stand between us and a roof over our heads, "I'm very pleased to meet you."

"And I'm very pleased to meet *you.*" Mr Mitchell lifted his cap and responded heartily. "Though I don't know ..."

"This lady is with the playactors who've just come over from Kesh this morning," explained his wife.

"Ah, the playactors!"

"Yes I'm one of the playactors and this is another, Wee Jim."

"Ireland's greatest young comedian," Mr Mitchell announced to the whole street.

"You've been reading our bills."

"I have indeed. And I can tell you me and the wife will be over there to see one of your plays before the week's out."

"I'm very pleased to hear that Mr Mitchell, bring your friends. By the way, I'm Mrs Mateer and my husband is the boss of the company. This is young Jim, my son, and this little rip down here is his sister. Say good morning to Mr Mitchell, Eileen."

Eileen tilted her small face upwards, opened wide two large brown shining eyes and said, "Good morning, Mr Mitchell." The man's face immediately lit up as though he'd been given a five pound note.

"Ah, that's a lovely wee girl." He bent down and gently took hold of her hand. She didn't draw back. "A great wee girl. And how are you Eileen, how are you?" Men always responded to Eileen's overtures like that. She was an expert at handling the opposite sex. Of course, she had been practising on her daddy for the best part of two years.

"William," Mrs Mitchell looked down at her husband, "Mrs Mateer and her husband and their two children are looking for lodgings and Sam Mullen recommended us."

Mr Mitchell didn't quite know what was expected of him, so he stood up and scratched the back of his head. "Oh, Sam Mullen."

"Yes. And I said we don't usually take in families."

"No, that's right."

"But we do have a big spare bedroom".

"Oh aye, we do indeed."

"And we'd be no bother." Mother came in on the landlady's side.

"Oh no, I'm sure you wouldn't." Mr Mitchell looked uneasily at his wife.

"So I said I'd have a word with you William."

"Certainly, certainly."

"And *I* said," mother gathered Eileen up in her arms, "that we'd take a little walk ... you're home for your dinner, Mr Mitchell?"

"I am."

"And nobody should keep a hard-working man from his dinner. So we'll do a couple of little errands and come back. In an hour maybe?"

"Och, *less* than that." Mrs Mitchell regarded her husband.

"Oh aye, less than that," he agreed.

"Half an hour then?"

"That'll do fine. So come away into the house William and get your dinner. And you'll call back later, Mrs Mateer?"

"We will." We moved off, and as we did heard her explaining.

"It will only be for the week William. And sure the bedroom's empty anyhow. And she's a very nice woman."

"Oh, she is that."

"And the children are that polite."

"Oh, that's a great wee girl."

"And the wee boy too, so well spoken. I tell you, they' re a right pair of wee angels."

Well! Polite, respectable, and in other people's houses and in the presence of strangers we were quiet, but angels we were not. Although I quite looked the part at times, for though sturdily built, like my mother I had a pale, pallid complexion. I was also, by nature, a little reserved and not in the least aggressive. Given the chance, however, and providing I wasn't wearing my decent clothes, I kicked footballs, threw stones, chased rabbits, searched for birdnests, and often fought, verbally of course, with my little sister. She, on the other hand, never bothered to pretend if she didn't like the landlady or anybody belonging to her. Even if it started a row she would play mother off against father when she had something in her sights. And if female cunning and conniving didn't appear to work, and she only had mother to contend with, she'd throw herself down on the floor and yell, kick and scream like a fiend out of hell. And talking about fiends ...

In a town I've long since forgotten, there was a spinster living alone who definitely didn't like children. I think she only agreed to take us in because she needed the money. What she thought about us, me and Eileen, was clear right from the beginning. So I smiled, flattered, stole round on tip toe and was excessively polite ... a right creep. But then I didn't want any trouble with her or the rest of the family, *our* family. It was easy for Eileen to be independent, she was a little girl. I was the elder brother, and if there was any trouble when mother wasn't about, even if Eileen was the cause of it, I got the blame. And to be thrown out by the landlady would have been bad enough, but to incur the displeasure of my father was something, even when I had reached the so-called years of discretion, I always tried to avoid.

What happened on this occasion was the direct result of a situation that continually presented itself to my mother when she was working, I mean in the theatre or actually on stage ... the problem of what to do about us. Landladies, and fortunately they were in the majority, who had children of their own were usually understanding and obliging. And when I started to work regularly, at about five years of age, I would go to the theatre with my parents and stay there till the show was over, so the problem was cut down by half. Though for me this was far from an ideal arrangement, because when I got tired or bored I would climb into an open trunk (the combination of greasepaint, mothballs and damp is a smell I'll always remember), go to sleep, and when roused be extremely ill-tempered. Father's answer to this, and he was genuinely concerned that I should not be deprived, at least not of sleep, was that I should go to bed for a couple of hours in the afternoon. When the sun was shining! When everybody else was running about! Eileen of course was too small to take to the theatre, and anyway if she didn't sleep, she'd talk, sing or suddenly dash onto the middle of the stage. She was such an extrovert, such a show-off. I had to be pushed or dragged on stage, but if she wasn't watched she'd be right in the middle of things singing, dancing and playing the mouth organ all at the same time.

So, on this particular night, although I hadn't actually started to work regularly on stage at that point, mother decided to take me with her to the theatre, while Eileen, on the clear understanding that she would be fast asleep and no problem at all, was left with the landlady, Mrs Brown. Now I hardly need to mention that Eileen had taken an instant dislike to the landlady. Nevertheless, she got into her cot without any trouble that evening and was fast asleep when mother and I, father having gone on ahead, set off for the hall. About half an hour after we had left and the show was already under way, however, the youthful sleeper awoke, called for her mammy, got no answer, called for her daddy, still got no answer, and then, feeling she'd been totally abandoned, began to yell. The landlady stuck it for a few minutes and then threw down her sewing, stumped up the stairs, opened the door of the bedroom and called out,

"Your mammy's not here, and your daddy's not here. And if you don't stop that noise *this very instant* ..." The noise stopped. The lady waited. The silence continued so she retired and shut the bedroom door. Immediately, with grim determination, Eileen opened up again.

"I want my mammy, I want my ..." The door flew open again and the menacing figure of Mrs Brown advanced into the room.

"Now I've told you ... your mammy's away acting on the stage and your daddy too, and if I get one more word out of you ... *you'll get smacked*."

Again there was an abrupt cessation of hostilities. The landlady stood and glared in silence for a few moments then she turned and made for the door, but before she could get out of the room, Eileen indignantly protested.

"I want my mammy."

The landlady swung round and took a couple of steps towards the cot by the window. As she did so the infant sat bolt upright, stretched out a small arm and a tiny accusing finger, and declared with all the passion she could muster, "*Stand back! Lay a finger on this child and by God will you!*"

I don't know where she got the lines, but they had a traumatic effect on Mrs Brown who stopped dead, stared in horror and disbelief at the small face and the large round eyes glowing in the darkness, and then backed off, shut the door, and vowed she'd never go anywhere near that child again. And on the last day when mother had settled up and was saying goodbye, with Eileen (who had slept in the dressing room for the rest of that week) in her arms and me standing meekly by her side, Mrs Brown expressed the full depth of her feelings regarding the incident in the bedroom.

"And I tell you this, Mrs Mateer, that boy by your side is a saint, *a saint*, and one day he will join Jesus and the angels in heaven. But that girl ... that girl ... *will come to a very bad end*."

Father actually laughed out loud, and he didn't often do that, when told that his dear little girl would come to a bad end. And mother, who saw that I was within hearing at the time raised an eyebrow, her voice, and declared, "But the little boy, the little boy is a saint." Then, as she turned back towards father I heard her add under her breath, "The sly little sod!"

We all got digs in Pettigoe, and very good digs they were.

3

Setting Up Shop

The men had already set up the box frame on stage when mother and I returned to the hall. Father was up the ladder securing one of the scenes while grandad was down below, in front of the stage, carefully and systematically coiling short lengths of stay ropes that had not yet been used. As well as an actor and wrestler, grandad had been a soldier in the fourteen-eighteen war and always left things in tidy heaps and straight lines – a practice that never failed to infuriate my father.

"We've got digs!" mother called out as she made for the small room behind the stage that would serve as our communal dressing room.

"Ah, good girl, good girl." Grandad immediately stopped what he was doing but father carried on working.

"Nice digs. The widow's taking you and mam, and a Mrs Mitchell is taking us. Cheerful lady, Mrs Mitchell. Doesn't mind kids. I think we'll be alright."

"Good girl, good girl." Grandad removed his gold-rimmed spectacles and proceeded to clean them with the cuff of his shirt.

"And I've brought you some bread and cheese and a bottle of pickles."

"Ah, pickles, pickles!" Grandad replaced his spectacles and rubbed his hands together. "A real working man's lunch."

"And there's milk, sugar and a bottle of Camp Coffee."

"That's the stuff to give the troops. That's the stuff ... Eh Bob?" Grandad raised his head and peered at the top of the ladder for confirmation, only to find that father, who had neither acknowledged our arrival nor responded to anything that had been said, had descended, picked up the end of a scene and was impatiently waiting.

"Ah, right Bob, right." Grandad swept an arm and his shirt sleeve across his sweating brow, scrambled onto the stage, fell over (he was very short-sighted) and finally got his hands on the other end of the twelve foot batten that father was holding. "Right Bob. Right Bob."

This was always the trouble when working with father. If he started a job nobody was supposed to stop, even to draw breath, until he had indicated that the operation was finished. And the other thing that was very difficult to contend with was the fact that he rarely told you what he wanted you to do. You were supposed to watch, follow, and even if he did something totally unexpected, know exactly what was in his mind and come in dead on cue.

"I'll light the primus." Mother disappeared through the doorway of the dressing room and almost immediately reappeared and presented me with the battered old aluminium kettle which, together with the primus, a set of chipped enamel mugs and a spoon, represented our complete travelling kitchen. "You run to that house across the road and ask for some drinking water, *please*."

"Alright." I took the kettle and started off, then at the bottom of the ladder I paused, looked up and ventured, "Can I stay and help in the hall?" Father didn't immediately answer so grandad chimed in on my behalf.

"Yes, let him stay Bob, he'll be no trouble, will you, Jimmy?"

"No. I'll stay at the back of the hall. I'll sort out the seats." I knew that father, when working, never tolerated hangers-on, backstage, front of house or anywhere else. Besides, I wanted to sort out the chairs and the long backless forms, I liked creating order out of chaos.

"Yes, let him stay," mother added her weight. "The landlady's making a snack for me, mamma and Eileen and that'll be one less. Let him stay in the hall, there's enough to eat."

"Alright, alright," father agreed, then irritably directed his attention to his helper down below. "A rope, a rope, I need another length of rope."

"Right away, Bob, right away." Grandad dashed off to one of the small heaps he'd constructed while I raced across the road to get a kettle of water. When I got back mother had fortified herself with a Park Drive and was down on her hands and knees in front of the stove.

"Damned thing," she said as she shut off the valve, pumped up the fuel, struck another match and then drew back swiftly as a three foot flame shot up into the air. "I hate this thing."

"It's not warmed up," I told her.

"It's probably *bunged* up, that's what's the matter with it." She opened the valve again, waited until the flame died down, then prodded the nipple a couple of times with the pricker. "Now, we'll try again." She shut the valve, pumped the fuel, lit a match, drew back, swore, repeated the performance a few more times until suddenly the yellow flame dropped, turned blue and the primus purred into life. "Right! Put the kettle on." I did so. Mother got to her feet. "Where's the card table?"

"It's here." I pulled out the green baize-covered, folding table that was used nearly as often off stage as on, and mother quickly laid out the provisions and the enamel mugs, and gave her final instructions.

"Now, tell your father when it's boiled."

"Yes."

"Then I'm off." She picked up her coat, bid her adieus in the hall and went back into the town.

When the kettle had boiled, it didn't take long, I informed father and he and grandad joined me in the dressing room for lunch, which was a brief, and for the most part silent and unceremonious affair, though grandad did make an effort to finish his off in style with a Woodbine. I had tried on several occasions, when he asked me to run and get him a packet of five, to get him to change to Park Drive because I wanted the cigarette cards but he said they were too mild and he liked a good smoke. Father at that particular moment didn't want to smoke at all, so as soon as he had eaten he went straight back onto the stage, grandad hurriedly following in his wake, while I made my way to the back of the hall. Father had let down the Actdrop before going to lunch and I paused, before starting on my own job, and regarded the familiar scene.

It consisted of a large country house, or maybe it was a hotel, with a raised garden, a stone parapet, and a flight of steps that seemed to come right down into the hall. The house stood on the left with the gable facing the viewer and the front visible, but diminishing in perspective. Behind there was a blue sky with white clouds, a blue-green sea, and on either side, coming down from the corners to frame the picture, the leafy branches of trees in full summer. The windows were latticed, the front door had a porch, the gable was covered with vigorous creepers, and the garden and the parapet with colourful plants and flowers. And down right, behind the trunk of a very large tree, standing close together and just visible, there were two figures.

I wondered, as I often did, who these two people – clearly a man and a woman – were, and what they were doing there. They seemed to be talking to each other, or maybe they were just looking at the sea. But where did they come from? Where did they belong? To the house, or from somewhere else? The same longing always comes over me when I look at the few traditional cards that are sent to me at Christmas. The same feeling, nostalgia I suppose, the same fascination as I examine closely the solitary woodman drawing firewood; the tiny cottage, dark and inhospitable save for the warm, reassuring light that shines out of one window; people coming out of a snow-covered church; children in bonnets and scarves running along a lonely country road or skating across the ice on a frozen pond. Who are these people? What sort of lives do they live? The two figures on the Actdrop, though of course I knew it was only a painting, the work of my father, always seemed like real people to me. Indeed, I would often stand, as I did at that moment in the small hall in Pettigoe, and concentrate with all my might in the belief that if I looked long enough the figures would move, turn round, speak …!

The Set

The box, or main frame that father and grandad had erected, and which was designed to support all the scenery, consisted of eight, three by three inch timbers, fifteen feet in length. Four of these, each in two shorter lengths bolted together so that the overall length could be reduced if required, served as uprights. The remaining four, entire lengths, were then attached to the top of the uprights, two across full length, and the other two either projecting beyond the proscenium, or the uprights at the back, depending on the depth of the stage. (And of course stages or platforms came in all heights. Once we built one of fish boxes.) The frame was assembled, bolted loosely, while lying on the stage and then eased up into position, two or four legs at a time depending on the number of hands. The bolts were then tightened and the whole structure secured by stays running from the top of the frame to the floor, stage, or side of the hall. If there was enough room we then ended up with a working stage fifteen feet across, nine feet deep and twelve feet from the stage up to the Flys. The height and depth could be altered by a few feet, but the fifteen feet width remained constant because of the length of the scenes. In very small halls no matter how we reduced the frame we often found we had little space at the side of the stage, and no room at all to cross behind the Backcloth to get to the opposite side. And even if we could manage a few inches, behind the Backcloth that is, bottoms undulating what was supposed to be a solid wall during the play was something that could send father right through the roof. However, we could cope with most halls, although about a year later, when we left the lakes, worked our way up to the north coast and crossed the worst stretch of sea round these islands, to play on Rathlin, we were confronted by a situation that nearly defied father's imagination. But then Rathlin was unique whatever way you looked at it, and our visit there the experience of a lifetime.

The Scenes

After the frame had been erected, the scenes were lifted up and placed in position. They were painted on canvas, fifteen feet across by twelve feet high, and each was nailed at the top to a flat batten and fitted at the bottom to a wooden roller. So, when the batten had been laid on top of the frame and the canvas unrolled until it rested on the stage, by means of ropes and pulleys the scenes could be raised or lowered as required. All the scenes were constructed like this save one, the Backcloth, and this had no roller, simply two flat battens, so once in position that scene remained down – providing, of course, it had been unwound by hand in the first place! And thereby hangs a tale of disaster and the near destruction of a young actress's reputation ... but later.

The canvas scenes themselves, apart from the Actdrop, were painted on both sides, though only one side could be used during the production. The drawing, designing and painting of these had been executed by the boss of the company himself ... quite a long time ago I would say. Although in one wild part of the country when father suddenly decided he wanted a *new* scene, I was permitted to witness, at a safe distance of course, the creation of one of his works of art. First he hung the fifteen by twelve foot canvas up in a barn, with the permission and help of the farmer, surrounded himself with bags and tins of powdered paint of various colours, mixed a pot of size made from flour (a concoction which when left around for a couple of days smelt like nothing I would care to mention), and set out buckets of water and an assortment of brushes which included one large, long, soft-haired broom. Then he outlined with chalk what he wanted on the canvas, removed his coat and hat, took hold of the broom, dipped it into one of the buckets – now containing water, size and whatever colour he required – and attacked like he was leading the Charge of the Light Brigade. Father, when he had decided on a project always advanced like that, because the job had to be done in the shortest possible time, if it wasn't then he lost interest and it never got finished.

Once all the scenes were in position the sequence from front to back was as follows: First the Actdrop, usually referred to as the Curtain; then about five feet back came the Front scene, which depicted either a street or woodland, depending on the plays for the week; then the Back scenes, consisting of a kitchen, drawing room and another outdoor scene; and finally the Backcloth, a dreary affair used for prisons, cellars and the like. And after the scenes, in the wings, set at an angle to mask the sides of the stage and allow easy entrance and exit, were positioned four twelve foot high by four foot wide Flats – canvas nailed to light wooden frames and held upright by "U" shaped irons that hung upside down from the box or main frame. The Flats were painted on both sides, indoor and outdoor scenes to match whatever was being used on stage, and being light they were easy to handle. To hide the upper frame, rolled-up scenes, headlights and the area above the stage, several long, narrow strips of what I suppose had once been blue material, the Flys, were tied on with string. And finally, draped either side of the frame, down to the floor and across to the sides of the hall, making sacrosanct the stage and everything beyond it, we hung heavy, much-faded (I suppose they had been a deep red originally), moth-eaten (we checked the size of the audience through the holes) curtains. All that was necessary after that was, first, to provide lighting ... if we were lucky and in a large town we had electricity, but in most of the places where we played we had to use oil – tilley lamps (vaporised paraffin), or plain oil or even hurricane lamps. And after the lighting ... music.

The Orchestra

In the early, more prosperous days, and there must have been better times, the company had a piano and a set of drums. Father was able to employ a pianist, plus a drummer who could sing and play small walk-on parts. But the pianist ran off with the comedian one day, and although I didn't miss the lady who played the piano, "Wee Teddy", that's what everybody called our comedian, was a terrible loss, and his departure pushed me into a role I never wanted to play. Like my father, Wee Teddy was a Belfast man, but unlike my father who came from the east of the city, Teddy was a catholic and came from The Falls - not that anybody cared in those days what part you came from. He was a very good comedian, a natural. Indeed, his career probably started the day he was born, continued at school, developed when he took to singing in dance halls and pubs, and finally matured when he went on the stage. Children in particular loved Teddy (they used to follow him in the street), not just because he was funny but because he was small, and small in a rather peculiar way. By that I mean he was the only man I have ever known who was taller sitting down than standing up. It was his legs. The top half of his body was perfectly formed but his legs were extremely short, undeveloped. To compensate for this, however, apart from making people laugh, he had a rather handsome face and lots of black curly hair. The pianist, who was in fact a cousin of mother's and therefore English and more of a heathen than a protestant, took to him right from the start. She herself was quite normal in appearance, though a bit fat, a bit plain and a lot older. It was clear to the rest of us from their first meeting that Ethyl had a great notion of Teddy, and as time went on the notion increased until she fairly came to dote on the man. *He* didn't mind, which didn't surprise us, but what did surprise us, was that one afternoon without any prior warning, the pair of them came back to the hall and announced they had got married and were leaving the company for good! The drummer went about the same time to find a better job, or at least one that enabled him to eat three meals a day. And father, unwilling to carry any unnecessary luggage, put the instruments in store for the time being, and the company moved on. Not long after we had left the town of Fintona where the store was, right in the heart of Tyrone, it rained, the river rose, the doors of the store caved in and the piano and drums sailed off to …! Well, where does the river that flows through Fintona end up? So with the musicians gone, and now their instruments, that was the end of our orchestra.

Father, however, never a man to lie down under adversity, also disappeared one day without saying a word to anyone, and returned several hours later carrying in both arms a contraption which none of us was ever allowed to go near. It consisted of a medium-sized suitcase which housed what he called a gramophone pickup and amplifier, and a roughly-made cabinet in which had been fitted a loudspeaker. And when he, to our amazement (though father was very good with gadgets) got the whole thing together and put on a record, we and our audiences had songs and music that I can still hear in my head and feel in my heart to this day. I never found out exactly how the thing worked, I wasn't particularly interested, and of course, as I said, no-one else was allowed to touch it, but occasionally father would send me to a garage to have his "wet" battery recharged, and so I presume that this, together with his "dry" batteries, was what amplified the sound. Though the same power didn't drive the turntable! Oh, how often have I heard the singer trail off, change from tenor to a basso profundo, and caught sight of father, shirt tails flying, racing to the machine to give it another wind while out in the hall the audience cheered. The records were all 78s of course, some second-hand but some new, being purchased in Belfast at such high-class emporiums as The Cliftophone and The Castle Music Salon. And these recordings formed part of the culture of our day. British and American culture that is, if I'm not misusing the word, for only occasionally did we play Irish songs sung by Irish singers, though father did have at least two records of his great favourite, Count John McCormick. But mostly our collection was of dance bands and popular songs of the twenties, numbers advertised on the record labels in the following manner:

Telling it to the Daisies and *Dancing with Tears in My Eyes*, sung by the crooning troubadour Nick Lucas.

Honey and *My Dear*, sung by a soprano, in English, Mildred Hunt.

Big City Blues from The Fox Movietone Follies of 1929, sung by Annette Hanshaw.

Tiptoe through the Tulips from The Gold Diggers of Broadway, sung by Mick Tabon and Mack Taylor

When All's Said and Done, sung by Pat O'Dell

For You, written by Dubbin and Burke and sung by Jack and Jill

Kiss me, Weary River and *Coquette*, sung by Layton and Johnston

And finally, though where this came from I'll never know,

Zulu Wail, written by Skinner and Bilbo and played by The Golden Gate Orchestra.

These then were the disembodied voices, accompanied by the music of their times, that drifted out through the doorways of Orange, Hibernian, Masonic and Parochial halls, down village streets and across desolate landscapes to dissolve into the darkness of a Celtic night. And the audiences didn't complain. They had heard all the old comeallyes like *Eileen Oge*, *The Bard of Armagh*, *The Irish Jauntin' Car*, *Mother Macree* and *The Rose of Tralee* countless times. And of course when we did an Amateurs' Night they had a chance to resurrect everything that had been composed since Brian Boru. No, the audiences we played to wanted something different, and something different is what they got.

And something different is what *we* got too, that is me and father, in our double act on our first night in Pettigoe.

4

Curtain Up

"Three minutes." Father put his head round the dressing room door.

"Right." Mother got to her feet.

"And a packed house."

"Good." She carefully stubbed out her cigarette and put what was left back in the packet. "Maybe I'll be able to pay mama back some of the money we owe her this week."

"Maybe."

Father withdrew and mother lifted up and placed on her head a small hat with a feather that reminded me of Robin Hood, checked her make-up, smoothed down the tight-fitting, slinky skirt that hung a couple of inches below her knees (knee-length or above would have been quite appropriate for her number but mother took after grandad and was short and none too happy about her knees), picked up a long furry boa and moved out to join father at the side of the stage. I got up from my seat on the prop basket and looked out from the dressing room door. Mother was standing in the wings and father by the Actdrop with his gold-plated pocket watch in his hand. The watch had belonged to his father and might have reminded him each time he pulled it out and regarded it of the more honourable way of life – his mother had intended him for the church, like two other members of her family – he might have enjoyed in respectable East Belfast. But father never looked back, never regretted anything he had done, and all that concerned him at that particular moment was that the curtain should go up on time. He was quite fanatical about things like that. If the curtain was to go up at eight, then no matter whether there was an audience of five hundred or only five, it went up on time. Any moment now he would dash back into the dressing room and turn off the music, so before that could happen I nipped in behind the Backcloth and made my way across to the prompt side from where I could watch mother's act and have a peep out into the hall.

The house certainly sounded full ... loud voices, stamping of boots, scraping of chairs, and even as I put an eye to a hole in the curtain there was a loud thump and a gale of laughter as a group of men at one end of a form squeezed up until several of their companions seated at the other end fell off onto the floor. It was noisy, but the noise was good natured and though loud was not totally unrestrained. And the place was packed to the door. All the reserved chairs at the front were occupied by the Elders and the well-to-do of the town. There were no spaces on the hard, backless and very uncomfortable forms that comprised the bulk of the seating in the hall. And right at the back against the wall there were men in overcoats and cloth caps who were prepared to stand during the entire performance. Grandad was hovering in the aisle at the side of the hall, I could see the light glinting on his spectacles. He was there to douse the two tilley lamps as soon as the music stopped. And grandma, her long, pale, soulful face illuminated by the light of a candle that stood on the upended script box, a box weathered, stained and built more like an ammunition case than a receptacle for scripts, was still on the door.

The music stopped. Grandad, who had been standing tense and alert, his head on one side (he was a bit deaf as well as short-sighted) immediately turned round, put out the lamp on the window ledge by his side and hurriedly made his way across the front line of chairs to deal with the one on the other side of the hall. There was an expectant buzz from the audience as the house lights went out, an increase in the rustling of sweet packets, some coughing, a little whispering, and then silence, complete silence, save for the purring of the tilley lamps that stood along the front of the stage.

The curtain went up and the audience got their first glimpse of the stage and the scenery behind. There was another little ripple of noise, then silence. Mother, at the side of the stage, lifted her head, took a deep breath, and carrying her boa in her hand walked on, made her way to the footlights and politely addressed the assembly.

"Good evening ladies and gentlemen, and let me just say, on behalf of the company, that it is a great pleasure to be here in the beautiful little town of Pettigoe. And to see in the hall tonight so many ladies and gentlemen ... particularly *gentlemen* ..." She paused and there was just the ghost of a murmur. The audience weren't sure how or whether they should respond at all. Mother continued. "Though to tell you the truth, to be perfectly honest," in a confidential tone she addressed a section of the audience, "I'm rather *off* men just at the moment." There was a giggle from the ladies at the front and a slight rumble from the boys at the back. "I mean, men can be really horrible at times." The rumbling increased. "Even the nice, handsome ... and I have to admit there are some nice, handsome, big Irishmen out in the hall this evening." The boys warmed up. "And of course the real reason why I'm so bitter, so hard on the male sex just at present is because ... well ... the truth is ... I've just been jilted."

"Aaaah!" A wave of mock sympathy rolled up over the footlights.

Mother sniffed. "And he was such a nice man, such a handsome man, so tall, dark and ..." She looked out into the hall and pointed. "Rather like that young man sitting beside that older man with the curly hair and the glasses." The audience were with her all the way, so she warmed up. Mother liked playing to the gallery, it was her favourite part of the house. "Oh, you can laugh, but it's a very, very sad story really," she dabbed her eyes. "And I'm quite heartbroken and miserable and I can't put it into words but ... I have a little song, and if you are all nice and kind and *quiet*," she hushed them down, "I'll tell you the whole sorry tale." She had another little sniff, straightened her hat, slung the boa over her shoulder, and without accompaniment, and in what would have been accepted in that part of the world as a common London accent, began to sing:

"I used to be as happy as the birdies on the trees
That's when I was courting and my mind was well at ease.
I used to be so happy with me Henry by me side
Looking forward to the day when I would be his bride.
But now he's chucked me over and I'm full of mis...er...y
Someone's been and done me out of William Hen...er...ee."

Chorus:

"He used to say that I was his Mary Ann
And I used to think that he was my young man.
But mother caught his eye and they got married on the sly
And now I have to call him Fa...ther."

Mother was a good comedienne, or to be more precise, a good soubrette. That was how she started her career, in her teens. She was born while grandma was playing and travelling with *her* mother's company in a Portable theatre in the Midlands before the First World War; and I suppose she was carried on stage when a baby was required, as was my sister; she may even have been pushed on in a pantomime at a very early age as I was myself. Though unlike me she always had a home to go back to. The Portable theatre, unlike our Fit-up company had its own prefabricated theatre, stage, lights, seats etc., and was accompanied on tour by horse-drawn caravans so that the artistes and their families always had somewhere to live. Mother travelled with her mother and grandmother until school age, and then when her grandmother retired and went back to her roots in the Derbyshire Peak District, mother went to live with her while grandma and grandad moved on. She didn't *have* to go on the stage. Though there was one memorable occasion, which she often related, when the professional child in the company who was to play Oliver in *Oliver Twist*, fell ill and there was no time to find a substitute. Mother was on school holidays and back travelling with her own mother at the time, so she got the job. A job that grandma was determined mother would carry out in a thoroughly professional manner.

Now to me grandma was the most gracious, gentle and wonderful person in the whole wide world. Mother clothed us, washed, chastised and made sure we were fed … mother looked after us. And father was my hero. But it was grandma I loved. She, however, just like my father, was a thorough professional, and the theatre and its priorities always came first. She may well have been as gracious and spiritual as I imagined, indeed she must have been special because everybody, including fellow artistes, referred to her as The Lady, but behind the ethereal front there was a realist, and down that long, straight, elegant spine ran a band of steel. So when she decided mother should play Oliver she had no illusions at all about mother's ability as an actress. There were considerable shortcomings. To begin with, mother had difficulty in remembering her lines. And she didn't improve a great deal as time went on (fortunately most of her work was done in father's company). Long speeches were always beyond her and she would "top and tail" them as she put it, that is, learn the opening and the concluding sentences, and what came in between was anyone's guess and varied from one performance to the next. The rest of the company just had to get used to her. Though in her favour it had to be said that she was always cheerful, knew her faults, never created "scenes" and never dried up. It was too bad about the playwright, of course, or an inexperienced actor playing opposite who had no idea where the dialogue was going or when he would get his cue.

So grandma had accurately assessed mother's potential long before she even set foot, professionally that is, on the stage; she was no child prodigy; she couldn't remember her lines; and on top of all that, she was fat. But there was no-one else to play the part and grandma had given her word. So the lines were relentlessly drilled into mother's head, her excessive puppy fat was laced in or disguised as much as possible, and she was warned that if she didn't make a decent job of the role she would get thumped. For myself I could never imagine grandma being violent under any circumstances, but mother swears the threat was made and she earnestly believed it would be carried out.

Opening night then, the play got under way, mother remembered her lines and acquitted herself in an acceptable fashion until she reached the part where Oliver, in this particular version, escapes from the Beadle and the workhouse. To do this mother had to climb through a window and make her escape out onto the stage. The window was quite low, but to allow easy access a box had been placed behind it. And so, at the given time, in the semi-darkness, with the audience holding their breath in case the Beadle would creep up behind Oliver and *pounce*, mother carefully stood on the box, took a firm hold of the frame, put a short, stocky leg outside the window and then … *got stuck.*

Well … the idea of poor, frightened, under-nourished little Oliver escaping from the misery and deprivations of the workhouse and getting stuck in a window of reasonable proportions would have been more than even a sympathetic audience could have been expected to swallow. And of course professionally it was a situation that could not be tolerated, indeed could not be allowed to take place. So grandma, who had followed mother's every line and move and was in fact standing behind her at that precise moment, immediately took hold of mother's other leg, the one still inside the window, put a hand on her generous bottom, and pushed. Mother fell out of the window, sprained her ankle and had to hobble through the rest of the play in considerable pain.

However, nothing like that happened during her first number in Pettigoe (The Fates had got me in their sights). Her act went down a treat and she took her bow, blew a kiss to the boys at the back, skipped off, quickly removed her hat and boa and then, in a more sedate manner, returned and begged for silence.

"Thank you. And now, ladies and gentlemen, I want to introduce the youngest member of our company, Ireland's greatest young comedian, Wee Jim. On his first night, however, instead of one of his usual comic numbers, which I hope you will hear another time, he would like to sing for you one of your own very dear old favourites – *The Rose of Tralee*. So, ladies and gentlemen ... Wee Jim."

Mother made her exit Left. I walked on Right, dressed in long black trousers, a sort of waistcoat with sleeves, and a white blouse with a black bow tie. I bowed to the audience, clasped my hands in front of me in the time-honoured tradition, and with a quick look out of the corner of my eye to make sure mother was in the wings in case I got off on the wrong key (she was there), began my song.

> "The pale moon was rising above the green mountain.
> The sun was declining beneath the blue sea
> When I strayed with my love to the ..."

Suddenly a man's voice rang out from the back of the hall.

"That's a nice song, a very nice song young fella, but *you* can't sing it."

Heads turned, chairs creaked, there was a slight commotion somewhere in the vicinity of the doorway and then silence. The voice, of course, was my father's and this was part of our act. I waited a few moments until the heads turned back in my direction, then in true professional manner and without making any comment, started my song again, from the beginning.

"The pale moon was rising above the green mountain." I took a short breath and waited for the second interruption, but it didn't come, so I continued.

"The sun was declining beneath the blue sea." I paused again, waiting for the heckling that would bring father out into the aisle, up onto the stage and on with our act. But the hall was as silent as the grave. What on earth was he waiting for?

"When I strayed with my love to the pure crystal fountain ..." Nervously I glanced into the wings but mother had gone, grandma and grandad were obviously back in the dressing room, there was no sign of father and I was out there on my own.

"That stands in the beautiful vale of Tralee." Oh, why didn't he come in? Why didn't he shout? I didn't know the words of the second verse, I'd never had to sing more than a couple of lines before. He'd interrupted me at the beginning so why was he silent now? Was he talking to someone? Had he nipped out for a pee? Oh God, come to my aid, help me! But nobody was listening, except the audience. And the act must not collapse, the show must go on, so in desperation, facing what to me appeared to be total catastrophe, I started the song, yet again, from the beginning.

"The pale moon was rising above the green mountain." Immediately I could feel the unease of the audience. They knew the song better than I did, they sensed something was wrong, that I'd been put off, or forgotten my words. They were very sympathetic but nothing could conceal the fact that *they knew.*

"The sun was declining beneath the ..." Then came a voice out of heaven itself.

"No, no, no, young fellow." It was father, thank God, oh thank God, and I'll never forget to say my prayers again, never.

"I've been listening to you and you've quite a good little voice but ..." He climbed up on the stage and as he came towards me I noticed his tie was crooked, his hair stuck up at one side, and beyond the line of his greasepaint, at the back of his collar, his neck was quite red. But he was there, on stage, and the act could go on, developing along the lines that my voice was untrained, father was a hypnotist and with his help I could become a really great singer. I agree to the experiment, he hypnotises me, I sing (merely mime the words), and instead of a thin, uncertain treble voice, out into the auditorium pour the strong, rich, mellifluous notes of this beautiful soprano (my grandma standing in the wings). The payoff coming when the verse is finished, father takes the credit, and then grandma pokes her head on stage and calls out, "*Was that alright, Jimmy?*"

There was applause out in the hall but back in the dressing room there was righteous indignation.

"Where were you?" I challenged father. "Where were you? I didn't know the second verse. I had to sing the first verse all over again and they knew, *they knew.* Why didn't you come in?"

"Well," father was almost apologetic, which was very unusual for him, "when you started your song I *did* come in."

"I know, I know, I heard you. But after that?"

"Well after that I started to ease my way through the crowd standing at the back of the hall in order to get out to the aisle, when suddenly a long arm came in between two heads, a large hand took hold of me by the scruff of the neck, a deep voice growled in my ear, 'You leave the wee fella alone and let him get on wi' his song,' and I was outside the hall and the door was slammed in my face. *It was the R.U.C.*" The dressing room erupted, so loudly they must have heard it out in the hall. "It took me ages to get back inside and convince him it was all part of the act. And the rest of the time listening to his apologies."

After the variety the Actdrop was lowered, a brief announcement was made, *and then came THE PLAY.*

5

The Play

Culture was not a subject much discussed in my youth, indeed it was not a word I ever heard used, certainly not with regard to the plays we presented. Shakespeare, of course, would have been considered cultural, but we didn't offer Shakespeare (we'd have played to empty halls and died of starvation if we had); though both grandma and father had worked in Shakespearian companies, and even little Eileen could have quoted you a couple of lines, due to the fact that when father took his turn pacing the floor with her as a baby he recited whole speeches from *Hamlet* to lull her to sleep. For myself, apart from coming in on father's midnight soliloquies now and again, or having a few moral precepts (the only moral teaching father ever resorted to) like, "Who steals my purse steals trash", "Costly thy habit as thy purse can buy", or, his favourite, "This above all, to thine own self be true", positively directed at me, I had no experience of the Immortal Bard.

Shakespeare wrote for Elizabethan audiences, in the language of his day, and I came to him in my own good time and appreciated that what he had to say applied to all mankind. Though I often wondered, as actors had to live and audiences had to pay, just how much access the common people had to his philosophy even in his own time. For commoners like us, in our day, Shakespeare with his archaic language and tales of English kings and queens had little to offer. Audience and actors therefore had to come together and work in a medium, a culture, more suited to their needs. And I know there are people, more educated and more sophisticated people, who would say that the word culture should be reserved for a process that aims at something ethereal, high-minded, and does not concern itself with mere entertainment. But *was* what we provided mere entertainment? And if so, where did the material originate? And more important still, as the theatrical experience is a live one, did the audiences bring no sense of history, no personal experience ... did they not react and give life, meaning and relevance to something that was not just an event but part of a living process? Well, I can tell you the answer to that. I *will* tell you the answer to that, in due course, because at one point, with one play, the audience left us, the actors, in no doubt at all about their idea of values and their awareness of culture when they found themselves participating in a cultural process that was totally alien to their own.

The plays in our repertoire, and our attitude to what was in those plays, didn't develop in a vacuum. We, the playactors, came from a variety of backgrounds, and we were travelling people, as were all the other small companies that toured Northern Ireland at the time. Though, strangely enough, when I come to think about it, we only once, in my few years' experience, ran across another Fit-up company. Either we were among the last on the road, or father planned and skilfully avoided competition of any sort. I'm inclined to the former idea because the economics of our life left us with very little choice of movement, either we moved on as far as our limited resources would permit, or we went back, but move somewhere we must. And as we moved we carried our past with us. And not just *our* past!

The Source

Companies like ours drew their material (though of course where we worked had a positive influence on our work) from two different sources, and embraced two quite separate traditions: The Legitimate Theatre, so-called because at one time you had to have a licence to produce plays, and your productions were subject to scrutiny by the Lord Chamberlain; and the Music Hall, which seemed to have a much freer hand, though I've no doubt the City Fathers and the Church expressed their opinions on what went on there from time to time. The Legitimate Theatre, and we still considered ourselves as essentially that, had been the preserve of the upper classes until the Industrial Revolution got well under way. The Music Hall catered for the people down below. Both traditions flourished in the cities, and then as time went on and the middle classes prospered, were carried out by repertory companies into southern towns and flourishing holiday resorts. They did not, however, reach up into the industrial areas of the north until the Portable Theatre, at the end of the last century, started to operate among the miners; and probably about the same time the Fit-ups (the last word in mobility) began to pioneer the rural areas, the Highlands and the uncharted territories beyond.

The Culture

Both groups, therefore, carried with them not just the plays and the culture they represented from the cities, but the entertainment that was offered in the Music Hall, the culture in fact of the working class. A culture that travelled well. Indeed, Londoners, cockneys who had never moved away from the sound of Bow Bells, could recite monologues, sing songs, and tell you jokes they'd got from places of entertainment like Collins Music Hall in Islington, while the audiences we played to in village halls in remote parts of Ulster were laughing, crying and enjoying exactly the same fare, the same culture. A culture that, now it embraced the traditions of the Legitimate Theatre as well, was very much concerned with morals, values and the problems of the day. For the most part Victorian morals, values and problems of course, clearly set out in plays like *East Lynne* – where the wife of a respectable gentleman, though seduced by an upper-class scoundrel, is banished from the family home. So terrible was the sin of adultery rated at the time, her only child dies in her arms and is not even allowed to recognise that the woman who nurses him is his mother.

The standards were clear and unmistakable, but they were not absolute. Transformation was already taking place. Indeed, before grandma joined us, when she was playing in England, the company she worked for put on *East Lynne* but played it (her terminology) "backwards". That is, though they played the play straight, no messing about with the plot or dialogue, in the casting they selected the biggest man in the company to play Little Willie, the smallest to play the local cop, and so on.

We didn't consider our audience had reached that sophisticated stage yet. They got *East Lynne* exactly as it was intended. And so when – pale-faced and lying in the arms of a veiled governess who was in fact my mother (both on stage and off), I coughed my last, dropped my head, and the distraught woman threw back the veil from her face and cried out, "Willie! Willie! Speak to me ... Speak to me ... He's gone ... Dead, dead *and never called me mother*" – there were cries of real anguish from the women in the audience, and even the farm-hands shuffled their boots, sniffed and cleared their throats. They identified, even though the characters were not of their country or class. They accepted the play, the plot and the standards. Though it has to be said that the levels, the depths, the standards of many of the plays presented were every bit as questionable, and biased, representing one class or one shade of opinion, as they are today. But then economic pressures applied in those days as they do now. *We* couldn't afford to pay Royalties. We already had to pay, or were supposed to pay, Entertainment Tax on every ticket we sold. And of course the amount of material, the plays, available to us *free of cost*, was enormous.

The Plays

Over one thousand plays – "Free acting drama for the representation of which there is no legal charge" – could be purchased, cost one penny per play, from Dicks Standard Plays, situated off The Strand in London. This list included *East Lynne*, *Uncle Tom's Cabin*, *The*

Colleen Bawn, *The Shaughraun*, *The Octoroon*, *Hard Times*, *Frankenstein*, *Sally in our Alley*, *Ten Nights in a Bar Room* and *The Maid of the Mill*, etc. Another source, though not quite so readily available in the form required by the theatre, was provided by The Daisy Bank Productions of Manchester. Here, for threepence per copy (inflation had even got to the Penny Dreadfuls) you could obtain a fully detailed account of the life, or life and criminal trial of Charles Peace, Maria Marten, Crippen, Maria Monk or Burke and Hare. And from these pamphlets a writer or professional actor could easily knock-up a play, based on a real live happening, one that had already taken hold of the public's imagination. Indeed father and his juvenile lead once, while touring in Lowland Scotland, sat up for two days and nights, illuminated by candlelight, fortified by bottles of beer, and turned out a play so "red hot" that when they presented it a weekly newspaper, which just happened to be running a remarkably similar story at the same time, threatened to sue. In father's defence, when confronted by the paper's representative, he put forward the claim that this was a "free country", adding very quickly, however, that in his opinion the play would probably help the paper to sell *even more copies*! The play was a success and the paper didn't sue.

*

Back in the smoke-filled, body-heated, cheerful atmosphere of the village hall in Pettigoe it didn't appear as though, apart from the R.U.C. incident, we were likely to have any trouble at all. We had moved *The Mormon Peril* to Friday and the audience laughed their heads off at *Cattle Smuggling on the Border*, a play specially written by father. They thoroughly appreciated also his comic verses on the same theme, and when they got the hang of it, heartily joined in the chorus of a parody set to the music of that fine old sentimental ballad, *Springtime in Old Ireland*. This number was presented by me, dressed in long baggy trousers, a cloth cap and carrying a blackthorn stick. It went something like this:

"Round the corner in the Free State near the Border,
Stands a heifer that is known as Mary Jane,
And a bull known by the name of Beefy Barney
With their drover they are waiting down the lane, oh the la … ne."

Chorus:

"When it's night time on the Border we will get the heifer through
Twill be payday in North Ireland but not for the Rev … en … ue.
Oh, my great big Beefy Barney
In spite of P.C. Carney
When it's night time on the Border we will fetch your fa … mil … eee."

The play had everything the audience wanted: Old feuds raised, old scores settled, adventure, love across the divide (the geographical not the religious), and what enchanted them most, it ended with the Customs and Excise officers thwarted, and the decent ordinary citizens of the town (the smugglers) coming out on top.

The Man who Won the Irish Sweep also went down very well. I've a feeling this too was written by my father, but I'm not sure. It was about an ordinary working man who wins a fortune, gets above himself, loses all his real friends, gathers round him a parcel of parasites and snobs, and is miserable until he sees the light, gives up his airs and pretences, and returns again to the real values and the genuine old friends of his youth. What he did with the money, if there was any left, I can't remember.

Ten Nights in a Bar Room was another thoroughly successful play and one with a very high moral tone. It's set in England. The hero, Joe, a working man who has taken to drink, squandered his money, lost his job and neglected his family, is on the way to rack and ruin until he is saved, dramatically, by *me*.

The crucial scene is the inside of a pub filled with a drunken mob, which includes Joe who now, without even the price of a drink, is having serious trouble with the publican. Back at home, as we have seen in a previous short scene, the cold, hunger and misery experienced by his family has reached such a point that Joe's little boy, even though it is snowing and he has no coat and holes in his shoes, leaves his mother and baby sister and goes out searching until he finds the pub where his father is drinking. Joe is practically on his knees begging for alcohol when the door is eased open, all heads turn, and there in the doorway stands the child who, in a small, plaintive voice, and through the medium of a song, begs his father to come home.

"Oh father, dear father, come home with me now.
The clock in the steeple strikes one.
You promised, dear father, that you would come home
As soon as the day's work was done.
Come home … Come home … Oh father, dear father, come home."

Joe is touched, ashamed, and then angry as his drinking companions taunt him with being henpecked, and so he shouts at the boy.

"Go home. Get back to your mother. *Home!*" Dejectedly, and wiping the tears from my eyes, I leave the stage. Joe turns, picks a fight with the barman, throws a bottle which misses and goes hurtling off stage. There is a thud, the sound of breaking glass (I drop a small tin tray loaded with bits of metal), a cry of pain, and then, blood pouring from a terrible gash on my forehead, I stagger back into the pub. I am seriously hurt. And the tragedy doesn't end there because of course in the next scene I die. However, this brings Joe to his senses and he signs The Pledge, gets another job, becomes a respectable citizen and they all live happily ever after. The audience adored the play, and as half the population of Northern

Ireland, then as now, was strictly Tee Total, they found the message most reassuring. I just found it sad. But not nearly as sad as *Darby and Joan*.

It's strange but I never got used to, never managed to distance myself from the emotions in our plays. I suppose that's why I never became much of an actor and took on the role of observer instead. No matter how many times I watched father, mother, or my grandparents from the wings, no matter how often I reminded myself that they were only acting, I still got deeply involved. The *idea* always seemed to get to me much more readily than the reality ... it still does. Of course, my family were professionals, they were good, and like the audience out front I accepted the thoroughly artificial nature of the theatre. I suspended my reason and voluntarily offered my imagination ... but then that's what audiences are supposed to do.

Darby and Joan, as far as I was concerned, was one of the saddest plays I had ever seen. Charles Armitage, the son of a local magnate, lends money to an elderly couple who own a small farm and cannot pay their mortgage. This ingratiates him with their only daughter whom he marries and then instructs never to go anywhere near her parents again. Not content with that, he also falsifies the I.O.U., increasing the amount, so that the old couple are ruined completely. And as though that piece of foul-mindedness wasn't enough, when he learns that his wife has gone secretly to visit her parents, and because she has no money of her own has given them an expensive ring to sell, he accuses them of theft. The old couple are turned off their land and out onto the open road. The old lady is ill, and the old man, in desperation, swallowing the last vestige of his pride, convinces his wife that their only hope now is to go to their son-in-law and beg for help.

The curtain rises on a scene set in the grounds of the villainous Charles (they were often called Charles for some reason or other). From the wings I watch grandma and grandad who play the old couple, hatless, coatless and leaning on each other, totter onto the stage. Grandma falls, she can go no further. Grandad gets down beside her and, in order to lift up her spirits, reminds her that they still have each other. Then they sing. And this just about finishes me ... my eyes fill, there's a lump in my throat, and how I am going to deliver my own lines I just don't know. The two quavering voices rise up, more or less together.

"Just like Darby and Joan
In a little world of our own
We'll build a nest, out in the west
Be it so humble we'll never grumble.
And when summer has flown
And the grey locks have shown,
Fates may betide us ... but true love will guide us,
Just like Darby and Joan."

Almost before they can finish, father, tall, arrogant and with a heartless sneer on his face, strides in and demands they get off his land and take their scurrilous bodies elsewhere. The old man begs for shelter. Father is adamant. The daughter comes in (mother) and *she* begs for shelter. He won't move. Finally, the grandchild enters (although in the play I don't know they are my grandparents) and pleads:

"Father, please help these poor old people."

Charles weakens (what passes for weakness in his book), and as we are all standing in the stables by that time, says they can spend the night there.

"But father," I point out, "it is cold in the stables."

"Well, there's a horse blanket over there, give them that."

"Yes father." I walk across the stage, take up a position half way between father and the helpless old souls, lift up the blanket and then, instead of giving it to the old couple, I proceed to tear it in two. Father protests.

"I said give them the blanket."

"I intend to, father."

"So why are you tearing it in two?"

"Well, father, they are cold and so I will give them this half of the blanket to keep them warm. The other half I will keep to give to you when you are old and cold as they are."

Curtain. And oh, dear God, the loud unrestrained sobbing that rose up on the other side of the curtain nearly annihilated me. But there was reconciliation, a happy ending, everybody was pleased, and on Friday night we did something totally different: *The Mormon Peril.*

Now a play about religion you might think would cause at least a week's rioting if presented anywhere, at any time, in Ireland. But father reasoned that it wasn't *their* religion, and it had a very exciting plot. Incidentally, this was one of the very few plays that actually had the name of the author on the script. It must have been a fairly modern work, although I hope the author was dead at the time. Dead a long time too, because I never heard anything about Royalties. But then that wasn't my concern. The play was set in an industrial town in Lancashire and so Lancastrian accents were needed which was no problem to us, and which we considered would give our audiences a "taste of the exotic", something they usually enjoyed. The period was just before the First World War and the plot dealt with current prejudices against the Mormon faith. So, if there are any genuine believers of that faith reading this account at the moment, I would like to make it clear that I wasn't even in the play. And also, if racial and religious discrimination had been a crime in those days nearly everybody would have been locked up in jail.

The heroine is a Lancashire lass who wants to get married but is desperately trying to raise money in order to procure an operation for her mother who is going blind. She meets an American, Mr Silas Hooker, who is in England on business matters. He is an Elder of the Mormon Church and as such is only too pleased to explain the more attractive aspects of his religion. He is also willing to come up with the money for the operation, providing (he is also a business man) the young woman agrees to work for one year as a secretary (not a millhand, mark you) in his textile firm in the U.S.A. She jumps at the opportunity, pays for the operation, leaves her fiance, catches the boat from Liverpool and ends up in Salt Lake City *where* ... to her horror she finds out, when the small print on the agreement is read out to her, that she has in fact sold her soul to the Mormons and her body to a man who already has more wives than King Solomon. There is no escape; she has taken the money, signed the paper, given her word, and she now stands alone and defenceless in a darkened room awaiting her lord and master (who declares she is the Soulbride of a Mormon!) to claim his rights.

Now how would you expect the audience in a village hall, in the heart of Christian Ireland, in the days before even "the villains of the silent screen" had flickered across their consciousness, to react to goings-on like that?

*

"Cut it out!" A tall figure rose up out of the darkness of the auditorium and pointed an accusing finger at the couple on the stage. The actors froze, then the man, about to reach out for the woman, dropped his hands.

"That's enough!" A second figure rose up and joined the first. "We won't have it."

"No, we won't have it." A full-blooded chorus from thirty or forty male voices backed up the protesters. The actors on stage glanced at each other then moved apart and waited for the uproar to die down. When it did, the first speaker, who was still on his feet, addressed them.

"I am the Member of Parliament for this area and I am now putting forward a formal protest on behalf of the people in this hall. We are horrified and disgusted by what we have seen up on that stage this evening. We do not want plays of that nature and so I demand on behalf of the people in this hall, and in this town, that this performance be stopped immediately. *Now!*"

There was applause, confirmation, and the stamping of feet as the Member of Parliament sat down. The actor on stage (actor, manager and boss) indicated to the actress playing opposite that she should leave, which she did, straightened his tie, adjusted his jacket, then moved down towards the footlights to confront the audience.

"Ladies and gentlemen, it would appear that in presenting this play of ours this evening we have offended some of you."

"You have offended *all* of us." Another speaker rose up from a different part of the hall. "I am a councillor on the U.D.C., and I would like to say that I fully support our M.P. What we have seen up there this evening is thoroughly disgraceful and we will not have it."

"But sir ..." Father was determined to make a stand. There were the night's takings to consider, the venues that lay ahead, and besides, the choice of play had been his. "With respect, this is a very well-known, well-tried, highly-acclaimed play and we have got through to the beginning of the second act! What part of the play has given you offence?"

"*All of it.*"

"Well, if that really is the case, all I can say as manager of the company is that I am sorry, and if you care to make your way to the paybox at the back of the hall I will see that your money …"

"NO, NO, NO!" The hall rose as one man … and one woman.

Father stood his ground still protesting. "But ladies and gentlemen, ladies and gentlemen, this play has been passed by the Lord Chamberlain himself."

"*We will not have it.*"

"It was written by a highly skilled, much respected playwright … has been produced in London and played all over England …"

The M.P. took the floor again and shouted above the din.

"It may well have been played in London, and it may well be fit for the people across the channel, but it is not fit for *us* and we will not have it."

"*No, we will not have it. We will not have it.*" The floor and the ceiling of the town hall vibrated to the sound of harsh voices, hard hands and heavy boots. Father waited and when he could make himself heard had one last try.

"Very well, ladies and gentlemen. Your Member of Parliament and your esteemed Councillor have, in a dignified and democratic manner, expressed views on your behalf. Now I would like to try and resolve this problem by following the example they have set. I would like to take a vote on the matter."

"Right. Take a vote. Go ahead, take a vote."

"How many of you out there in the audience would like us to continue with the play?"

Not a hand. Not a vote.

"Then it's off." Father looked up, the curtain came down, and as the audience roared their approval he made a rapid exit and joined the rest of the cast who were huddled together in the wings. After a few moments, when the noise had diminished, or at least acquired a less menacing tone, he came back out in front of the Actdrop. The audience immediately hushed and waited to see what he had to say.

"Ladies and gentlemen, I would like to say on behalf of myself and the rest of the company that it was never our intention to upset or offend anyone in this hall, or in this town. We are actors and have come here hoping to earn your patronage, your good will, and to provide you with entertainment of the highest order. We appear to have failed in our duty this evening and so … in order that you do not leave this hall disappointed, and in order that we will not be denied the pleasure of your company now and in the future, if you will be patient for another few minutes, we will change the scenery, change our costumes and present you with another play … *The Monkey's Paw.*"

*

The incident just recounted did not, as you may or may not have guessed, take place in the village of Pettigoe. And the play at the root of the matter was not *The Mormon Peril* but another play, by another playwright, entitled *Other Men's Wives*. In a copy of the "Belfast Telegraph" dated, Monday, 15th December 192*, with the heading:

"Irate Theatregoers
Other Men's Wives annoys (the town of) X
We won't have it ..."

you will find a full report, together with the names of the M.P., the Councillor, the company and the town where all this took place. Oddly enough, though it makes sense if you understand your audience, the keen theatregoers of that town had seen on the two previous nights: *Maria Marten*, a play about a young woman who is seduced, made pregnant, strangled and buried in a barn; and *The Ripper*, a tale about a psychopath (the Whitechapel murders) who tracked down women of easy virtue and in his own time and for his own amusement carved them up. Here too, there had been murmurings but, as the "Belfast Telegraph" reported: "... and though there had been some adverse comments in the town anent [against] these productions, no steps were taken by the audience ... On Saturday night however it was evident from the beginning that *Other Men's Wives* was not meeting with favour ..."

The play, modern and sophisticated, was about adultery, as the title suggests. As such it was considered a flagrant attack on the sanctity of marriage, and the good citizens of that town would not tolerate it.

The Mormon Peril, on the other hand, as presented by us in Pettigoe in the more recent past, was a success. Father was perfectly right, it wasn't *their* religion. Besides, everything came right in the end because two friends of Lillian (the white slave) who had smelt a rat from the beginning, followed their friend out to Utah, infiltrated the Mormon community, thwarted the lecherous Elder, Silas B. Hooker, and "browt lass safely back te Deepdale, where ... an' ah'll tell thee summat for nowt ... she got married and lived happily ever after".

We ate well in the small border town of Pettigoe, had nice dry, clean beds and made friends. And on the morning of our departure, when I came down to my porridge and found that the whole household was buzzing with the news that a herd of cattle had been pushed across the border the previous night, right alongside our hall, and were now safely grazing in green fields somewhere in the North, my cup simply ran over.

I flew out of the house, raced across the border without saying "good morning" to the man in the Customs Office, got down to the river alongside the hall, and sure enough ... *footmarks, hoofmarks!* The muddy river bed was churned up and covered with the signs of last night's activity … cattle, smugglers, and some even larger footmarks which I presumed were made by the R.U.C. I was thrilled! Though my spirits dipped sharply when, back in the town, I learnt that only half a dozen scrawny cows had crossed the river at that point and were immediately pounced on and impounded by the Customs men who were lying in wait. But they soared again when our informant added that, of course, a *bigger* herd of really first-class beasts had been safely smuggled across the border on the same night, only a bit further down-stream.

I was happy in Pettigoe and didn't want to leave the town or the river. But it was time to move on, so we followed the lakes out to the Atlantic Ocean and then came back again to the village of Kesh where The Fates, and the evil that had been building up on account of *Sweeney Todd* – there was a jinx on the play – awaited our arrival.

6

Sweeney Todd and the Jinx

Schooling was always a problem for travelling people who had children. Not that it seemed to worry father a great deal, he didn't appear to mind whether I went to school or not. Which was surprising considering his own mother had been a schoolteacher and he had been better educated than anybody else in the company. It may have been, as I was fairly bright, he thought education would take place naturally, by means of osmosis! I can't think he wanted me to grow up an illiterate! Quite the reverse, because when I first drew his attention to the fact that I had acquired some literary skill by pointing to, and reading from, a large advertisement for stout which had the caption *Guinness Is Good For You*, he was delighted and told everyone. Still, the decision as to whether I went to school or not, he left, like everything else to do with us kids, to my mother. She too had a better academic education than I ever got because she lived permanently with her grandmother during part of her childhood; and even went on to a "finishing school". Father was very amused about the "finishing school" and remarked more than once that it did mother no good at all. He added that he wouldn't have expected it to do her any good, and that anybody other than my grandma, who had paid for the education and was determined to make something out of mother, would have known that the only thing likely to get finished during an operation like that would have been the school. Mother was no more interested in my being educated than was father. *Her* main concern was that we didn't appear different to other children, and that she was never disgraced by having to confront a Schools Inspector and explain my non-attendance.

Going to school, as far as I was concerned – and I calculated that by the time I was nine I had attended fifty-nine of them – was just one of those unpleasant things that had to be endured, like having your hair washed and water poured in your ears and soap poked in your eyes or up your nose. Every time we moved and the prospect of yet another school, another teacher, another classroom of grinning, leering faces, loomed ahead I prayed for at least one of the following: that the school was a protestant one and had closed early (before July 12th) for the summer holidays; or it was catholic and had worked through the Twelfth and so had a longer holiday at the other end; or that it was autumn, "potato gathering" time, and *both* schools were off for at least a week; or if all else failed that I was ill. And I had my fair share of complaints in those days I can tell you: measles, scarlet fever, whooping cough, ringworm, and for a long time cut hands and battered knees that wouldn't heal. I really couldn't see the sense in my going to school. I'd learnt to read without their assistance. My grandma taught me to sing when I lived with her for a while just after my sister was born. Mother showed me how to move on the stage. And because of father I had a fair vocabulary and could talk my way into and out of most difficult situations. It was an unnecessary worry, although I had to admit some schools were better than others, and some teachers ...! Well, again Kesh came up with some interesting variations regarding teachers, schools and digs.

To begin with, we already knew Mrs McNally who was offering to put us up in her cottage which stood some little way out of the village. "Us" being mother, father, Eileen and myself. And Mrs McNally had children who went to school which to me was a genuine blessing because mother never introduced me to my latest school or teacher, I just had to turn up and introduce myself. In Kesh, therefore, even if they hadn't broken up for the summer holidays, and there was every likelihood that they had, I'd have friends and we could all go off to school together. So I was quite hopeful when we turned up on a Thursday afternoon (we had to leave our previous hall half way through the week because of some local function) and met the entire McNally family, goats, chickens and all. Though at the beginning it looked as though we were going to have a problem regarding the school, or rather regarding one of the teachers.

"Maybe we could find somewhere else for a day or two?" Mother, as usual, was in charge of negotiations, although father, for some reason or other, was also present but stood outside on the doorstep cleaning his pipe.

"Not at all, not at all," Mrs McNally protested.

"But how can you manage?"

"Don't you worry about how I can manage."

"We could easily go into the village you know."

"Now you talk about going into the village and you'll upset me."

"Well, that's the last thing I would want to do, but ... you have your own family to think of."

"Now listen, I've worked it all out. It's only for two nights and then Maureen here will be away home."

"That's right." A beautiful young woman who I had never seen before came out of the bedroom and joined in the discussion.

Harry Wynn (Grandad)
A Black Belt, a Heavy, and a most terrifying Sweeny Todd

Louie Bates (Grandma)

1914-1918. While her man goes to war grandma takes his place on the home front

Jim with his grandparents

"Then you can have *her* bedroom."

"Well, that's most kind of you, but I still don't see …"

"Then listen and I'll tell you. Now!" Mrs McNally took the floor. "Me and Pat (her husband) will take the baby and wee John in with us. Jeannie and Margaret, my other wee girls, can go up to the loft … we'll make them a bed on the floor … we've done it before, they love it. Then you and your husband can have the children's room … there's space for the cot for your own wee girl. And Maureen here says that your wee boy can sleep with her."

Father suddenly took an interest in the proceedings and entered the kitchen, while the young lady, who must have been in her very early twenties, smiled, stretched out her arm and laid a hand on the top of my head.

"You won't mind sleeping with me for a couple of nights will you, Jimmy?"

"Oh no … no." The idea didn't appeal to me at all. I didn't like sleeping with other people, but one had to sleep somewhere and above all one had to be polite.

"Now that really is most kind of you." Mother was exceedingly grateful.

"Not at all." The young lady removed her hand from my head and put a protective arm round my shoulders. "School breaks up tomorrow and on Saturday I'll be away to my own home for the holidays. It's no hardship. Indeed, it'll be quite an experience," she looked across at Mrs McNally who grinned, "having a young man in my bed."

Father took his cue, pretended to be uncertain, and enquired, "And is this an experience you're likely to extend … I mean, is it an invitation you're likely to offer …?"

"No it's not." The young woman blushed.

"Don't be so rude," mother reprimanded. She then turned to the landlady. "Aren't men awful?"

"Oh, terrible," Mrs McNally laughed, "terrible." Then everybody laughed though I didn't think it funny. And to my embarrassment father didn't leave it at that.

"So you're the schoolteacher then?"

"One of them." The poor lady had gone quite red.

"And this young fellow," father looked down at me, "would be a pupil in your class?"

"That's right." To cover her confusion she began to fuss over me. "And tomorrow I'll take him in with me and introduce him to the rest of my wee gang. You'd like that, wouldn't you, Jimmy?" This was another idea that didn't appeal to me, but again I was polite.

"Oh yes."

"Well, I don't know," father turned and looked at Mrs McNally, "I've heard of pupils taking apples to their teacher but going to *bed* with them …!"

There was more laughter and jokes and I wished father would give up and go away. But there was worse to follow because the next day John McManus, our juvenile lead at the time, and father, got together and threw handfulls of grass in through the schoolteacher's window which landed on her bed. I was ashamed. I had never seen my father behave in such a silly fashion before. Oh, he had faults, he was quick-tempered and he drank a bit, but I never saw him chase after women. Though he was a handsome man, he'd been a dandy and known lots of girls in his youth, my aunt told me. But he was married now, and this was silly. It never occurred to me that the young teacher might have felt flattered or even got enjoyment out of the game. And anyhow, shortly after the incident I myself was fully occupied with another young female, Jeannie, the landlady's eldest daughter who was about my age but much more experienced in the ways of the world. Jeannie led me down to the end of the garden to see the goats and the chickens, then up to the loft where she showed me her bed, explained the facts of life, particularly the differences between wee boys and wee girls, and later that week took me for a long walk. A walk that nearly brought one young career to a very tragic end.

Jeannie and I became very close friends and I had no objection at all to playing doctors and nurses and getting to know her intimately. But going to bed with the beautiful young schoolteacher was another thing entirely. On the first night I edged so far across the bed, so that her body wouldn't touch mine, that I lay against the wall which was cold, and woke up a couple of times. Although I was fast asleep when the young lady came to bed, and up in the morning and away to my mother's bedroom to wash and dress before she was even awake. On the second night I kept clear of the wall and went to sleep almost immediately. Although I was conscious, at some point, of the teacher pulling the bedclothes round my shoulders, very carefully, very gently; she sensed that I didn't like being touched. The following morning was Saturday and by then I was getting quite used to the sleeping arrangements. Indeed we were both sitting up in bed chatting away when there was a knock on the door and in came Mrs McNally with a tray.

"Breakfast!"

"Great!" The young lady took hold of the tray and laid it partly on her lap and partly on mine.

"For me too?" I looked at the two cups and saucers with amazement.

"For you too."

"A boiled egg." Mrs McNally and the young lady laughed.

"This is marvellous." I'd never had breakfast in bed in my life. Apart from once when I was ill and didn't want anything to eat.

"Isn't it now? Hold onto the tray." Maureen leaned across, eased me forward and made the pillow comfortable at my back. Her arms were bare and sunburnt. Her body was warm. And there was lace all round the top of her nightie.

What a breakfast! And what a tragedy that youth, as somebody once said, is wasted on children and fools.

*

Opening night in Kesh and the hall was packed to the door. The audience knew the sort of entertainment we would provide, they knew us, and there was nothing but excitement and boisterous good humour out front. Backstage in the dressing room, however, things were different. There had been words, and now there was an uncomfortable silence as we made-up and got ready for the show. Mother at the card table sullenly poked a hairpin into a small jar of solid eye make-up, ran it through the flame of the lighted candle and applied it to her lashes. Grandad, seated on his camp stool and using their costume basket as a table, rubbed in number five and stared hard at his reflection in the mirror. Father was by the door while grandma, who had completed her own make-up and dressing, was at the other end of the room attending to me. I could make myself up, apart from the finishing touches, and I had already rubbed in the boiled lard we used as a foundation, worked in the white number five and the flesh coloured number nine, but then either mother or grandma had to finish off my eyes, mouth, and in this case give me a red nose. I can't remember what words had passed between my father and mother, or what led up to the outbreak, but suddenly, without any warning, father said, "And by the way, *Sweeney Todd* is off."

Off! Everybody turned and looked at him in amazement.

"I'll think of something else to put in its place."

"But what ...? Why? That's outrageous!" Grandad was incensed. Not just because father had suddenly sprung the news on the company, but because *Sweeney Todd* was his favourite play and the part of the infamous barber his star role.

"And just why is it off?" Mother laid both hands on the table.

"None of your bloody business," came the reply.

"Well, I think it is some of my bloody business." Mother swung round to confront father but as she did so grandma called out from the other side of the room.

"Lily!"

"But he can't just say it's off," mother protested.

"Lily!" Grandma didn't raise her voice, but mother took heed and didn't say anything further. Grandad, however, wasn't going to be silenced.

"But Lily's quite right. He can't just take it off."

"Now Harry," grandma spoke softly but firmly. She was always the peacemaker, always the voice of reason at times like this. Grandad, however, was very angry.

"But Louie, it's one of the best, the greatest dramas ever staged. And what's more," he turned and jabbed a finger in father's direction, "it's on the bill."

"Then we'll take it off the bill." Father calmly brushed some talcum powder off the sleeve of his jacket.

"But this is outrageous, outrageous." Grandad started to his feet but grandma reached out and laid a hand on his shoulder.

"Sit *down* Harry."

"But Louie, what about the cast ... the company?"

"*Sit down!*" Again her voice was low but it had the ring of authority and grandad couldn't ignore it, so he sat down. Grandma then continued in a quiet, soothing, reassuring manner. "There is no need for tempers and histrionics from either of you two." She looked at mother and then back to grandad. "If Bob has decided to cancel the play, then I'm quite sure he has very good reasons."

"What reasons?" enquired grandad.

"Well, at the moment I don't know, but I'm quite sure he wouldn't take this action without considering the matter thoroughly. After all *Sweeney Todd*," she beamed light and reason across the room, "as we all know is a very popular play."

"Too damned popular," father responded.

"But it is also," grandma admitted, "a very unlucky play. We've had quite a few unfortunate incidents recently."

"Disasters you mean," mother corrected. Grandma glared at her but went on sweetly.

"And we actors don't like tempting The Fates, do we Robert?"

"That's got nothing to do with it," father retorted. But it had. Grandma had hit the mark. Actors believe in The Fates and so take whatever action is necessary to avoid incurring their wrath. Grandma once gently reproved me for whistling in the dressing room. Ladies were not allowed to knit in that part of the theatre either. And even father, who instantly smashed down any suggestion of magic, extra-sensory or Spiritualist powers (and grandma, as it happened, was a Spiritualist) wouldn't mention the title of a play, if it came in the dialogue, before the opening night. Actors are very superstitious, but then so are fishermen, farmers and anyone whose living depends on the vagaries of the weather and the humours of their fellow mortals. But father wouldn't admit the jinx had anything to do with his plans to cancel the play. He simply ended the discussion by saying, "I'll think of another play," and left the room.

Grandad immediately hit the basket with both fists, jumped to his feet and began to pace the room like an animal in pain. "It's outrageous, outrageous. Sheer damned, pigheaded arrogance." Grandma smiled gently, stood back and let him get on with his act. Grandad's face was streaked with number nine – he hadn't finished his make-up – and he looked just like a Red Indian on the warpath. "Not a hint, not a word, not the slightest intimation … Just off … *off!* And it's one of the finest plays ever put on the stage Louie. I've played the part of Sweeney Todd in theatres, *real* theatres, not tin huts and chicken houses, in Reading, Bristol, Nottingham, Dundee …" He stopped opposite the card table. "By God Lily, I've had the audience on the edge of their seats, I have knocked them in the aisles. Some of them actually told me they were so terrified they couldn't go out in the yard, or even into their bedrooms alone after the performance. This is a crime against the theatre Lily, a crime against the profession."

"I know dad, I know," mother took out a Park Drive and leaned towards the candle, "but it's not just the play. To be frank, I don't care what he puts on or takes off, what gets me is that he never *tells* you, never considers anybody else, and he should, he *ought* to. I've a damned good mind …" She half rose but again grandma's voice rang out.

"… to stay where you are and keep quiet."

"But mam, we can't let him walk all over us."

"Now listen, and you too Harry." Grandma nodded in the direction of the door. "I see our juvenile lead had the good sense to clear off before all this started."

"Yes, and what about him mam? He's in the company, he's in the cast, what about John?"

"Listen to me." Grandma moved down stage centre. "In the first place it's Bob's company and he can do as he pleases."

"He *can't* do as he pleases," mother shouted.

"Keep your voice down. It's enough to have a wild Irishman to deal with, but a fishwife for a daughter is something I will not tolerate. As I said, Bob is the boss and if you argue you'll simply get into a row and then your dad and me will get drawn in."

"But why doesn't he *tell* us?" mother complained.

"And what's he got against *Sweeney Todd*?" grandad growled.

"Well, my belief is that he considers the play unlucky."

Grandad snorted.

"It is unlucky Harry, and I think that's the reason, but he won't admit it. And anyway," grandma went on, "fighting or nagging will only make matters worse. My advice is to say nothing. We've got a whole week and when I can get him in a more reasonable frame of mind …"

Grandad whipped off his glasses and stared in disbelief. "You'll never get that man in a more reasonable frame of mind Louie."

"When I get him in a more reasonable frame of mind I'll have a quiet word and see if I can get him to change his mind. In the meantime say nothing, to anybody. If I find either of you getting at Bob, or trying to drag in young John, you'll hear from me. Leave it!"

"Aaaagh!" grandad sat down and went on with his make-up. "Bloody arrogant Irishmen!"

"*Beginners!*" Father poked his head in at the doorway. "Come on Wee Jim." I quickly followed him out to the side of the stage where he instructed John to pull up the curtain, and then went on and announced my number. The audience gave me a round of applause when I made my appearance in tartan trews, waistcoat, glengarry, a gnarled stick, and of course a red nose. The song was one I'd learnt from a comedian who had once worked with our company. He was a Scot who drank a great deal and had a habit of collapsing in the doorway of pubs gasping "Brandy! Brandy!" And he often got it too, free. As usual I sang unaccompanied.

> "When I was but a little laddie years and years ago,
> My mother used to dress me up in kilties don't you know.

But later on my mother said, some trousers you must wear,
Dad's ould ones came in handy so she cut me down a pair."

Chorus (*and a march round the stage*)**:**

"Oh, I never shall forget that morning
I felt as proud as any millionaire
As I walked away to school to learn the golden rule
In the trousers that my father used to wear.

We had a master at our school, a man I used to hate,
One morning just for fun I drew his picture on my slate.
But when the master saw it he said, come out boy to me,
And then he gently turned me upside down upon his knee."

Chorus:

"Oh, I never shall forget that morning
He whacked me hard but still I didn't care.
I only had to grin at a great big sheet of tin
In the trousers that my father used to wear."

There were a few more verses about bulldogs and the girl next door and I got another hearty round of applause when I came off. John was next with a straight song, an Irish ballad, which went down very well with the girls. He was a very good-looking man was our juvenile lead, tall, broad shouldered, and lots of black curly hair. He was also a catholic, although not from Belfast but somewhere in Tyrone I think, and he knew all the old Irish songs like *Killeter Fair*, *The Ould Brown Knowe*, and the one he sang that night in Kesh (one I hadn't heard before), *The Old Bog Road*. I can't remember any of the verses now, indeed I can only call to mind a few odd unconsecutive lines, but the sound of his sweet, clear, true voice, and the simple sentiments expressed in his song I will never forget.

"My feet are here on Broadway this blessed harvest morn,
But oh the ache that's in them for the place where I was born.
My mother died last springtime when Ireland's fields were green
And the neighbours said her Waking was the finest ever seen.
There were snowdrops and primroses piled up beside her head
When they carried out her coffin down the Old Bog Road."

Oh, the silence in the hall. The emptiness outside. And the longing, the heartbreaking longing of the immigrant for somewhere … for something … something that never was.

After John, and the last number before the play, father went on and did one of his monologues. And his monologues were good. When he was on I was always over at the prompt side, down on my knees watching and listening to every word. Father liked reciting these ballads, and there weren't many things, as far as I could see, that made him happy. He enjoyed swimming of course, when that was possible, and Eileen always seemed able to cheer him up. But he didn't laugh or smile a great deal, unless he'd had something to drink. Doing his monologues, however, was something that gave him great satisfaction. Some of them were comic, some tragic, and some were very exciting. My favourites, and I knew many off by heart, were:

Gunga Din

"... 'e'll be squattin' on the coals
Giving drinks to poor damned souls
And I'll get a swig in hell from Gunga Din."

The Pigtail of Li Fang Fu

"... He was dead and his death was fearful
With features of ghastly hue
And snakelike around his throat was wound
The pigtail of Li Fang Fu."

Shannaghan's Ould Shebeen

"Shure this is the tale that Cassidy told
In his hall of sheen with purple and gold.
Told as he sat in an easy chair
Smoking cigars at a dollar a pair."

And the one that thrilled, chilled and enthralled me crouched in the wings, and the audience sitting silently out there in the darkness of the little hall in Kesh: *The Yukon Trail.*

Father announced his own number, turned aside for a moment, then moved out towards the audience. With his hands he drew pictures of desolate wastes, and with his voice lulled and lured us into his tale.

"By an old wood shack on the northern track
Where the snows of Alaska fall,
There are dead men's bones and the cold wind moans
With the howl of the wolves in counter tones,
And God's hand over all.

A lonely man staked out a claim that never seemed to pay,
When late one night a stranger came who had chanced to lose his way.
They supped and smoked and talked awhile and then a silence fell,
And each man thought of a woman's love and a woman's fond farewell."

It goes on to tell how the men discover they both love the same woman. They fight. One man is killed and the other, in digging his grave inside the hut discovers ... *gold!* He thrusts the body outside and frantically goes on with his digging.

"He could hear the sound of the wolves outside and trembled in every limb
As they fought and tore at the cabin door at the thing
That had breathed but a while before,
Then madness came to him.
A loaded gun, a muttered prayer, a shot that rent the startled air.
Then dawn came up and peeped in there by the lonely Yukon trail.

By an old wood shack on the northern track
Where the snows of Alaska fall,
There are dead men's bones and the cold wind moans
With the howl of the wolves in counter tones,
And God's hand over all.
There are two lives paid for a love betrayed
And the broken vows that a woman made
In a far off English vale."

7

The Jinx *continued*

On Monday night we presented *Hard Times*: a play about miners and poverty, mine-owners and greed, and the love that crosses boundaries and conquers all.

On Tuesday it was *Robbie Burns:* the life and loves of the Scottish poet with songs sung by John and poems recited by father. Father considered Burns the greatest poet ever, and the line "an honest man's the noblest work of God" as the truest saying ever said.

Wednesday it was *Trilby*: the well-known story about poets and painters living in the Latin Quarter of Paris. And about the "more handsome than beautiful" tone-deaf model, Trilby O'Ferrall, who is hypnotised into becoming a great opera singer by the wicked Svengali.

Thursday it was *The Face at the Window*: this was the tale of a murderer whose every attack was preceded by the sound of a wolf howling and the appearance at the victim's window of a deathly face. I played the face. The play ends when the detective who has relentlessly pursued the killer, tracks him to his lair, discovers his identity and finishes him off.

Friday it was *Sally in our Alley*: about a sweet Lancashire lass, my mother, who is tyrannised and in one scene flogged ("Offstage if you please Bob, and I'll yell as hard as you like") by her bruiser of a father, played by her better half. Grandma sang the song made famous by Gracie Fields. The play ends happily because Sally's lover stands up to the old man and they are allowed to get wed.

And finally, on Saturday night, we gave them ... *Sweeney Todd*!

Now, ever since father's announcement that the play was "off", nobody in the company had dared mention the subject. During the course of that week we just watched and waited but no alternative was given, the bills remained unchanged, and after Friday night's performance it was clear that father had changed his mind. So the jinx got to work.

Mother woke up on Saturday morning with a bad throat, though she didn't lose her voice. Grandma had an attack of neuralgia which stayed with her all day. Grandad complained of a bad back, a legacy from his wrestling days in the booths. And the only members of the family who appeared to be trouble-free were father and myself. But then, we were to be the principal actors in a short drama, or rather two short dramas, that somebody was busily writing "out there".

Of course, it would be silly to lay all the blame for what occurred at the feet of *Sweeney Todd*. The company, apart from John, had family problems, which wasn't surprising. Having your in-laws working, and in some cases living in the same room with you was hardly a recipe for happiness or marital success. And quite apart from that, father had taken a dislike to grandma even before she became his mother-in-law. Indeed even before he set eyes on the attractive young actress who, after a whirlwind romance, was to become his wife. It seems he had applied for a job with a repertory company that was touring somewhere in the north of England at the time. He was accepted, and in his first play found himself acting opposite an actress who had a lot more experience, and maybe talent, than he had himself. Grandma, unlike father, had been born into the business.

She had started her career in her mother's Portable theatre, working for a while alongside another young actor – who incidentally became mother's godfather and went on to make a name for himself – Will Fyffe. And during her time there her father, a musician called Bates (and grandma used her maiden name in the profession), taught her to sing and play the piano. After which he left the running of the theatre to his wife, a tough old lady by all accounts, and went off to conduct the orchestra at the Grand Theatre, Halifax, for ten years or so. Grandma, therefore, could sing and play several instrument, after a fashion. Not that her ability to sing or play the piano would have annoyed father in the slightest because he was tone deaf and couldn't sing a note. But she was not only a singer, musician and character actress, she was also a thoroughly dedicated professional like himself. He would never have admitted that of course, but on at least two occasions I overheard him telling people, who were not in the business, that his wife's mother had once worked in a theatre at West Bromwich (Staffs.) where the company stayed for thirty-six weeks, presenting four different plays a week. This meant, as he pointed out, going on stage in one play at night, having supper and reading through a new play into the small hours, sleeping for a while, rehearsing the new play in the afternoon, then after another couple of hours rest going on again at night and acting in a *third* play. I believe he secretly admired her, and his initial resentment may have been due to professional jealousy. Although mother maintained, and she always scratched beneath the barrel when looking for motives, that father disliked grandma because in their first play together she had to throw a glass of wine over him … *and she never missed*. It cost him a fortune in laundry bills.

Father's dislike of grandad, however, was another thing entirely; there was no hint of professional jealousy there. Grandad presented himself as a character actor, a heavy, and father considered he was a ham, which I suppose was true. And which I suppose was the reason why, when he played the part of the demon barber, he had the audience screaming in their seats. So it had nothing to do with professional jealousy, or even the fact that their characters were totally incompatible. Father had something more tangible, more concrete and more reprehensible to back up his dislike of his father-in-law. *He* maintained that not a fortnight after grandad had joined his Fit-up company the old man had totally, completely, and quite deliberately, wrecked an entire play. Now I can't remember the title, or what that play was about, but the scene where the catastrophe took place was an experience none of us was ever likely to forget.

A party was supposed to be taking place, in a large house, set in extensive grounds, somewhere in England. At the height of the festivities a young woman, who has been acting strangely and is clearly in a very depressed condition, disappears. The guests are concerned and search the house but she can't be found. They also search the gardens, in the failing light, but still there is no trace. They fear the worst and are just about to call the police when suddenly the gardener (grandad), in a very agitated state and clearly with something important to tell, makes an entrance. (I think this was the only appearance and the only lines he had in the play.) Immediately he has the attention of the guests, and the audience, and his announcement was designed to bring down the curtain.

Now grandad had recently acquired a set of false teeth. How people obtained false teeth in those days, if they weren't well-off, I don't know. You could rummage through piles of spectacles in Woolworth's and choose a pair of glasses that suited you, but obviously it wasn't quite so simple with teeth. Also obviously, no matter what it cost, an actor, even a heavy like grandad, couldn't go on stage without teeth. So he acquired a set and they were a very poor fit. Naturally he was assured they would settle down eventually, and in the meantime he used a fixative and his tongue to keep them in place. But they really were a terrible fit. That night, however, as he stood in the wings, hours ahead of his time, he was confident that at last he had got his dentures thoroughly under control. And sure enough, when his cue came he dashed on stage and flawlessly announced:

"I've found her."

"Where?"

"In the shrubbery."

"In the shrubbery?"

"She's dead."

"*Dead!*"

"Yes." Grandad held up a revolver. And then what he should have said ... what he intended to say ... indeed what he *tried* to say as his teeth came down, his tongue went up and a volume of spit sprayed everyone in sight ... "*She's shot herself.*" Well, it didn't come out like that. But it certainly brought down the curtain. It brought down the *house*. And while the audience was falling about in the auditorium the entire cast on stage had surrounded father in an attempt to stop him choking the gardener to death.

What happened during the performance of *Sweeney Todd* that night in Kesh, despite the family history I've just been relating, had nothing whatever to do with grandad. He gave a splendid performance, as usual. And the play started off very well. We had a packed hall, a wonderful audience, it was our last night and everyone seemed to have recovered from their complaints. Even father, though he didn't say a great deal, seemed in a reasonable mood.

The play, set in Fleet Street in Victorian times, as I'm sure you know, opens in the cold, dreary, dimly-lit barber's shop where Sweeney Todd plies his trade. The curtain rises to reveal grandad standing by the barber's chair on the Right, and his soapboy, Tobias (played by me) downstage Left.

TODD: *(All smiles and benevolence)* Tobias!

TOBIAS: *(Quickly and anxiously)* Yes, Mr Todd?

TODD: Tobias, I would like you to run a little errand for me.

TOBIAS: Yes, Mr Todd, certainly, Mr Todd.

TODD: Here is a sixpence *(Holds up a coin and I nervously approach)*, a whole sixpence. And what I want you to do is run down to the little shop at the corner, ask for an ounce of Mr Todd's tobacco, get the change and come straight back here as fast as your little legs will carry you. You understand?

TOBIAS: *(Takes the coin)* Oh yes, Mr Todd, as fast as I can.

TODD: Now you won't dally, or hang around the street corner?

TOBIAS: Oh no, Mr Todd.

TODD: And of course you would never even dream of taking the sixpence and running off?

TOBIAS: Oh no, no, never. I'll go straight to the shop and straight back and I'll run all the way.

TODD: Good, good. *(Puts his hand on my shoulder)* Ah, you're a very good little boy Tobias. A very *poor* little boy but a very *good* little boy. Tell me, where is your mother, Tobias?

TOBIAS: She's in heaven sir.

TODD: And your father?

TOBIAS: He's in heaven too.

TODD: And have you seen them in heaven Tobias?

TOBIAS: Oh no, sir.

TODD: So how do you know they're there? Did someone tell you?

TOBIAS: Yes, that's right, Mr Todd, someone told me.

TODD: And you believed it?

TOBIAS: It was a lady!

TODD: Hum! Well, let me tell you something Tobias. Never believe anything that anybody tells you. The truth is your mother's dead, your father's lost, you are an orphan and I am your father and mother and I give you board, lodging and washing. Is that not so?

TOBIAS: Oh yes, Mr Todd. You are very kind to me.

TODD: And when you are finished here – if you should live that long – you will have a profession as good as, indeed even better than, one in the Law. And you will owe it all to me, you understand Tobias?

TOBIAS: Oh yes, Mr Todd, I understand.

TODD: Good. So now you will run down to the shop, get my tobacco, come back with the change, and on the way you will not talk to a soul, you will not breathe a word … you will *never* breathe a word of anything that's said or anything that goes on inside this shop.

TOBIAS: Oh no, no, nothing. I won't ever say a word, Mr Todd.

TODD: Because if you do, if you do *(suddenly changes mood, whips out an open razor and holds the blade to my throat)* I'll slit your throat … from ear to ear … *I'll polish you off.* Do you hear, Tobias?

TOBIAS: *(Terrified)* Oh yes, Mr Todd, I hear, I hear, I won't talk to anybody, I'll never talk to anybody, and I'll come straight back.

TODD: *(Releases me and is all light and sweetness again)* Then off you go Tobias, and I'll sit here and count the minutes till you come back. *(I exit Left, quickly, because grandad is very convincing. He sits down in his chair and looks lovingly at the open razor in his hand.)*

The razor, of course, was a prop, but the first time grandad (who'd only recently joined our company at the time) went on stage as the barber and took hold of my hair and laid the blade to my throat, father, who happened to be in the wings, suddenly realised to his horror that the razor was real. And that grandad wasn't wearing his spectacles. And that without his spectacles he was blind … so blind that when he volunteered for the army in 1914 they wouldn't let him go anywhere near the Front. He'd have been a much greater danger to *us*, as my father once remarked, than to *them*. There was a terrible row when he came off stage. Grandad said his professional reputation had been "impugned". Father said (he was the next customer to sit in the barber's chair) that if he wanted his throat cut he could do it himself. So the razor grandad was using that night was a very realistic imitation made by father, who was playing the part of a sailor home after a long voyage with plans to marry his sweetheart, and dreams of a prosperous future on account of a handful of pearls which he has safely tucked away in his belt. He tells all this to the barber who, soaping, shaving and weaving his cut-throat about prattles on:

TODD: Ah well sir, it is indeed fortunate for you that you have come in here this morning. For though I do say it myself, there isn't a shaving shop in the whole city of London that shaves, finishes and, most important of all sir ... *polishes off* the customers like I do myself.

And "polishing off", as you've guessed, refers to the point where the barber slits the sailor's throat. After which he pulls the lever that operates a trapdoor and precipitates the body into the cellar where his accomplice, Mrs Lovett, *who owns a pie shop*, is waiting to collect.

Now, this business with the trapdoor presented certain technical problems. The townhalls, village halls, schoolhouses and such that we played in didn't offer anything as convenient as a trapdoor on the stage. And father was determined to make the murderous act look as realistic as possible, so he worked out a very simple routine. He took an ordinary kitchen chair, covered it with canvas or some other material, and placed it on stage, but close to the wings. At the point then where the barber cuts his throat and opens the trapdoor below his seat, all father had to do was tilt back his chair, roll over, and take both himself and the chair off stage. It worked very well and looked very realistic. But in Kesh there was a problem with the piano. Not our piano I would add, which had long since gone, but the one that belonged to the hall. There was no room for it in the dressing room, father didn't intend to use it and didn't want it left out in the hall in case it got damaged, so he had to move it off stage, but at the side where he did his act. This meant that his movements were a little restricted, but by rehearsing and marking clearly the place on stage where the chair should stand, the problem seemed to be resolved.

So Sweeney Todd grinned, grimaced, gloated and worked himself up to the moment where, with a fiendish yell and a slash of the razor he cut the sailor's throat, pulled back the lever and father howled, tilted, rolled over and then ... *hit his head on the side of the piano.* Grandad didn't notice a thing. But grandma, playing Mrs Lovett, who was standing on the opposite side in the wings waiting for her cue, saw that father was injured, out cold, and dashed back to the dressing room, calling out to mother.

"Quick! Bob's hurt himself ... hit his head ... I'm on." Then she dashed back and made her entrance on cue. Mother flew out of the dressing room and rushed across the back of the set to find father lying where he had fallen.

"Oh my god!" She moved his feet in case they were on stage and could be seen (the show comes first), then she whispered in his ear and slapped his face but he didn't move. She tore back to the dressing room and returned with a bottle of water which she poured over his face. As most of this went into his mouth and up his nose, when he did come round he thought he'd been drowned. His first action was to put a hand to his head. Then he looked at the piano. Then he regarded mother who was anxiously peering down from above, and his first words were,

"You moved that bloody piano."
"I *didn't*."
"Somebody did."

*

Sunday was a beautiful day. The air was sweet, the sun was shining and the fields were unbelievably green. It was about eleven o'clock in the morning and the entire McNally household had gathered outside the cottage and onto the middle of the road. Not that Mrs McNally, the children, or myself were going anywhere in particular, but Mr McNally was setting off for church, and father and mother (taking Eileen with them) were heading for the hall. We were due to move out early on Monday morning so they had to take down the scenery and pack all our stuff. Most of our travelling was done at odd hours, sometimes even late at night, because the lorries we hired were always driven by the owners who had to fit us in between jobs, or travel in their spare time.

There was a great deal of noise and activity outside the cottage as those who were migrating towards the village slowly moved off. The children all shouted and waved as though their father was going to Japan. And as *my* father had related his experience of the previous night, and mother had capped it by saying that father believed *she* had moved the piano, and if she had not then it was done by Sweeney Todd, jokes and wisecracks were flying in all directions. Everyone was in the best of humour. Mind you, the McNally family found everything we did exciting, humorous or at least worthy of comment. And we were in good heart because business had been good and despite father's encounter with the piano the final curtain had come down to great clapping, cheering and stamping of feet. The walk home after the show was also an experience I remember with pleasure… the lonely road, the silent hedges, and the night air filled with all the smells of the countryside. Supper was on the table when we got back to the cottage, everybody was ravenous, and nobody, not even the children, got to bed or to sleep until midnight. But to get back to Sunday morning.

By the side of the road Jeannie waited until my parents and her father had moved out of earshot and watched till the rest of the children had wandered off to find something interesting to do, then she came across to where I was standing and whispered.

"Let's get away before they see us."

"Where are we going?" I whispered back.

"A secret walk."

"Oh." The idea appealed to me.

"Quick!" She took hold of my hand and we started off along the road but didn't get far before Mrs McNally called out from the doorway.

"Where you going, Jeannie?"

"To show Jimmy the old cottage down the loanen," Jeannie lied without hesitation, she had no intention of going anywhere near the old cottage, "before he goes away."

"Alright, but be back in time for your dinner."

"We will." We walked quickly away from the cottage and the village for a short distance then Jeannie ordered, "In here, quick."

"Right." I clambered in between the bars of an old iron gate.

"And keep down." She lowered her head and began to run. I followed and we raced along the bottom of a hedge that separated the field from the side of their garden. I say garden because that's what the McNallys called it, but in fact it was just a small area of rough ground filled with potatoes, chickens, goats, children, and a very exciting pile of old farming implements. When we reached the end of the hedge we climbed over and edged through what Jeannie called a dyke (a low bank with a hedge on top), jumped across what she termed a sheough (a ditch with water in it) and found ourselves in a meadow filled with tall, creamy-white flowers that smelled so sweet and so strong that I can never encounter the smell without remembering the place and what happened there.

"I'll miss you when you go, Jimmy." Jeannie slowed up now we were out of sight of the cottage.

"I'll miss you too." I put a handful of the meadowsweet, though I didn't know its name then, up to my nose and drank in the scent as though it were wine.

"Will you really?"

"Oh yes, I'll miss you very much." Though I knew, even then, I wouldn't miss her half as much as she would miss me. My way of life didn't permit me liking, and therefore missing, anyone too much.

"Where are you going to on Monday?" Jeannie also picked a handful of flower heads and put the heady mixture to her nose.

"Omagh I think."

"And will you ever come back to Kesh again?"

"I don't know, we might, father likes it here and business is good, but I'm not certain."

"You know you're different from all the other wee boys I know, Jimmy."

"Ah well, I've travelled a lot." This, I felt sure, was the reason for my superiority.

"No, I mean you're polite, and you never use any dirty words ... Me mammy says she'll miss you too."

"Your mammy is a very nice lady."

Jeannie was silent for a few moments and then she sighed.

"Oh, I suppose after the holidays are over Maureen will come back to stay with us, and she's good fun but... I wish you could stay, Jimmy."

"I have to go. But never mind, I'm here now and this is a beautiful walk. Where are we going?"

Jeannie stopped dead, turned and looked into my face to see how I'd react, then replied, "To the river."

"Oh, *great!*" I was genuinely pleased and surprised. "I wanted to see the river before I left."

"I know, that's why I've brought you. But you mustn't say a word to a soul because we're not allowed to play there and if me da knew I'd brought you he'd skin me alive."

"I won't tell your father, I won't tell anybody, but I'm glad you brought me Jeannie. I love rivers … there was one at Pettigoe. I think rivers are very exciting. Where is it?"

"A bit further on … down that wee hill." We walked to the end of the meadow and then into another small field, at the end of which I could see a line of bushes and small trees.

"Is it there?" I pointed.

"Yes."

"Where does it come from?"

"Oh, from the far side of the village and then it winds round and goes away down… Do you see through those trees… the bridge?"

"Oh yes," I looked where she was pointing, "a stone bridge."

"That's right. But we're not going that way because you come up to the road there. This way." She walked on, I followed, then when we got to within a few yards of the bushes she put out a hand to prevent me going any further. "It's there."

"Where? I can't see anything." I took a step forward.

"*Mind*, Jimmy."

"It must be a very small river, Jeannie."

"No, it's not all that small. *Mind!*" She stretched out an arm but didn't move from where she was standing.

"I'm alright, I'll be careful, don't worry." I moved cautiously through the long grass towards the bushes. "I mean *you* know where it is, but I can't see … ah yes I can. *There* it is." The water was below me; dark brown, still, lying against the opposite bank. "Oh yes, though I still can't see the bottom at this side."

"Mind Jimmy, for God's sake!" Jeannie was biting her fingers.

"I'm alright, I'm yards away from …" The next minute the ground went from beneath my feet and I dropped straight down through the lush vegetation and into the river. I went under, and almost immediately came up again kicking deep water and clawing at the grass and weeds above my head.

"*Jimmy!*" There was a shriek from Jeannie and when I looked up she had crawled forward on her hands and knees and was peering down at me. "Oh … help!" She took one look, turned (obviously with the intention of running home for assistance), and in that split-second I knew, for certain, that if she left me I'd drown.

"*Jeannie!*" I yelled with all the power and authority I could muster. Then as I could feel myself slipping back into the river I dug my feet into the bank, tightened my fingers round the weeds, sobbed "Please God, please God …" and looked upwards again. Jeannie's face was above me, several feet above me. "Now listen to me …" I was calm, my life depended on it.

"Yes, Jimmy?" Her face was ashen.

"Do exactly as I say."

"Yes, Jimmy." She started to weep.

"Lie down on your stomach." She dropped flat. "Hold on to that bush." She took a firm grip on what may have been a small willow. "Now stretch your other arm down as far as you can." She reached down and I reached up but there was at least a foot between us and I was slipping again, so I yelled, "I'm going to jump ... dig in your toes ... *now!*" I lunged, kicked at the bank, clawed at the weeds, grabbed hold of Jeannie's hand, she pulled, and the next minute I was lying on the bank by her side.

"Oh my God, Jimmy," she sobbed. "I thought you were drowned."

"And I would have been," I rolled over onto my back, "if you'd run off and left me."

"But I was only going for help."

"I know, but I couldn't get out, and there was nothing but grass to hold on to."

"I was heart-scared."

"So was I." I sat up.

"Are you alright, Jimmy? Are you alright?"

"Yes, I'm alright. But I'm cold."

"Let's go home." We both leapt to our feet and ran, raced, like Old Nick himself was after us.

When we entered the kitchen and Mrs McNally caught sight of me and heard from Jeannie what had taken place, she went into action like a helmsman confronted by a tornado. "Out ... out!" she yelled at the children crowding in the doorway. "Margaret, get them round to the back. Take wee Eileen with you." Then to my utter amazement (I could see now where Jeannie got her ready answers) she shouted after the departing youngsters, "Jimmy fell into the sheough." But to my mother, who was coming up to the front door at that moment, she whispered in a hoarse voice, "He fell in the river and we've got to get him dried and changed before Pat gets back or he'll skin the lot of us. Bring some dry clothes."

"Oh ...yes ... certainly," mother hesitated so Mrs McNally pushed her in the direction of the bedroom.

"Quick!"

"Yes, but is he alright?"

"Just cold." I reassured her.

"Then up to the fire with you." Mrs McNally put a hand at my back. "And get his dry clothes. And you Jeannie, get out onto that road and watch for your da."

"Yes mammy." Jeannie flew out to the road and mother came dashing back with an armful of clothing.

"We'll have to get him changed and his clothes dried," Mrs McNally vigorously poked at the fire, "because if Pat gets to know about this he'll kill Jeannie. Oh, this is a terrible thing, Mrs Mateer, a terrible thing to happen... and on your last day."

"Oh, it's not that bad," mother tried to calm the distressed woman. "Don't worry, there's no harm done."

"No harm! He could have been drowned, both of them could have been drowned. What about shoes?"

"Well, I'm afraid these are the only shoes he's got at the moment."

"Never mind, we'll put newspapers in them." She then turned on me. "Get these off." I had already removed my shoes, socks, jersey and shirt, and mother was about to help with my trousers, but before either of us could lift a finger I was stripped naked and Mrs McNally had grabbed a towel and was making a serious attempt to rub all the hair off my head.

"I could kill that Jeannie," she threatened, "murder her! She knows fine well she's not allowed to go near the river, she's been warned, they've all been ..." She broke off as Jeannie reappeared in the doorway, and I made a desperate attempt to cover my shame. "Is he coming?"

"No, there's no sign of him yet."

"Lucky for you girl, lucky for you. Whatever made you take Jimmy to the river? What in heaven's name made you do such a thing?"

"Well ..." Jeannie, miserable and dejected, looked in my direction and I just couldn't let her take all the blame.

"I asked her to take me, Mrs McNally," I volunteered.

"Aye, but you didn't know Jimmy, you had no idea ... that river is narrow but it runs deep. And up near the bridge water comes in underground and there's a whirlpool! God in heaven Jeannie, if he'd gone in there he'd never have come out alive. Oh, get back out on the road. And *remember*!" Jeannie turned back. "If anybody wants to know why Jimmy's clothes are in front of the fire ... *he fell in the sheough.*"

"Yes, mammy." Jeannie departed in haste.

But nobody mentioned the washing. The younger children prattled away about Jimmy falling in the sheough, but the two men, when they returned from the village, paid very little attention. I don't think they even noticed the washing drying in front of the fire. So father was never told about the incident, he never knew, and I don't think my mother realised either just how near I had come to drowning among those green and pleasant fields. And I'm sure nobody ever mentioned the subject to Mr McNally.

Early the next morning before even our landlord, who worked for the council, had gone off to his work, the lorry loaded up with our scenery pulled up outside the cottage and the whole family, some with eyes half-closed and sticky with sleep, came out to see us off.

"Goodbye ... Good luck ... Come back soon!" There were shouts and waves and tears streamed down the cheeks of the little girl (probably, if she was spared, a grandmother by now) who had reached down the steep river bank at Kesh that Sunday morning and saved my life. We moved on, heading north, into Tyrone.

8

"Support Humanity, not its Imitation"

TONIGHT
See and Hear the Real Live Drama!
We are here in person. We spend money in your town. Hall Owners, Shopkeepers, Landladies, Printers, Haulage Contractors, all benefit by our visit. Why pay to see shadows on a sheet and hear the echoes of voices that have spoken perhaps years ago? Your shadow and echo company arrives in a tin box; orchestra, actors, scenery and properties all under the lid. They require neither food nor lodgings. They spend nothing. Yet *your* money goes abroad to keep these phantom stars in luxury. And at the best they are but imitations of the real thing. Do *your* bit to wipe out unemployment
See a BIG, Once Nightly Programme at Twice Nightly Prices.
6d and 1/3d

We are here now in person

*** THE BROADWAY PLAYERS ***

In Drama, Music, Variety and Farce
SUPPORT HUMANITY, NOT ITS IMITATION

(Printed by Gray, Printers and Stationers, Strabane)

We posted these bills, as well as our normal playbills, all over the towns of Omagh, Dungannon, Cookstown and Strabane. A Mr McLean, Billposter, sent in his account: "Posted all leading roads from same (Cookstown) on 13th March 1930. Charge 8/-" And the Irish National Foresters Benefit Society rented us a hall in Cookstown for three nights: "Total cost £4, including lighting (electric)" *Electric!* They were sizeable towns by Northern Ireland standards, populations of between five and six thousand souls apiece. And whether the cinema had already got to all, or any of those places at that time I can't remember, but if they hadn't, and I feel sure there was at least one of them in the area, then they were heading in our direction, and fast.

My grandparents had already been squeezed out of the affluent South (of England), the industrial Midlands and North, and into the Lowlands of Scotland by the movies. While my parents with their Fit-up company (grandma and grandad had worked in larger, much less mobile Repertory and Stock Companies before joining us), had been forced up into the Highlands, out of the more prosperous counties of Antrim and Down, and now found themselves working in the more remote parts of County Tyrone. Not that the towns I've just mentioned were cut off from the outside world, indeed they even had railways in those days. But for us this was the last stand before heading out into the lonely borders of Donegal, across the Sperrin Mountains and up towards Derry, playing in such places as Clady, Feeny, Dreen, Killeter, Killen, Six Mile Cross, Five Mile Town, Gortin, Desertmartin, Tintagh and Lissan. There weren't even villages in some of those townlands, just isolated cottages and a hall. Where people came from and they didn't always, I'll never know.

We no longer had any choice in the matter. All we could do was run before the storm. Recession, depression and poverty were facts of life to us, we were used to them, but with the advance of the cinema, The Pictures as everybody called them, the end of our way of life was in sight. Competition wasn't the name of this game, it was annihilation. And not just for us. Thousands of professional and talented people, actors, musicians and stagehands, were now facing ruin – no alternative employment, no dole or sick pay – starvation. This was the grim and more realistic drama that was being enacted off-stage. Live theatre was being squeezed out of the cities, even the buildings themselves, in some cases, were being converted into Houses of Shadows. And in "The Stage", the weekly paper that kept everyone in touch and informed about the theatrical scene, scores of artistes declared that they were willing to play anything, work anywhere, travel anywhere, even to the boglands of Ireland ... if you sent them the fare. But the monster that forced us out of the towns also drew sustenance from the boglands. It was a desperate struggle for survival, and father fought it with everything he had, and in every way he could.

"*We need more publicity*," he declared on our last tour of Scotland before returning to Ireland for good. "We've got to sell our wares, we've got to advertise." So the entire cast walked and talked and put up bills. But it wasn't enough. "No, something more direct, more dramatic, is needed." So he and three other men in the company dressed up as cowboys, and using the lorry they'd hired to shift the scenery, drove down the main street of one quiet town waving revolvers and firing off blanks. They came to within an ace of getting arrested for a breach of the peace. Father then had an even better idea and in the next town he crept round under cover of darkness and posted up, even outside the police station, a poster which read:

> £500 REWARD
>
> WANTED ... A tall dark clean-shaven man aged approximately 28 years. Last seen wearing a dark suit, a black hat, and carrying a small bundle concealed beneath his jacket. Reported to have been seen walking quickly away from the spot where the latest *Ripper Murder* took place. The above reward, offered privately for information likely to convict the perpetrator of the gruesome and amazing murders, failed to bring the culprit within the hands of the law. In an exciting and surprising manner this abnormal slayer is at last run to earth by the author of the sensational play ...
>
> JACK THE RIPPER
>
> Presented by The Broadway Players ... In This Town
>
> You simply *MUST* see it

The police tore down the bills. Father put them up again. The police gave chase. Father escaped and hid in the hall. The police got bored, or maybe saw the humorous side because father swore he saw two of them in the audience on opening night.

His next stunt, with the same play but in a different town (and he would never have tried this in Ireland) was designed to stir up the press, but initially the audience, before the curtain went up. The doors were closed, the house lights went out, the audience settled down to enjoy the performance. There was a hush. Then suddenly from the back of the hall came a piercing scream and a young woman (mother) dashed down the gangway followed by a man (father) brandishing a knife. Mother reached the safety of the curtain but father never got anywhere near it because two members of the audience leapt to their feet, grappled with, and bore to the floor the would-be assassin. Father wasn't hurt, and the men apologised, but he never tried that stunt again. Nor did he attempt to gain the attention of potential audiences by offering them any more controversial plays. You remember what happened when he tried *Other Men's Wives* in Ireland! Well, when he presented a much better-class of play altogether, *Damaged Goods* by the French writer Brieux, boldly announcing, "If you don't want to know the facts of life don't come", he had similar trouble with the Elders of the Presbyterian Church. The play was about venereal disease.

So if you can't beat them or join them ... copy them. Well, of course this was something the live theatre, Repertory and Fit-up alike, had been doing for some time. Although with *Jack The Ripper* our small company had exploited the drama of the Whitechapel murders and presented a stage play long before the cinema came up with *The Lodger*. But in general it worked the other way round and successful screenplays came to life at a later date on the stage. *Dawn*, for instance, was a stage play about Edith Cavell, the nurse who was executed by the Germans in the First World War for helping wounded British soldiers to escape. Lil Wynn (mother's stage name) played the part of Edith Cavell.

Orphans of the Storm was another drama I believe first appeared on the screen, though I never saw the film and it was mother who told me that Lilian Gish and her sister had the star roles.

Shadow of the Cross: this was a play we advertised as:

THE BROADWAY PLAYERS
In a great spectacular & picturesque
production of Truth & Beauty

A poignant and vivid story of the struggles
of the early Christians upholding the faith
they loved against steel, fire and callous
persecution.

Beautiful costumes of the period * Special Scenery

Don't miss this Grand Dramatic Triumph

(Handbills, Printed by Gray of Strabane)

Mother said *The Shadow of the Cross* was our version of another film called *The Sign of the Cross*. She also believed that *Midnight Wireless S.O.S.* (about Crippen) and *The Maid of the Mountain* may also have started on the screen, but she wasn't sure. About *Sonny Boy*, however, she was certain. And so was I. For *Sonny Boy*, the song and story obviously taken from one of the first great movie musicals (*The Jazz Singer* starring Al Jolson), was not just a success as a play, it was a milestone on the open road of my life. I had made my stage debut at an even earlier age, but it was in this play that I had my first speaking part. This was the beginning of my acting career, a career which by one of those perverse twists of fate had nothing to do with my father's Fit-up company, and still less to do with my father who was outraged, "bloody child labour" he fumed when he heard about the event. You see it was grandma who first put me on the stage. But to go into that we have to leave The Broadway Players and go back for a couple of years.

9

Don't Put Your Grandson on the Stage

I was separated for quite a long period, I have no idea just how long, from my father, mother and a new baby sister. This was some time between my third and fourth birthday. Where exactly we were at that time I don't know except that it wasn't in Ireland. My mother was unwell. And a member of the company had left suddenly and taken half the cast along with him. I think it must have been in Scotland (we crossed the Irish Sea at least twice to my knowledge), or maybe it was in the north of England, Durham or somewhere like that. Anyhow, wherever it was, the company was stranded, high and dry, there was no money and so it was decided to send me off to my grandparents who were working elsewhere. At a later date Eileen (she would have been about four then), was also farmed out to an aunt when we crossed over to the Island of Rathlin. But her stay was short because father wanted her back. Mine was of much longer duration, so long that I didn't want to return to my parents. Although my leaving, my departure from them was something I remember only too well.

The station, whatever station it was, was large, the engine was huge (steam of course) and father was seeing me off. I was to go to Reading. My ticket had been paid for by grandma, and grandad was to meet me at the other end. I was unhappy about the arrangement, a long journey and going alone, but a stiff upper lip was called for and so I didn't complain.

"Here's a carriage," father looked in at the window and then opened the door. It must have been very early in the morning because there were very few people about. "In you get." I clambered aboard and then stood in the doorway. The carriage was empty. "You can sit by the window and look out." I didn't notice the large suitcase on the rack above my head. "You've got your sandwiches?"

"Yes." I held out a small paper bag in which mother had put some corned beef sandwiches and a couple of buns.

"And your parcel?"

"Yes." I put my arm round the small brown paper parcel that contained my pyjamas and a few other articles of clothing.

"And what about your sixpence?" Father was obviously trying to lift my spirits because he didn't usually rattle on like this.

"It's here." I touched my trouser pocket and felt for the coin he'd tied up in my handkerchief before we left the digs. "I've got it."

"Good, good. Now I've seen the guard and he'll look in and see you're alright. Do you know where you're going?"

"To Reading."

"That's right. To your grandmother."

"But how will I know when I get there?"

"The guard will tell you."

"Where is the guard?"

"Well, I don't know..." father looked round "... seeing about things I suppose."

"He doesn't know what I look like."

"No, but I've told him, I've explained ... and there isn't another little boy travelling on his own."

"He might forget to tell me when we get to the station." I began to show my anxiety.

"No he won't forget."

"But he doesn't know me and if I don't get off at Reading the train will go on ..."

"No, no, no, don't worry."

But I did worry, and father didn't look all that confident himself.

"I don't want to get lost."

"You won't get lost, you can't get lost, look!" He reached in and pointed a finger at the large label that was pinned to the front of my coat. "There's your ticket. There's your name and your grandmother's address. And your grandfather will be waiting on the platform at Reading." (He wasn't as it happened.)

"But suppose grandad doesn't know me." Tears began to well up in my eyes at the prospect.

"Oh, of course he'll know you." Father looked a bit uncomfortable, he wasn't used to situations like this.

"I don't think I remember *him*." I hadn't seen either of my grandparents for at least a year.

"Oh, come on now, Jim," father didn't often use my name, and neither he nor my mother ever called me Jimmy, "you mustn't cry, big boys don't cry. And there's nothing to cry about. I'll come down and bring you back as soon as we get things sorted out. Wipe your eyes." He held out a rather grubby handkerchief and looked round for some sort of assistance, the guard I presumed. "Ah!" he spotted the bookstall, "I'll tell you … wait … I'll get you a comic." He hurried along the platform, bought a comic from the lady on the stall and came back to my carriage. "There you are. That'll help you pass the time."

"Thank you." I took the paper. "Here's your hankie."

"Right. So you'll be alr…" The engine suddenly erupted, the train shuddered and my carriage began to move backwards. "You're off! The guard's blowing his whistle … he's waving his flag …"

I leaned forward and looked father full in the face, but there was so much concern and embarrassment written there that immediately I sat back in my seat and fought the tears more on his account than mine. Offstage, apart from being angry, or when he was playing with Eileen, father never showed any emotion.

"I'll come and fetch you." He reached into the carriage which had stopped moving backwards, but he didn't shake hands or touch me, or anything like that, he just patted the seat and then took hold of the door. "I'll come and fetch you. You'll be alright. *Read your comic*."

Obediently I raised my paper and studied it intently – *upside-down*, as father told me many years later. The door slammed, the train moved, forwards this time, and I was off.

Fortunately before the full impact of being separated from my parents and carried out into the great unknown hit me, a lady, the owner of the suitcase, returned from the dining car where she'd been having breakfast and we immediately became friends. She asked me who I was travelling with, and when I said no-one and showed her my label she then inquired if I was hungry, to which I replied yes. So she went back out into the corridor, along to the dining car and returned with a tray of tea and toast. I was just tucking in, feeling that things were going better than I expected, when to my disappointment I learnt that the lady would be leaving the train before Reading. However, as she had barely finished telling me this when the guard looked in and assured me he'd see me off at the right station, my spirits rose again and I finished my breakfast, my second breakfast that morning, quite contented. I don't remember anything else about the journey, maybe I slept, but my arrival at Reading was an event not likely to be erased from my memory.

"*Reading!* Your station young man." The guard, out in the corridor, pulled across the sliding door and put his head into the carriage. "Now wait till the train stops and then get off. Your grandad will be waiting."

"Thank you very much," I was on my feet. "I'm ready." I'd been ready for quite some time, with my comic in my pocket and my parcel under my arm. At two previous stations I had gone out and asked people who were waiting in the corridor if this was Reading, to be reassured that it was not. This time there was no doubt. We had arrived.

There were people all over the platform and when the train finally came to a standstill they all began to get on, and those on the train began to get off. Someone opened a door near me and so I got as close to it as I could, but I didn't get down to the platform because

I wanted grandad to see me. Though I couldn't see him. *He wasn't there!* So I started to climb down, then fearful that he would be looking up at the train and not down at the platform, I got back up again. Only to be hit by the terrible thought that if the train started to move I'd be carried off and never seen again. Then the guard blew his whistle and I panicked, jumped, fell, picked myself up again, looked round and caught sight of grandad … his gingery head, gold spectacles and long brown leather coat. He came hurtling out of the stationmaster's office and onto the platform like a bullfighter looking for … or rather like a *bull* looking for something to charge. His fists were clenched, his mouth was working and his head was swinging from side to side. Then *he* saw *me*.

"Ah, Jimmy, Jimmy, I thought you'd missed the train, I thought you hadn't come. I couldn't see you anywhere."

"I saw you grandad."

"Ah, I thought there'd been a hitch, that you'd missed the train. I went into the stationmaster's office to see if there was a message. Gimme your hand." He took a firm grip with one hand and with the other grabbed hold of my parcel. "And your parcel. Did you have a good journey?"

"Oh yes, very good. A lady on the train gave me tea and toast."

"Tea and toast, eh? Ah, that's the stuff to give the troops, that's the stuff. Are you hungry now?"

"Oh yes. I had sandwiches too, but it was a long time ago."

"Right, then we'll get you back to your grandma. She's making a big tea, and there's custard pie. You like custard pie?"

"Oh yes."

"So let's get home. But just a minute." He stopped abruptly outside the stationmaster's office, put his head in the doorway and called out, "It's alright, it's alright, he's here, this is him." He pulled me round to his front. "This is my big grandson. He's fine, he's O.K. We're off."

So we went home to grandma and …

"Oh, *there* he is! Give your old grandma a big kiss. *There* he is! And a big hug. Oh, he's his grandma's boy … he's his grandma's big boy!"

And of course I was. Apart from the fact that she was the only one who ever showed me any real affection, staying with grandma meant no change of digs every week. Though we must have moved at least twice during that visit because I remember being in Nottingham, and when I left to go back to my parents we travelled out from Bristol. It also meant a limited number of landladies, no sharing of beds, I had my own bed for weeks, maybe months on end. And finally, though this didn't interest me in the slightest, I got lots of new clothes. There was a navy blue sailor's suit with long trousers for weekdays, and a spotless white version of the same to be worn on Sundays. With hats to match … *H.M.S. Hero* round the band just like the advert on Players Cigarettes. Grandma also made me a pair of velvet shorts and several white blouses. She was an expert seamstress and created many of our theatrical costumes. And when she was satisfied with my outward appearance she got down to the matter of my *inner* health.

Extract of Malt, Halibut's Codliver Oil, Andrews Liver Salts, Californian Syrup of Figs ... and in the middle of all this I was taught to say my prayers and clean my teeth (and some good must have come out of that because I still have most of my own teeth). When I eventually returned to my parents and my father caught sight of me and heard my English accent (though when travelling in Scotland I became a pure Scot and he didn't complain) he nearly had a fit. Child abuse was not a phrase I ever came across in those days, but had it existed father would certainly have used it. *Cissy* was as far as he got. And a right little Lord Fauntleroy I must have appeared; fussed-over, dressed-up, paraded. And the odd thing was that grandma hadn't done this with any of her own children as far as I could find out. Quite the reverse, because mother assured me *she* was drilled, disciplined and quite often thumped. But grandma never laid a finger on me, and although I lived a sheltered life in digs and dressing rooms and was too young for school, I did get into scrapes at times. But she never walloped me, she never shouted, so I would have done anything – *even go on the stage* – in order to please her.

And I didn't want to go on the stage. I wasn't an extrovert like our Eileen, nor was I an introvert who needed the theatre and the stage in order to expand. I never wanted to be an actor, and it was a standing joke in the family that once when I came off after a performance and a member of the audience praised me and asked, "So what are you going to do when you grow up, young man?" my reply was, "I'm going to settle down." All I ever wanted, all I ever asked for, like Garbo, was to be left alone. But that grandma obviously couldn't do.

I must have been somewhere between two and three years of age when my parents, who hadn't yet formed their own company, went to work in a rep. in Lancashire. My grandparents, just as it happened, were also working in another company not far away. So it was decided that I should go and stay with them for a couple of weeks, and it was during this short period that grandma first introduced me to the stage. My father, I believe, would never have done this. I don't think he saw me as having anything to do with his business. Or perhaps, remembering his own childhood, he considered I was too young. Or maybe he was just angry because *she* made a decision that should have been his. I don't know. Grandma, as I said, had been born into the business and so I suppose it was quite natural that the ten-year-old girl she lost had been playing in *East Lynne* only a few days before she died. Though the second child she lost, Tommy, had been left with his grandparents until he was fifteen, and as far as I know he never once set foot on the boards. Mother too wasn't pushed very hard in that direction; though that may have been because grandma didn't consider she had sufficient talent. So why did grandma use me? And *how* did she use me? Ah well, that was one of my earliest recollections.

Grandma and I were sitting in a dressing room (I think, according to my researching, it must have been in the Municipal Hall in Colne, a vast place), and she was coaxing me to do something for her, something to which I agreed.

"*That's* a good boy, *that's* a good boy. So we'll just get you out of these clothes and into something more colourful." My shirt and trousers were swiftly removed and replaced. "And what I want you to do for your old grandma is to sit on the stage with all the other little boys and girls, just for a couple of minutes at the beginning of the play."

"Will you be there too grandma?"

"Oh yes, and grandad, and the manager's little girl, we'll all be there."

"Alright then."

"That's the boy, that's grandma's big boy. And we'll just put a bit of make-up on your face because if we don't, when the lights go up on the stage you'll look like a ghost and frighten everybody. That's it."

She made up my face and I didn't ask to look in the mirror, and she didn't seem to think it necessary. The next thing I remember was being hurried upstairs and onto a stage that seemed to me to be in total darkness. There was a great deal of shuffling and whispering and stepping over feet, but eventually I was set down at the front of a small group of children who had been planted down stage Left.

"Are you alright, Jimmy?" whispered grandma.

"Yes, thank you," I whispered back.

She disappeared. Lights went up on the stage (the curtain had already been raised), I blinked, got used to the glare, looked round and... *all the faces were black!* Topsy, Eliza, Uncle Tom – it was *Uncle Tom's Cabin* and nobody had told me, nobody had explained, and I had no idea that my face was black like everyone else. Wherever I looked, even at the two little piccaninnies on either side of me, the faces were black as pitch. I yelled, got to my feet and headed straight for the wings. It was a very unprofessional beginning.

I was used again in the same town, in the same company I presume, only this time I was assured beforehand that I wouldn't even have to go on the stage. All I had to do was stand in the wings beside grandma, and when she said "scream", I was to scream. This didn't seem a very daunting prospect, and I had let her down in *Uncle Tom*, so I agreed. Came the night and we stood in the wings waiting for our cue, and when it was delivered grandma put her hand on my shoulder and whispered "scream!" I opened my mouth and gave out what must have sounded like a rather painful squeak. Grandma leaned a little heavier on my shoulder and hissed in my ear "scream!" I tried again but what issued forth this time could barely be heard on stage much less out in the auditorium. And everybody on stage was waiting. "*Scream!*" Grandma nipped my bottom hard and I screamed ... and screamed ... and screamed, and had to be rushed down to the dressing room and pacified. I wasn't showing a great deal of promise.

After the plays there were pantomimes and I went on in *Jack and the Beanstalk*. In this show the manager's daughter and I had to sit huddled under a table (hidden from view by a long tablecloth) and when the giant reached down into the open-topped table and hauled us out through the brown-paper crust of a gigantic pie, all the children in the audience gasped, and then cheered as we escaped and fled towards the wings. Finally grandma asked me to go on in *Babes in the Woods*, dressed as a girl because the manager's little daughter was ill, and here I drew the line, I protested, it was too much. However, in the long run I did as she wanted. And of course, you would say that was inevitable because I was a small child and loved and needed my grandmother. But grandad, I noticed, also did what grandma wanted. And despite the fact that he was a strong, grown-up, bruiser of a man, there was never any fighting, arguing or shouting about the matter. So how did she do it?

Well, as a child I never asked such a question, it was a fact and I accepted it as children do. But years later, when I was turning things over in my mind, it dawned on me that the answer didn't lie entirely with grandma, it lay in the relationship, the rules laid down before the pair of them got wed. Grandma, it appears, felt sorry for grandad: he'd had a hard life, and his father was a scoundrel who even pinched the money grandad was saving in order to get married. And the other thing that seemed to attract grandma was the fact that grandad wasn't really a very inspiring actor. Oh, he made a wonderful job of Sweeney Todd and Simon Legree (the slave trader in *Uncle Tom*), but had it not been for grandma, who made it clear to anyone who was interested in employing her that they would also have to take Harry (even if all they could offer was a job as stagehand), he would have been out of work a lot of the time. Having said this, having given the lady a very generous, a very altruistic character, I'm well aware that grandma was no saint, and her relationship with grandad was based on one very fundamental rule, which was, that she was The Queen and his role was to cook, clean, hump luggage, guard and protect this fine and rare talent from all the irritating and unpleasant little problems that occur in everyday life. Just the same it was a very satisfactory arrangement, a very happy arrangement as far as I could see, providing ... *providing* grandad accepted his role and stayed in his place which now and again he did not.

There was an incident once when they were both on stage seated at a table, grandma demurely, her eyes lowered, and grandad leaning across earnestly declaring his undying love. His overture expands, rises up, and just as in opera when words can no longer express what the lover feels, he breaks into song. Now grandad was no great singer, although unlike father (who according to mother, on one occasion and for some inexplicable reason, opened his mouth and completely wrecked a choir of Welsh miners), grandad could sing in tune. And he'd played this role and sung this love song many times before. On this occasion, however, though he got through the song nicely enough, when he came to the end – grandma still sitting, hands on her lap and eyes on the table – he quite unexpectedly held onto the last note. And not only did he hold onto it but, having taken quite a deep breath, he introduced some sort of embellishment, a quavering, which went on for a considerable time. When eventually it stopped, grandma raised her head and looked across the table at her lover, and he looked at her, hard, his little piggy eyes gleaming behind his gold-rimmed spectacles. He'd surprised her! She hadn't expected this. She was the one with the imagination, she was the one who always said how things should be done, but this time he'd got there first, and she'd have to admit it.

Grandma, true artist that she was, gave not the slightest indication that anything unusual had occurred. She just looked into his eyes, tenderly, lovingly, as the part demanded, and then carried on to the end of the scene, to the end of the play, without making any comment. Grandad fairly writhed with impatience but he was determined that she must speak first, so he restrained himself and said nothing. The rest of the cast cleaned up after the performance, said goodnight and went back to their digs. The pair were left alone in the dressing room, in silence, a silence that grandad could no longer endure. He coughed, but before he could speak grandma brought up the subject.

"Harry!" Her approach was very casual.

"Yes Louie?" Grandad smirked but responded in the same vein.

"Harry, what did you do to your song tonight?"

Ah, ah … it was out!

"Well, Louie," grandad leaned back nonchalantly in his chair and put his fingers in his waistcoat pockets, "I have been studying this song for some time now and it seemed to me that it lacked something, something that would lift it up and carry it off. And just as it happened, the other day I picked up a magazine which had an article in it about music and singing. And as I was reading this article it suddenly came to me, it flashed across my mind, and I knew exactly what was wrong … what was missing. Well, I didn't say anything to you at the time Louie, I just thought, I just practised, and then tonight," he opened his arms, turned, and waited for the applause, "*tonight*, Louie …"

"You mean, Harry," still there was nothing in her voice or demeanour that indicated either criticism or praise, "that that sound … that quavering … that bleating …"

"*Right* Louie," grandad thumped the table, "that quavering, that bleating if you choose to call it that, *that* was what this love song needed in order to give it pathos, tragedy, beauty. *That* was what it lacked, and *that* was what I gave them tonight."

Grandma slowly got to her feet, walked to the door, languidly took down and pulled on her long black top-coat with the high fur collar, while grandad watched her like a hawk. How long could she hold out? How long before the great lady would have to swallow her pride and *admit* it? Then she spoke.

"Harry …"

"Yes my love, my dearest?" Here it came.

"Harry, if you ever" grandma paused, put a hand on the door handle, raised herself to her full height, turned, and looking down her long, aquiline nose said quietly, "if you *ever* make a horrible noise like that when we are on stage together again, I shall simply get up, walk off, and *stay* off until you have finished."

Grandad got back into line.

Ah, grandma was in a league of her own. As a child I was in no position to judge her ability, but in later years when going through family effects I came across a few programmes and press cuttings that gave me some indication of her incredible range as an actress. For instance, she played male leads when all the young men were away at the war (1917) at The Lyric, Hammersmith (working in Will Casey's company). And she played them so well that after one performance an army sergeant came to the stage door and demanded to see her exemption papers. She and the manager played the soldier along for a while and then grandma raised her voice to its normal pitch, removed her wig so that her long black hair (dyed, as she went grey early on) fell to her shoulders, and they all enjoyed the joke.

She then did an 18-week stretch playing what she termed high-class comedies in the Tower Circus, Blackpool.

In the Victoria Theatre, West Stanley, Durham, she had the title role in *Jenny Omroyd of Oldham*. "Jenny, played by Louie Bates, is a typical Lancashire woman full of common sense with no time to waste on sloppy sentiment, but with a heart of gold." That was how she was billed by Alida L. Richardson, who ran the theatre and became a great friend of grandma.

In the Municipal Hall Repertory Theatre in Colne, Lancs., she and the rest of the family came together in a Frank Fortesque production of the famous play *Journey's End*. Grandma played the part of a colonel as there are no parts for women in the play.

In West Hartlepool, working for the George Walkley Repertory Company (a company, incidentally, that had family connections because the boss's wife, Monica Holmes, was related to grandad), grandma enjoyed a repertoire we could never have afforded in Ireland: "At the Palace Theatre, West Hartlepool, twice nightly:

Hindle Wakes
Blackguard of the Queen's Regiment
Women and Wine
Passion's Hour
Simple Simon's Baby
Lady Windermere's Fan"

Finally, there was the role she played at the Cosy Theatre, Dunoon, a role she didn't choose but a role she was forced to play on two separate occasions. On one occasion, two Scottish newspapers headlined the event as follows: "Death of child actress" and "Child actress's last call". While from Lady Lauder's secretary (Lady Lauder, the wife of Sir Harry) came a card edged with black, dated November 1st, 1925, which read: "I have been instructed to convey Lady Lauder's sympathy in your sad bereavement. Enclosed please find note to help in tiding you both over. Yours faithfully, H.T. Vallance."

The story behind the letter of condolence was that grandma's youngest child Ivy, who was travelling and working with her parents at the time, had climbed onto a garden wall one afternoon and encountered a gardener at work. Proudly she informed him that she was an actress, that she was playing at the Cosy Theatre, and that he should certainly go there and see her. The gardener said he would, and he did, and he turned out to be Sir Harry Lauder. Tragically, only a few days after her portrayal of Willie in *East Lynne*, the little actress got diphtheria, died, and was buried in Dunoon. Only two years before that grandma had lost another child, Tommy, who was fifteen and died of rheumatic fever. She didn't even get to his bedside.

So maybe it was the loss of both Ivy and Tommy that made grandma treat me as she did. Maybe I got the love and affection she felt had been denied to her own children. Maybe. But that didn't stop her pushing me on stage in Reading, Nottingham, Bristol, or wherever it was, in *Sonny Boy*. Though by this time I was a professional, I was four, and the play was an outstanding success. As I've already mentioned, it was based loosely on the film *The Jazz Singer*, and at the end of the play, dressed as a minstrel with his face blacked up, the singer comes on stage to do his number. Behind the singer and entertainer however, there is a man whose world has collapsed: his wife has left him, his little boy has died and he is on the verge of a breakdown. He moves down stage, starts to sing, falters, starts again, falters again, then falls to his knees and bows his head. He's finished, as a singer, as a person, it's curtains. *Then!*

A spotlight beams up onto a box close to the stage. The singer looks up, the audience looks up, and there, poised above the hand rail (securely held by the legs I might add) appears a small figure dressed in white, with arms outstretched, who calls out (no pinching or prodding needed to get my lines across to the audience this time), "Sing up daddy ... Sing up for Sonny Boy."

There's a great sob out in the auditorium. The singer responds, dashes the tears from his eyes, rises to his feet, reaches out to the audience and sings:

> "You came from heaven and I know your worth
> You made a heaven for me right here on earth.
> So when friends forsake me, let them all forsake me,
> I'll still have you ... Sonny Boy."

Curtain, applause, line up, and more presents and toys than I had ever seen, or was ever likely to see again in my life. They all went to the hospital next day, apart from one toy which I was allowed to keep, a Zeppelin, a model of the Airship R.101 which tragically blew up with the loss of 48 lives later that year.

Then it was back to father, the Fit-up and Ireland. Only this time when the Liverpool boat bumped against the quay in Belfast we had my grandparents on board with us. The Broadway Players would never again cross the sea to tour in Scotland, our destiny was to plough on, play on, until the final curtain came down in a remote spot in Co. Down. And before that point was reached my grandparents would have returned to their own land ... and why they joined us, why they ever agreed to throw in their lot with us was a mystery to me at the time. I mean, why, when father was so difficult and always fought with my grandparents, why, when grandma could have got work in England (she managed even in the worst of times), why did she and grandad agree to come to Ireland and live a hand-to-mouth existence in father's Fit-up company? The answer, simple enough, yet one I only recently discovered, was that they came because father's company couldn't have existed without them. He needed at least two more actors but he couldn't afford to pay them proper wages, or any wages at all at times. And of course it was grandma – father wouldn't have admitted it and certainly wouldn't have asked – who made the suggestion, and grandma who made the decision. They would come with us to Ireland. And though the arrangement was doomed from the start, it kept our company going for a while longer, and it was an experience, as grandma once remarked, "the experience of a lifetime." And quite a long step from The Lyric in Hammersmith and the Playhouse in Nottingham, out into the bushes and among the boggy mountains of Tyrone.

10

Dungannon and Into the Workhouse

We didn't all end up in the workhouse, only mother, and she anticipated, expected, *knew* it would happen or something like it. It wasn't the first time we'd been in the town, we'd been all round this area before, and though I couldn't recall much about our previous visit to Dungannon, mother remembered it only too well.

"Oh, not Dungannon," she groaned when she heard of the booking. "Not Dungannon!"

"Yes," father said "and for a whole week." Business had been bad and we couldn't afford to book halls in most of the larger towns for more than three nights. "I think there's a market, so there should be a few people about."

Father was hopeful, but mother just wished we could go somewhere else. Her aversion to Dungannon, I might add, had nothing whatever to do with the town itself or its citizens, some of whom had been more than kind on our earlier visit. The reason why she didn't want to go back there was because on the last occasion she had been taken ill, the doctor diagnosed diphtheria, carted her off to the fever hospital and had her locked up for three weeks. Father also had good reason to remember the place because he was left without a leading lady, *we* were left without a mother to look after us, and the irony of it all was that when the tests finally came through it turned out mother didn't have diphtheria at all, just a terrible throat. But once inside the Isolation Ward she had to stay there for the specified time. The prospect of returning to the town, therefore, not only stirred up unpleasant memories, but it also gave her a very funny feeling, as she told us, clutching her throat and working herself into the role.

"You know my sister Ivy died of diphtheria. And I know I didn't actually *have* diphtheria, the doctor made a mistake, but I was locked up in that place and came out with this very strong feeling, a premonition, that if I ever set foot in Dungannon again something awful would happen to me." And it did.

For myself, though I had a vague recollection of mother being in hospital, I didn't remember much about the place itself, so on the first day, when everybody else was at work in the hall, I wandered off to have a look at the town. Now I don't remember exactly where the hall was situated but I do remember that I had paused to consider a long street that went down a steep hill ahead of me, when suddenly, on the opposite side of the road to where I was standing I saw this boy. *And he saw me.* And the moment he saw me he stopped in his tracks, he froze like a dog when it catches sight of another dog. Immediately I lowered my eyes and pretended to examine the footpath, but he still stared, then he shrugged, turned as though he would hurry away, turned and stared again ... and I knew I was in for trouble. I would be in that place for a week and every time I went out that boy would be waiting. I should have faced up to the inevitable, but at that particular moment I didn't feel like facing up to anything, so foolishly I turned and went back to the hall, where I found mother looking even paler than usual (she had a very pale, almost flawless, complexion), holding her head and complaining to father.

"You know I think it must be the 'flu. I don't feel at all well. In fact I feel terrible. I think I'll just go back to the digs, take a couple of Aspros and lie down for a bit. Maybe it'll pass." But it didn't pass, it got worse, and the next day father had to get the doctor, who, after examining her, put her into his car and drove her off to the hospital (the one the locals called The Workhouse, right opposite the fever hospital where she'd been the last time), because he said she was very ill and had pneumonia. So for the second time, in the same town, father was left without a leading lady and we were left without a mother or anybody to look after us. Of course, grandma was with us this time and offered to help, but father didn't want to be beholden to my grandparents on my account (not again), and he wouldn't let grandma within a mile of his little girl.

"I'll manage," he said, after he'd seen mother safely tucked away in The Workhouse, "I'll manage. Fancy being ill, twice, in the same bloody town!" Then he turned to me and put his hand into his trouser pocket. "Here, you run along to the shop and buy a loaf of bread, some marge and a tin of corned beef."

"A large loaf?" I enquired.

"Yes, I suppose so ... brown if you can get it. And I'll go and see the landlady... maybe she'll suggest something. Go on."

"Alright." I took the money, left the digs, ran along the street, and when I got to the spot where I'd paused to view the town the day before, there, waiting for me, was the boy. This time I couldn't back-off, nor could I run complaining to my father. With mother in hospital and Eileen already demanding attention he had his own problems. Besides, earlier on I'd faced the same situation and father had given me a lesson, one of the very few, a lesson I never forgot. That was in Dundee, just before my grandparents joined the company and we all set sail together for the Emerald Isle.

Mother had just brought me back from Bristol, dressed in my sailor's suit and carrying my Extract of Malt, Codliver Oil, and a pair of beautiful velvet shorts. Father had got a company together again (though not for long, they couldn't agree), and was booked into The Empress Theatre Dundee, with *The Life of Robbie Burns*. The play was complete with songs and poems, the songs sung by a newcomer, the poems recited by father who had the title role, and the part of Hielan Mary played by mother who studied her lines all the way back on the train. On arrival I was immediately debriefed, and debagged (the sailor's suit was never seen again), and as I was now considered old enough to look after myself I was allowed to play outside the digs in the street where, naturally enough, I came into contact with other children, other boys.

Now town boys, as I had already discovered to my cost, were not as friendly as village boys, who treated strangers with some regard and respect. On top of that my long stay with grandma, enjoying her protection, and imbibing the spiritual values she extolled, had completely unmanned me. The result was that I got pushed, kicked, had my sweets stolen, my shirt torn, and was forever running back to mother with another tale of woe. Which she didn't take very seriously, merely remarking, "Oh, you're alright, you're not hurt. You'll just have to keep out of their way." Though at one point she did refer the matter to father who either wasn't listening, and he rarely listened to anything mother said, or didn't consider the matter important. Then one afternoon when mother was out shopping and father had come back to the digs for something he wanted, I came running in wailing about the latest injustice and he couldn't avoid getting involved.

"What's the matter now?"

"A boy … a big boy … he pushed me against the wall … he hit me … he cracked my head." Father had a quick look and couldn't see anything.

"There's nothing there … a scratch maybe."

"But he hurt me."

"I expect he did, and I expect he'll go on hurting you, boys like that usually do."

"But I wasn't doing anything to him … only playing … and he pushed my head against the wall … and it hurts."

"Now listen here, Jim," father didn't often look as though he intended to spend a lot of time in discussing things, so I gave him all my attention. "You've been running to your mother complaining that boys have been hitting you."

"Well, there was another boy yesterday."

"Yes, but you can't go on running to your mother, or to me. I mean, what do you expect me to do, go out there and fight with their fathers?"

"Well …" I hadn't really though about this. Though if it came to it father *could* have fought their fathers because he was a fighting man and had a terrible temper. Mother wasn't afraid of much, but she was afraid of father at times. Not that I ever saw him actually hit her, but on a couple of occasions when she'd nagged him I did see him leap to his feet, clear all the dishes off the table and storm off to the pub. His temper worried me a bit too, not because I feared he'd hit *me* (he never laid a finger on me in his life, that was mother's job), but because the same sort of uncontrollable anger rose up inside me at times. Indeed once, when I was very small and there had been a clash of wills between mother and myself, I had picked up and hurled a bread knife at her head. For that I was thrashed with the back of a hairbrush and never forgot the incident, or the lesson maybe. Though whether the lesson was that violence begets violence, or there's always somebody bigger than you, I don't know. Anyway, fighting other boys' fathers wasn't what father had in mind.

"No, you can't go on running to your mother or me, you've got to stand up for yourself. I mean, what happens when you start school? What happens when your little sister gets into trouble and you have to protect her? You've got to be able to defend yourself. And I'm going to show you how you can do it. Take off your coat."

"My coat?"

"Yes, quickly." Father removed his jacket and laid it, together with my coat, over the back of a chair. "Now the first thing you've got to remember is that if you're confronted by a bully you must never show fear, bullies thrive on fear. And the next thing to remember is that if somebody is about to attack you, you must get into a position to defend yourself. Like this." Father took up the classic position. "Close your fists… no, not like that, you'll get your thumbs broken… across your fingers… that's right. Now, stick out your left arm, bend it a bit, and keep your fist up … that's right. Now, put your right arm across your chest to protect your solar plexus – that's the nerve centre, that and your chin … get hit there and you're finished, you're out. And keep your head down, your chin in, your left foot forward, your knees bent … and stand on the balls of your feet so you can move about like this." Father gave a very impressive display of ducking, dodging, weaving and delivering the coup de grâce. He'd been a keen sportsman in his youth, played football and cricket, and could run, swim, shoot and box. I don't know how much boxing he'd done in his time, but certainly he'd been in several fights since mother got to know him. Once, she said, when they were working in another company, the actor/manager and father had to fight on stage and during the rehearsal the boss had hit father hard and father had warned him not to do that on the night. During the performance, however, the boss got carried away, he considered the fight the highlight of the play, and he hit father very hard, and father knocked the man out cold. Mother and he both got the sack.

"Now you're ready to defend yourself." Father reached out and made a few minor adjustments. "And the best form of defence is attack, so make sure you get in there first. Like this …" He demonstrated. "A straight left to the jaw … that'll make him bend back and expose his solar plexus. Then come round with your right … not just your shoulder, your whole body … and hit him in the middle and that's the end of the fight. Now, you practise that."

"Like this?" I began ducking and weaving.

"That's right." Father pulled on his jacket as I began to dance round the room flooring every bully in sight.

"You do that and you won't have to keep running to your mother or me."

"But suppose – " a doubt came into my head, " – suppose he's a big boy and I can't reach up to hit him?"

"Well then," father was heading for the door, "use your feet, go for his shins."

"But suppose he's a very big boy?"

"Then hit him with a stick, a broom, anything that comes to your hand." Father had lost interest, the lesson was over, the problem solved.

So I practised in the digs, the dressing room, the theatre, and father put the matter out of his mind. Then one day, again it was in the afternoon, as he walked in at the top of the street next to the one where we had lodgings, he heard a child crying and saw a small boy being comforted by his mother. He walked on and when he got to the bottom of the street he saw another boy, also crying and running towards his father who had come out to the front door to see what was going on. "Bit of an epidemic this afternoon," father thought as he turned round the gable of the last house just in time to see a *third* boy running for his life and being pursued by yours truly wielding a large broom.

"Hey, hey!" He dashed over, disarmed me, disposed of the brush and got us both off the street and into the digs. "You can't go around bashing small boys like that."

"But they were going to hit me."

"Ah they were *small* boys, smaller than you. You can't go around bashing and bullying ... Do you want us to get run out of the town?"

There were no more incidents in Dundee, maybe I'd acquired a reputation. And I don't remember any other cases of bullying until we crossed the Irish Sea and I stood facing the boy on the street in Dungannon.

He was at least half a head higher than I was, had holes in his trousers, was none too clean and was absolutely delighted to see me. His face lit up, he waited, then as I approached he deliberately got in the way and accosted me.

"Who are ye lukin at?"

"I'm not looking at anyone," I replied.

"Yer lukin at me. What dae ye think ah am ... a freak ... somethin' oot o' a circus?"

"I'm not looking at you."

"Yer a bloody wee liar."

"I'm not a liar and I'm not looking at anyone, I'm just walking to the shops to do a message."

"An yer not from these parts."

"No, but I'm staying here for the week."

"An we dinae like strangers comin' in and lukin at us like we were dirt."

"But I'm not looking at you."

"Ye are."

"I'm not."

"Ye are, ye are." He stepped forward and took a handful of my jersey.

"Take your hands off my jersey."

"Why, what'll ye dae if ah don't?"

"Let me pass."

"What'll ye dae?"

"Let me go … let me …" I pulled his hand away.

"Right, ye wee shite!" He drew back his arm and immediately I took up the classic position, left arm out, right arm across my chest, knees bent, and started to weave. The boy's fist remained suspended in mid-air and he looked at me in amazement, incredulity written all over his face. Then he laughed, dropped his arm and lashed out with his right foot catching me on the side of the leg. I closed with him (he hadn't heard about Queensberry Rules), wrestled him to the ground (grandma's malt hadn't been wasted, besides I was never a weakling), got across his back and pushed his face into the ground.

"Now you listen to me."

"Let me up!" He struggled but I held on to him. "Let me up!"

"Now you listen to me. I mind my own business. I go my own way. I never bother other people so don't you bother me, because if you do – " I put a bit more pressure on his head, "you'll be sorry. Right?" He didn't reply but I felt sure the message had got through so I got up, brushed myself down and then calmly (I didn't want to precipitate another attack) continued in the direction of the shops. He let me get a fair distance away before he started hurling abuse, fortunately there were no stones handy, but he didn't follow me, and when I came back with the groceries he had gone. I was relieved and then extremely pleased with myself. Father could be proud, though I didn't intend to tell him about the incident because I didn't really think it was a proper fight. Just the same I'd stood up for myself, I'd sorted out my problem. Now we'd see what father had done about his problem.

"Brown loaf, half a pound of Echo margarine – it's cheaper than Stork – a tin of corned beef and the change." I set the items in front of father. Immediately Eileen, who had been taking a keen interest in the proceedings, reached up and enquired,

"Can I have my dinner now daddy? Can I have my dinner now?"

"No, it's not ready yet," father moved the loaf out of her reach. "It's not ready."

"But I'm hungry daddy."

"Yes, well you'll just have to wait. Your mother's in hospital and I can't do everything."

I couldn't see he had done *anything*, so I asked, "What did the landlady say?"

"About what?" Father looked surprised.

"About us! You said you'd have a word to see if she could suggest anything."

"Oh no, no, there's no use talking to the landlady, she's got her own family to look after. Anyway your mother could be in that place for weeks and we'll be miles away."

"Well, what are we going to do?"

"I'll send a wire to your Aunt Agnes in Belfast."

"To come and look after us?" This was a solution I hadn't considered.

"Yes, first thing in the morning. In the meantime you go down to the landlady and see if you can cadge some tea, sugar and milk."

"Oh no!"

"Just enough for now, and I'll sort things out after."

"Oh, alright." I hated asking for favours, and was no more anxious than he was to get involved in this domestic business. But I was hungry too, and cold corned beef was better than nothing, and nothing was what we were likely to get if it was left to father. He was hopeless about such matters. I mean, the last time he was left in charge of Eileen, when mother and I had gone to visit grandma who was playing in another town and stayed overnight, the result had been disastrous. "Daddy nearly got me drowned once," Eileen used to tell total strangers when the subject came up. "Yes, it was in West Hartlepool," mother always joined in because she never missed a chance of getting back at father, "and I was only away for one night."

What happened was that father was left to look after my little sister, and according to mother everything was arranged, there was really nothing for him to do. This being the case father had got up late the following morning (he was a terrible riser), dressed Eileen, though she insists she dressed herself because he kept putting her shoes on the wrong feet, and after the landlady had provided them with tea and toast (mother's arrangement), the pair of them went down to the beach. It was a beautiful sunny morning, what was left of it, so father removed Eileen's shoes and socks, tucked her little red dress into her knickers, played with her for a while and then left her paddling in about two inches of water while he sat down some distance away to enjoy his newspaper and have a smoke. Now he swore he had only just sat down and hadn't taken his eyes off the child for more than a couple of minutes when he heard a man shout, he looked up and saw a large wave and a small red bundle being swept out to sea. "My god!" He tore across the sand, dashed into the water, rescued the bundle and then had to cope not only with her screaming distress, but with the righteous indignation of the onlooker who pointed to a notice which warned of ebb tides and the like, and said father wasn't a fit person to look after a child.

Father's day off was ruined. He returned to the digs with cold feet and wet trousers, changed Eileen, dressing her in whatever was left of her limited wardrobe, and then decided, as he hadn't shaved that morning (and it was very unusual for father to go out without shaving), he'd make himself respectable before meeting mother and me at the station. There was a bathroom in the house, a rarity for us, indeed I don't think I *ever* came across one in digs in Ireland, and in order to make sure Eileen didn't get into any more trouble he took her in there with him and locked the door.

Eileen had completely recovered from her frightening experience, was in good humour and quietly amused herself by turning the bath taps on and off. Father couldn't see there was any harm in that, it kept her quiet, so he went on with his shaving. However, what father didn't know was that the plug was in the bottom of the bath and as soon as my little sister had collected a fair amount of water she clambered up on to the edge and fell in. Mother was absolutely disgusted, disgraced she said, when father met us at the station and she saw the odd assortment of dirty rags the child was wearing.

Father's incompetence, as far as domestic matters were concerned, was notorious, so we were both very pleased, me and Eileen that is, at the prospect of being looked after by Aunt Agnes. Aunt Agnes wasn't married but she liked children and was an excellent cook. What she would provide would be a great improvement on what mother usually dished up. She replied immediately to father's telegram: "Lily in Dungannon Hospital Stop Can you join us soon as possible Stop Will send fare Stop Reply paid", and said she would come but father needn't send the fare because Elizabeth, father's other sister who was a secretary, would pay for the ticket. Elizabeth wasn't married either, she and Agnes were the only two left of a family of nine (that included their parents) still living in the ancestral home. Another sister who had been training to be a teacher like her mother, died before she qualified. A fourth became a buyer in a large store in Belfast (Women's Lib didn't start yesterday) and moved out. A fifth went to Canada, as did Uncle Joe, though he didn't go to get married but to seek adventure. And father, of course, went on the stage. Agnes was the only one of the family who hadn't been trained for a profession, and when her mother died, at a very early age, she was left to look after the house (which had attics as well as bedrooms), and cook, clean and care for her father and any other members of the family still living at home. And this, of course, as I heard father once remark without even a blush, was because Agnes was too frail to go out to work!

She was a very small woman, my Aunt Agnes, with lots of dark tousled hair already streaked with grey, two large brown lively eyes (Eileen took after her in that respect), and a body so frail and fleshless that she had terrible trouble with her clothes. Her dresses drifted off her shoulders, her stockings wouldn't stay up, and one morning (according to mother who was most indiscreet about people's private affairs), when she was about to go into the local post office her knickers (she'd just bought a pair of French ones because she hated the way she looked and felt) fell down. She didn't panic, mind you, or faint, she was far too doughty a warrior for that, she just whipped them off, put them in her handbag and went home, after buying her stamps. She was little but she had courage, a sense of humour, and everything she possessed, including whatever energy was at her disposal, she gave to other people.

My aunt travelled up by train from Belfast and we got her out to the shops and then back to the digs where she cooked us a real dinner. We were very well looked after all the time mother was in hospital. As it happened, mother didn't do badly either because the day after she was taken in she passed the crisis stage and when asked by the doctor how she felt she said "hungry". "So what would you like to eat?" She requested a pork chop and this was provided. And for nearly two weeks – *she* said it was because she was a stranger and an actress, but I suspect it was because she told the nurses smutty jokes and made the doctors laugh – everyone treated her like a duchess.

Agnes stayed in Dungannon for the rest of that week and then moved on with us to our next venue. I don't remember where that was, but it couldn't have been too far away because mother had to catch up with the company when she got out of hospital. And during that time, not only did father get my aunt to look after us, but he also got her to go on the stage.

"Oh no Bob," she protested when he first made the suggestion, "I could never do that."

"Of course you could."

"But I've never been ... I've never done ..." she looked down at herself, "I'm not made for the stage."

"Oh, we'll soon fix that. There'll be something in Lily's basket to suit you."

"But I'm not an actress. All that dressing up and making up! I know nothing at all about acting."

"You go to the theatre."

"Oh yes I go to the Ulster Hall now and again, and the Opera House, and sometimes the Empire at Christmas. I like plays but that doesn't make me an actress. Besides, I couldn't learn a part, I've a head like a sieve, I can leave the kitchen and completely forget what I've gone for by the time I reach the bottom of the stairs."

"Oh, but this is only a small part, a few lines, and we're stuck Agnes, with Lily in hospital. Now here's the script. You play Constance, an ordinary young woman who becomes involved with a mysterious character who lives in a huge mansion."

"Is that *Bluebeard*?" I had been quietly following negotiations. You always needed to find out what was going on because nobody ever told you.

"That's right, *Bluebeard*."

"It's about a man," I explained to Aunt Agnes, "a hypnotist who invites young ladies to his house and they disappear and are never heard of again."

"Oh, that's great," said Agnes, "I suppose they all end up in hospital with broken arms or amnesia or something."

"No, it's a good play," said father. "And you're only on for a few minutes at a time with me. Have a look at the script."

"When is this to go on?" Agnes reluctantly took the ancient manuscript he was holding. "And what about rehearsals?"

"Oh, you've got a couple of days yet."

"*A couple of days!*"

"And we'll give you a run-through before the night. So all you have to do is read the script, the whole play's in there, then get an exercise book – I think I've got one back in the hall – write down the cues, that's the last lines of the person you're talking to, underline them, and then copy out your own part. That way you learn as you write."

"But there's half a page there!" Agnes opened the script and pointed to one passage. "I'd never learn all that. I have no memory I tell you, I'd forget and you'd be furious." She turned to where I was standing a decent distance away, "You know, when we were children your father used to write plays and dress us up and make us put on his productions in the front attic. Me and Elizabeth always giggled and got chucked out. And once when your Uncle Joe laughed he got thrown down the stairs."

"Oh, that's a long time ago," father laughed, "I won't throw you down the stairs this time ... there'd be nobody to cook the dinner. No, this is easy Agnes, a walk-on part, and if you do it, and maybe a little programme selling as well ..."

"Oh, but I do the programme selling. I do the programme selling." This was my territory. The programmes you see weren't really programmes as such, they were song sheets (parodies father had written), each one numbered, and at the end of the play there was a raffle and a prize. I got commission on the programmes I sold, and as I never got any pocket money and didn't get paid for acting this was the only opportunity I had to get my hands on some cash. And every penny I earned went into my post office money box, a small metal box that could only be opened in a post office. Money was very important to me in those days. I suppose there was a psychological reason, a need for security perhaps, because in later life, though I was always careful, I wouldn't go out of my way to increase my earnings, I had better things to do with my time. But as a child I was keen on money, and besides, I had worked out a scheme to maximise my earnings as a programme seller. When the curtain came down at the interval father would appear at the front and start selling, and I would get to work from the back. Now there were always men either sitting on forms or standing at the back near the door, so before the curtain actually descended (it depended on what sort of climax they'd worked up to – dramatic or otherwise) I would move quietly among the customers and start plying my trade. So you can quite understand that when father suggested another seller I was very unhappy. However, he assured me there was nothing to fear.

"Oh, it's alright, it won't affect your selling. Proper little tycoon he is. Aunt Agnes will just be standing in for me. So," he continued with the negotiations, "if you do the part, sell programmes and maybe do a stint on the door as well, I'll see if we can manage a small remuneration."

"Oh well," Agnes immediately showed some interest in the proceedings, "I wouldn't mind earning a wage." She was every bit as keen as I was when it came to getting her hands on some money. It hadn't been *her* choice to stay at home and keep house. And having to ask Elizabeth for every penny she needed irritated her immensely. So she agreed to go on. Although, as she found out to her cost, father hadn't fully explained or prepared her for what she had to do, or what she ought to expect when she found herself up on the stage.

Bluebeard was a play we didn't do very often ... about this eccentric who invited ladies, who subsequently disappeared from the face of the earth, onto his estate. Aunt Agnes was to play one of the women (grandma was the only other actress we had at the time), and as such she would be lured inside the great house, charmed, and told she could do anything she liked and go anywhere she pleased except for one room which was always kept locked. And in this room, as the audience and everybody else soon suspected, lay the answer to the riddle of the disappearing ladies.

Father had the star part, the only part ... he was Bluebeard. And he steadily builds up to the point where his latest victim, Agnes, now suspicious of his intentions and determined to find out what lies behind the locked door, manages to steal the key to the room. Now, in order to get the maximum effect and bring down the curtain, father had constructed the mystery room on stage. This he did by setting up a mock door and two large folding draught screens up-stage Left. So when the young woman, fearful but consumed by curiosity, throws open the door, the whole construction collapses and everyone can see what's inside. And what's inside is a semi-circle of pedestals and on top of each pedestal what appears to be a human head. Agnes knew, of course, what the play was about, but she hadn't seen what father had concocted on the other side of the screen. Consequently, when the atmosphere had been created, the tension heightened and the young woman (together with the audience) can stand the suspense no longer, Aunt Agnes inserts the key, opens the door ... And as she did so one of the heads, just an old wig stuffed with papier-maché but in the semi-darkness it looked rather horrible, fell off and rolled to her feet. She screamed, very realistically, which was what was expected. But what she didn't do was get out of the way, so the entire spare room came down round her ears and flattened her. She wasn't hurt, just shocked. Father, however, was very pleased and said it was the best curtain he'd seen in years. And after the play and the raffle came *The Farce.*

Father considered the farce an essential element in our entertainments, although he was strictly a tragedian himself, and mother said the comic roles he played were the worst she'd ever seen in her whole life. *Before* the play, in order to warm up the hall, we put on variety, but at the end of the night, no matter how sad, serious or thought-provoking the play had been, we always ended with a farce. "Send them home laughing," was father's philosophy, and the one I remember and liked best, the one we did in Dungannon with Aunt Agnes's assistance, was called *Who Died First?*

The plot was simple and outrageous, though not a whit less subtle than many of the television comedies dished up to more sophisticated audiences sixty years on, and a great deal more satisfying. Or were we all so much more innocent in those days? Like all the variety we presented it was devoid of any jokes that were blue, and there was never any blasphemy, that is, using the names Jesus and Christ as swear words. A large section of our audience blasphemed regularly and quite naturally, but father wouldn't tolerate it either on stage or off. I suppose it was his Presbyterian upbringing. Though when I knew him he wasn't what you would call a religious man, that is, he didn't go to church. Mind you, as we often had to travel on Sundays, and mother said her coat was a trifle shabby, we didn't go there much either. Though when we settled down and could live like everybody else she had us off to Sunday school, bible classes and church. But still father wouldn't go. And once, one Sunday when the three of us were dressed up and about to leave for the evening service, I did actually ask him, point blank, why he didn't go. He just grunted, jerked his head in mother's direction and said, "That's what happened to me the last time I went to church."

So, *Who Died First?* was clean, wholesome, and much enjoyed by both audience and actors alike. It was a game and everybody knew the rules and the roles that actors and audience were expected to play. Not that audiences directly participated ... hissed, booed, yelled "Look behind you," or anything like that ... they were far too well-mannered in those days. Though in a farce you might just get the odd comment and if it was apposite then it only added to the fun. Grandma and grandad played the two central characters, Mary and William O'Hagan, a right pair of old rogues who dodged, scrounged, and the last thing they would ever have dreamt of doing was pay the rent. Father played the landlord, Agnes was his wife, and the sketch opens with the landlord on his way to the cottage with the ultimatum: *Either pay the rent or get out.* The old couple see him coming and consider hiding or running away but finally hit on the idea of pretending that one of them, the old lady, has just died. So grandma stretches out on the bed and when the landlord enters he is confronted by a bereaved, grieving and distraught husband.

WILLIE: Oh, Mr Donovan sir, the rent, the rent, how can you think of such a thing and me distressed, distraught and out of my mind on account of how my poor darling Mary has just gone and left me.

LANDLORD: *(Looks at the bed)* Left you?

WILLIE: Given up the ghost.

LANDLORD: *(Horrified)* You mean she's not ... *(Takes a closer look)* she's not just ... ?

WILLIE: She's gone, Mr Donovan, moved on, passed over, kicked the bucket. She's dead.

LANDLORD: *Dead!*

WILLIE: This minute, the very minute you came in through the door looking for the rent. It was the strain sir ... the worry of it. Oh, my poor Mary, what will I ever do without you? *(Goes down by the bed and weeps)*

LANDLORD: Oh, this is terrible Willie, terrible, and so sudden! Oh, I'm sorry, very sorry indeed. I don't know what to say ... what to do. I'll just go home ... tell my wife ... I'll leave you.

WILLIE: That's right sir, you go home to your wife and leave me to my grief. Oh, she was such a wonderful woman, such a wonderful wife. Oh, my poor Mary.

The landlord leaves, without the rent, and when he's a safe distance away Willie gives the signal, Mary jumps off the bed and the pair of them laugh themselves silly. Then they decide to have a cup of tea, so Mary opens the front door in order to empty the teapot and is seen by the landlord's wife who is approaching with a bunch of flowers.

MARY: *(Slams the door and cries out)* Oh, Willie, we're undone, we're undone.

WILLIE: *(Has unearthed a gin bottle)* What do you mean, undone? What are you going on about?

MARY: Look out the window Willie. Look who's coming up to the front door.

WILLIE: Who's coming up to the front door? (*Crosses to the window*) Who's coming ... Oh dear God, it's the landlord's wife, Mrs Donovan, and she's brought a bunch of flowers for your grave.

MARY: And she's seen me Willie, she's seen me. Oh, what will we do, what will we do? (*There is a great deal of running about and arguing and then Willie comes up with another brilliant idea*).

WILLIE: Alright Mary, alright, I'll tell you what we'll do. If she's seen you, then *I'll* have to be dead.

MARY: You Willie?

WILLIE: Aye, *me*. I'll have to be dead.

MARY: But the landlord thinks it's me.

WILLIE: Aye well, this is the landlord's wife and she can think he's made a mistake. I'm the one that's dead Mary. *(Jumps on the bed and stretches out)* Let her in and then get rid of her as quick as you can because I can't hold my breath all day.

MARY: Right Willie, right. *(Mary goes to the door weeping, and confronts the landlady)*

LANDLADY: *(Exclaims in disbelief)* Mary! I couldn't believe my eyes. Mary!

MARY: Aye it's me, Mrs Donovan, what's left of me, it's me.

LANDLADY: But my husband told me ... my husband said ... I thought it was *you* that was ... that had died.

MARY: Oh no,it's not me, it's him, him there lying on the bed. My Willie, my own dear, darling Willie. He died of a heart attack Mrs Donovan, the minute your husband came into the house and asked for the rent, off he went.

LANDLADY: Oh, this is awful Mary, awful. And how could my husband have made such a mistake?

MARY: Oh, the heat of the moment, Mrs Donovan, the heat of the moment.

LANDLADY: Oh, I'm sorry Mary, really sorry and ... here's a bunch of flowers, and a couple of pounds to help tide you over. We'll both come to the funeral and if there's anything we can do let us know. I am very sorry Mary.

The landlady is ushered from the cottage and when out of earshot the old couple screech with delight and dance round the room. Then they both get stuck into the gin. When the bottle's empty Willie gets up, intending to throw it out of the front door, but in passing the window he exclaims,

WILLIE: Oh Mary!

MARY: *(Somewhat intoxicated)* What's the matter Willie?

WILLIE: Mary, it's the both of them.

MARY: The both of who? *(Staggers across the floor to join him at window)* The both of ...? Oh, the Donovans! The *both* of them. Oh, we're finished Willie, we're finished this time.

WILLIE: Aye, we're cornered.

MARY: We can't run.

WILLIE: We can't hide.

MARY: And we can't *both* be ...

WILLIE: *(Another brilliant idea hits him)* Oh yes we can ... that's the answer.

MARY: What's the answer Willie?

WILLIE: We'll *both* be dead!

MARY: *Both* be dead?

WILLIE: Aye, get on the bed, quick, stretch out and we'll both be dead. (*He joins her and they both prostrate themselves. The visitors knock a couple of times, then enter, arguing*).

LANDLORD: But I tell you it's Mary that's dead.

LANDLADY: And I tell you it's Willie. Mary met me at the door.

LANDLORD: And *Willie* met *me* at the door.

LANDLADY: She stood on that very spot and she said ... (*Catches sight of the two figures on the bed)* Oh, good heavens!

LANDLORD: *(Sees what she sees)* Dear God!

LANDLADY: They're both dead!

LANDLORD: You were right.

LANDLADY: And you were right.

LANDLORD: They're both dead.

LANDLADY: What an awful, terrible, tragic thing to happen.

LANDLORD: Together, at the same time.

LANDLADY: Well, it couldn't have been exactly at the same time because I saw Mary, when Willie was on the bed.

LANDLORD: Yes, and I saw Willie when Mary was on the bed. So one of them must have gone before the other. One of them must have died first, and I'd like to know who it was. *(Twitches from the couple on the bed)* I'd be very interested to know who it was. In fact, I'd give a five pound note to know *who died first!*

WILLIE *and* MARY: *(Sit bolt upright on the bed)* ***I did! I did!***

The audience roared, clapped, cheered, the curtain came down and they all went home. And it's a strange thing, but when I think back, when I visualise packed halls, the air reverberating with laughter and talk, the atmosphere charged with good-humour, expectation and promise, I don't feel any emotion at all. It's always the memory, and the feelings that go with the memory, of *empty halls* that I can never forget. After the show, with the chairs that started off side by side all over the place, and the forms that I had carefully placed in straight lines lying on their sides or upside down. The place littered with cigarette ends, sweet papers and song sheets. The air redolent of wet clothes, stale smoke and the sawdust and Jeyes Fluid that was scattered over the floor. The show's over, the hall's empty, the curtain's up and the stage is silent and yet … not dead. It's the emptiness and the silence that I remember. In some way they seem to fix and hold fast to the life, laughter, tears … to everything that has gone on before.

11

Sent to Coventry

Mother returned in fine shape after her holiday, as father termed it, in The Workhouse. Aunt Agnes got on the train, went back to Belfast, and we packed up and headed off into one of the longest, wettest and most miserable winters I can ever remember. Every journey seemed to be taken in darkness. Every road seemed to be more desolate and potholed than the one before. And we were cold … cold halls, cold digs, cold lorries. And wet … everything we wore, everything we possessed was damp and splattered with mud. I don't remember one single placename or village during that long, dreary period. The farms were isolated, the cottages were in the middle of bogs … it just seemed to me that we had lost touch with the rest of the world. And for the first time in my travelling experience (and mother said it was the same for her) not only did we have to cope with poverty and the weather, but with ill-will and bigotry as well. The problem began with the hall.

Most halls we now played in, and this Hibernian hall was no exception, were either made of wood, corrugated iron, or a combination of the two. It had a door in the gable facing the roadway, a stage about eighteen inches high at the other end, and a little ante-room at the back of the stage. It was small, you might have crammed in a hundred and fifty people, and it was in the middle of nowhere. Although there must have been people living somewhere in the area, hidden among clumps of trees, down long narrow lanes, or tucked away among the hills. There was certainly a chapel some distance away, and that meant people within walking distance, also a small school, and even a shop. The shop in particular I remember on account of the smell. The digs too, because we lodged in a house with an upstairs and not in a cottage, as was often the case, I can recall, but not much else. You see my movements and therefore my knowledge of an area were very restricted in winter. Winter days in northern parts are very short, and the children in the digs were often young like myself, or if older had gone off to school and so I had little contact with them. I was therefore confined to the digs, the hall, or now and again I might become more closely acquainted with a shop, as I was in this particular area, or rather a store, which fascinated me so much that I can remember it to this day.

It seemed to be partly below ground, a basement or cellar dug out from underneath a house. You had to go down a few steps into a vault that was so dark, even in daytime, that you could barely see the back wall. The ceiling was low, so low that I felt I could reach up and touch it. And the place was piled up with whatever the community needed. It smelled of a great many things, but the odour that predominated was that of dried fish. The fish, skate I presume, hung like tattered remnants of dirty grey carpet from the wooden ceiling, and I think you had to boil it before it could be used. But we weren't in that place long enough to enjoy the experience. This was a catholic community, hence the Hibernian hall (and the fish for Fridays), and at that time we were all protestants as John, Wee Teddy and Ethyl who married him and converted, had left the company. Not that that had caused us any problems in the past. Religion was never a problem to us in those days. And was it really religion that was at the root of the trouble we encountered? Well, you'll have to make up your own mind about that.

Father had booked the hall on a Saturday morning and we were due to open on the Monday night. The parish priest who ran everything in the community was away on business, so father made arrangements with the caretaker, paying him six shillings as a deposit on the rent. We moved into the area sometime on the Saturday afternoon, set up the scenery and got lodgings with no trouble at all. The caretaker, who had a wife and several children of his own, said they could take in father, mother and the two youngsters, while his eldest sister, whose family had grown up and gone away, "would be pleased to take in the old couple", my grandparents. We'd struck lucky. These were decent, honest, hard-working people – of course it was always working people who gave us lodgings and were willing to share everything they had. And although the house was small and full of activity, it was cheerful and spotlessly clean. They were all catholics in that area, and unlike some strict presbyterians we had encountered who considered play acting sinful, they were wildly excited about the theatre. We would get plenty of support. However, later on Saturday evening the parish priest, Father Corrigan, returned from his business, learnt about the booking (it was for the week), and that we had already moved in, and was absolutely furious. He, it appears, though he hadn't told the caretaker or anyone else as far as we could gather, had other ideas, other plans, and the hall should not have been let. He was very annoyed about the situation and stormed round to the caretaker's house where he confronted a very respectful but very excited household (entertaining strangers and the prospect of a whole week of plays was their idea of living), pulled down their dream world and gave the caretaker a good telling-off.

"You had no right to let the hall in my absence, Tom."

"But Father, I didn't know you wanted ..."

"No right at all."

"But Father," the caretaker's wife moved alongside and tried to give support to her husband, "Tom had no idea ..."

"Quiet woman," the priest silenced her. "The minute I'm out of the parish people start taking affairs into their own hands and I will not tolerate that sort of behaviour. They're all protestants I hear."

"Yes Father, I believe they are, but we've taken them in and they're all decent ..."

"Well they can't have the hall ... it's booked ... I have plans of my own. Where's the man, where's the boss of this outfit?"

"They're all down at the hall fixing things up Father." The caretaker looked round at the rest of the family who were standing meekly, like himself, before their pastor.

"Then they'll just have to *un*fix them. And I'm left with the job of going down there to point that out. I'm very upset Tom. I'm only twenty four hours away from the place and this is what happens."

"I'm sorry Father."

"So am I!" Father Corrigan marched out of the house, along the road, into the hall where we were putting the finishing touches to the scenery, and told father the deal was off. We would have to be out of the hall by Monday morning. Father was shocked, but he remained calm and politely pointed out that we had booked the hall in good faith, we had moved in, and *we* had no idea what the previous arrangements had been. And you know I don't think the reverend gentleman said what the previous arrangements had been, I don't think we ever found out ... mother certainly didn't remember. Anyway, father stuck to his guns and repeated that he was sorry if we had accidentally upset anyone's arrangements but we had arrived, we were here, and we would "open as arranged on Monday night".

"*To an empty hall!*" retorted the priest, angrily leaving the scene. And just to ensure that this was the case and prove that his was no idle threat, at Mass the following morning he announced his displeasure from the pulpit and ordered that no-one should put a foot inside that hall until he gave them permission.

Our poor landlady, when she returned on Sunday morning and told mother what had been said in chapel, was greatly distressed.

"Oh, Mrs Mateer," she said, "this is terrible, terrible ... Isn't it Tom?" She looked round at her husband and the rest of the family who were standing behind her dressed in their Sunday clothes, their shining, well-scrubbed faces clouded over with gloom.

"Oh yes it is," agreed Tom, "terrible. We were all looking forward to the plays."

"And to have you staying with us for the week. It's just terrible."

"It's certainly very unfortunate," agreed mother. "I mean, we've nothing else planned, nowhere else to go."

"Oh, we know that, we know that, you've just moved in, you've everything set up, and it's really hard on you. Tom's sister agrees with us, everybody we talked to on the way home from chapel agrees with us, but you see … you understand, Mrs Mateer … we couldn't go."

"Of course, you couldn't go after what Father Corrigan said, I quite understand that. But, as I'm sure you'll appreciate, we're in a difficult … a different situation. I mean, just at the moment we're all protestants in the company."

"Oh, but what difference does that make, what difference does that make? You're all decent people, and we wanted to see the plays."

"Yes, I know, but what I mean is … what I'm trying to say is … it's a pity, us being different, that Father Corrigan couldn't have found a way of compromising."

"Oh no, he won't do that, Mrs Mateer," the caretaker assured her, "he's a very strong-willed man is Father Corrigan."

"Yes, well, unfortunately so is my husband."

"No, he won't change his mind, Mrs Mateer," the landlady agreed with her husband. "And though I would never say a word against him … nobody would ever say a word against Father Corrigan because he's a great priest and a great man, but … well, we think maybe he's been a bit hard in this instance."

"Maybe …" her husband looked down at his highly polished boots, "but he won't change."

"No, I don't suppose he will," agreed mother. "And of course it's his hall and his right, but you see my husband …" she paused, looked round as though concerned about father who was upstairs, and lowered her voice. "Mind you, I shouldn't be saying this …" Then she went into one of her petty, cheap, blatant little acts of confidence and betrayal, pretending it was a secret and painting father in the worst possible light. Of course, something of the sort was necessary, and it was mother's job to clear the way before one of father's charges, or tidy up after he'd gone through, but if only she could have managed a little more subtlety, a little more finesse. Not that her audiences ever complained, indeed the more obvious the act the better they liked it. "To tell you the truth, Mrs Maguire, I've had a terrible night with my husband over this hall business."

"Oh *no*." Mrs Maguire lowered *her* voice. Mr Maguire stopped looking down at his boots, and the Maguire children quietly edged into the conspiratorial circle.

"Oh yes, I've had no sleep at all. I've talked myself hoarse trying to get him to see reason. But he's a stubborn man is my husband … a straight man, an honest man, but stubborn as a mule. Mind you I suppose he has a point when you try to see it from his side. I mean, *he* says we booked the hall in good faith and paid a deposit," she glanced in the direction of the caretaker and he nodded in assent, "so he thinks, he feels …" Again she glanced over her shoulder though everybody in the kitchen could hear father still snoring upstairs. "And you mustn't breath a word, you mustn't tell him I've said this."

"Oh no, no." There was head shaking, glances and mumbles all round.

"He's got to tell you it himself."

"Of course."

"Well, he thinks we have the right, and he says despite what Father Corrigan said in the chapel ..." There was a pause. The Maguire family waited with bated breath. Then mother delivered her punch line. "*He's going to open on Monday night as arranged.*"

"Oh, but nobody will come," wailed Mrs Maguire, "nobody will come."

"He'll open just the same."

So about seven o'clock on Monday evening we left Eileen asleep in the digs (the landlady was only too pleased to look after her), collected grandma and grandad and made our way along the quiet country road to the hall. The night was dark, we walked slowly, looking up at the sky for light and guidance. When we got to the beginning of the long, black, potholed cart track that led down to the hall itself, grandad, at the head of the column, took charge.

"Company halt!" he commanded. We all stopped, apart from father who just snorted and went on. Then he called out to me. "Jimmy!"

"Yes grandad," I replied from the end of the line where I was escorting mother.

"*Jimmy!*" His hearing wasn't much better than his eyesight at times. "Where is that dogsbody?"

"Oh, don't call him that Harry," grandma laughingly reproved him.

"Where is that tripehound?" Grandad ignored her.

"How dare you call my son a tripehound!" Mother joined in.

"Where is he?"

"I'm here grandad." I made my way to his side.

"Ah, right, right. Now, here's your lantern soldier."

"My lantern?" I echoed in surprise.

"Ah, you didn't know your old grandad had made you a lantern did you?"

"No."

"Well I have, I've made two, and here's yours." He pushed what felt like a glass jar into my hands and took out a box of matches. "Now let's see if it works." He struck a match, I held up the jar and he lit the small piece of candle he'd stuck inside. "There! How's that?"

"It's very good." Immediately the prospect of wandering around in the darkness became a great deal more interesting.

"I've tied a piece of string round the top so you can carry it. Now we'll light my one." He struck another match, applied it, the candle struggled, and then a second jampot glowed in his hand. "Now what do you think of that?"

"I think it's very good indeed. Now we can see where we're putting our feet."

"Right. Back to the end of the column soldier," he ordered. "Hold your lantern near the ground. And don't swing it about. Are you right Louie?" he turned to grandma.

"Yes corporal." (That was the extent of grandad's promotion as a stretcher-bearer.) Grandma took hold of his arm.

"Company advance."

Father was already in the hall by the time we got to the door, and by striking matches (I don't think battery torches had been invented then, or if they had they hadn't yet got to us) he'd located and lit two of the oil lamps. By the light of one we changed, made-up and got ready for the performance. By the light of the other father set up two more lamps, got the gramophone going, then instructed grandad to open the door so that the light could shine and the music could drift out into the darkness beyond. Then we waited ... and waited ... and waited. But nobody, not even one small boy, and there was always one small boy who couldn't afford the threepence but was curious to see what was going on, came near us that night. We stayed until nearly nine o'clock then father gave up, shut down the gramophone, blew out the lights, locked the door, and we went back to the digs.

Supper was a very silent, miserable affair that evening. The landlady's children were in bed, Mrs Maguire sat quietly sewing by the firelight, and Mr Maguire, with his feet on the fender, smoked his pipe and stared into space. There was very little conversation, and after we had finished our supper and cleared up we said goodnight and retired to our room. Eileen was asleep in her cot so I got undressed, and as the rest of us were sharing a bed, quietly climbed in and moved over towards the wall. Father took out his map, spread it on top of the chest of drawers, and by the light of the candle studied it intently, while mother, after getting into her nightdress, sat on the edge of the bed and tied her hair up with little bits of paper. Finally she broke the silence.

"What are we going to do Bob?"

"No business, that's certain," replied father. "The parish priest has seen to that."

"I wonder why he couldn't alter his arrangements."

"Because he'd made up his mind not to. And he's got no business ... and I've a bloody good mind to tell him so."

"Oh no, Bob."

"Well, what right has he to stop people coming to see the play if they want to ... and they all want to."

"I know. But you can see the situation, the way things are. What's the use of making trouble?"

"He's the one who's made the trouble."

"Yes, but it's his house."

"And it's our bloody living."

"Well, fighting won't solve anything. It'll only make things worse ... upset the landlady, and she's very upset as it is. You've got to be sensible Bob."

"And will that pay the rent, and the digs?"

"I don't know. Haven't we got *any* money left?"

"About ten bob."

"Well I've got another three shillings I've been saving for a pair of shoes." She turned and looked in my direction. "And maybe Jim has ..."

"Oh no," I shot up in bed. "You're not getting any of my savings."

"Shut up," father snapped, "you'll wake Eileen."

"But that's my money ... I'm saving up."

"Go back to sleep."

"But it's not fair, it's taken me years."

"Go back to sleep," mother reassured me, "nobody's going to touch your money." She turned again to father. "I'll talk to mam and dad in the morning and see if they can help."

"We'll have to move." Father again applied himself to his map.

"Of course," agreed mother, "but to where?"

"God knows! We're in the middle of nowhere. The Bog of Allen I should think by the look of it. And I thought getting this hall was a stroke of luck."

"And the digs ... they're really nice people."

"We're miles off the beaten track. And we'll have to get a lorry."

"What about the man who brought us here, doesn't he live somewhere in the area?"

"Yes, I think he does."

"Then why not try him? What's the nearest place on your map?"

"It's about ten miles away. I don't know whether it's a village, there are houses on the map, or just a handful of cottages."

"The Maguires would know. Why not ask them?"

"Yes, I suppose they would know."

"Pick two or three possibilities and we'll ask Mrs Maguire in the morning. She'll be only too willing to help."

"There's a Killy-something-or-other at the crossroads ... houses and I think a church. That's a bit nearer."

"Write down the names and if we get up early we can talk to *Mr* Maguire before he goes off to work. They've lived all their lives in this area, they'll know the district for miles around."

Father took out a pencil and an envelope and again peered at his map. "There's also a small village we passed on the way here."

"Write that down too, and then come to bed. I'm worn out. I feel like I've done a night's work. Come on, that's enough names Bob, come to bed." Father put the envelope and map back in his pocket, undressed and blew out the candle.

The next morning, Tuesday, we were up early, father had a talk with the landlord and then we had breakfast, toast, which was no simple operation as they didn't have a toast rack (many ranges in country houses had one) and we had to use a fork. The bread was fresh and the fire was not really suitable so either the bread broke and fell on the hearth, or the toast got done too quickly, in fact got burnt and impregnated with smoke. After we had eaten father put on his coat and hat and wheeled round his bike.

"Don't know when I'll be back," he said as he threw his leg over the saddle.

"Before dark I hope," mother went out to see him off.

"Oh, I'll be back before dark," he reassured her. And to our surprise, quite early on in the afternoon while we were still fiddling about in the hall, father walked in through the door.

"*You're* back early," mother greeted him.

"Yes." His face told us nothing but I had a feeling he'd sorted out something.

"Any luck?"

"Oh yes," he took off his coat and hat and turned to grandad. "Let's get on with the scenery."

"Right boss." Grandad had been itching to have a go at the scenery all morning but he couldn't do it on his own, and it was too heavy for the ladies.

"Well?" Mother put her hands on her hips and watched father climb up the ladder. "Aren't you going to tell us? What did you get?"

"A small church hall ... presbyterian I think."

"No trouble?"

"I saw the minister as well as the caretaker."

"Good."

"And the caretaker drives a lorry and can move our stuff."

"Great."

"He also gave me a couple of names to try for digs."

"Wonderful."

"Ah," grandma came out into the hall, beamed one of her gracious smiles and added her praise, "you can always rely on Bob to get the company out of a hole."

"When do we move?" Grandad had taken up a position on the opposite side of the stage, ready for action.

"Tomorrow morning at first light."

"That's the stuff," the old man thumped a fist into his hand. "That's the stuff, no hanging about."

"You did very well," mother looked at grandma and then returned to father. "What about food, did you get anything to eat?"

"The caretaker's wife gave me a plate of stew."

"Oh, you really hit the jackpot this morning." Mother laughed and turned to go back into the dressing room.

"Yes," father agreed and then added, "and when we've got the scenery down I intend to finish the day off by having a few well-chosen words with the parish priest."

Mother stopped in her tracks. "Oh no, Bob, you're not going to cause trouble!"

"No, no," father was very calm, a fair sign that that was exactly what he had in mind. "I'm just going to inform him that we're vacating the hall, thank him for his kindness and quote a short passage from the Bible."

"Oh no, you mustn't, you can't, oh no," mother protested. "Oh, why can't we go quietly, peacefully? Why do you want to fight with the man?"

"I'm not going to fight with the man, he's a priest. I'm just going to talk to him."

"Oh dear, dear," mother looked anxiously in grandma's direction, "we've got another hall, another lorry, digs ... Why does he want to upset everybody? And it's not just the priest, it's the landlady, she's nearly in tears over this business as it is. Oh mam, don't you think he should let it go this time?"

"Now Lily," grandma was much too wise to get drawn into an argument of that sort, so she moved forward and gently took mother by the arm, "you leave this matter to Bob."

"But mam, the landlady ..."

"He knows exactly what he's doing, and I'm sure when he approaches the reverend gentleman he'll be diplomacy itself."

"*You're joking!*"

"Come and finish your packing."

"But mam ..."

"Your *packing*." Grandma tightened her grip on mother's arm and led her away from the line of battle. The two men went on with their work in silence.

When everything was pulled down, packed up and made ready for the lorry, we left the hall. Grandma and grandad returned to their digs and we returned to ours. Father said nothing more about his threat to confront the priest, and of course mother, hoping against hope that he'd given up the idea, steered well clear of the subject. After tea, however, without saying anything to anyone father left his pipe on the table by the bedside, put on his coat and hat and went out ... to the parochial house. And when he got there ...

"Good evening." He raised his hat and greeted the housekeeper, a lady getting on in years, who came to the front door.

"Good evening." The lady had never met father but immediately guessed who he was, and of course she knew all about the trouble over the hall.

"Is Father Corrigan at home?"

The housekeeper looked uneasy. "He is, but I don't know ..."

"I wonder if you would be kind enough to ask him if he could spare me a couple of minutes ... my name's Mateer ... we booked the hall."

"Oh yes, yes, I know who you are, Mr Mateer." She hesitated and then added, "Will you just hold on a minute and I'll find out if Father Corrigan can see you?"

"Certainly, certainly." Father turned away. The lady didn't shut the door, so after she had knocked and entered an inner room he heard her announce his arrival. There was a short conversation, the sound of heavier footsteps coming down the hall, and father turned to confront the unsmiling cleric who appeared at the front door.

"Mr Mateer?"

"Yes, Father Corrigan."

"What can I do for you?"

"Well, at this late date not a great deal. I've just called to inform you that we will be vacating the hall early tomorrow morning, and we'll leave the key with the caretaker if that's alright."

"Oh yes, that's alright." The priest looked relieved.

"We opened last night as I said we would ... scenery, costumes, music, everything ready for a performance. We even stayed in the hall until nine o'clock but nobody came."

"No, they wouldn't." Father Corrigan looked grim again.

"And that, of course, was because in the chapel on Sunday you ordered them not to."

"Yes, well I explained the situation, Mr Mateer, but I'm afraid you didn't listen. The hall was needed, you had no right to be there."

"Oh, but we had every right to be there."

"Now I'm not going to argue."

"Every right because we booked in good time, in good faith, and paid a deposit of six shillings."

"Ah well," the priest reached into his trouser pocket and brought out some coins, "you can have your deposit back."

"Oh, but we don't want our deposit back, we occupied the hall, that's not why I'm here. I came here to tell you we booked, travelled, erected our scenery, and got lodgings with kind, generous-hearted people who wanted to come ... who *would* have come to the hall to enjoy what we had prepared for them, but you ordered them to stay away."

"Now I've told you," the priest grew angry, "I've explained ... I even came round to the hall to see you personally ... I had other plans and you should not have been in that hall."

"That is not the point Father Corrigan. You ordered your parishioners to withhold their support and by doing so you denied me, my wife and the rest of my company the chance to earn a living."

"Nonsense, rubbish, that has nothing to do with me."

"Oh, but it has. You denied us the right, the God-given right, to earn our daily bread."

"Now listen here Mr Mateer, I am a priest, I don't need a sermon, I don't need actors, travellers, particularly protestant travellers, to talk to *me* about religion."

"So it was because we were protestants that you denied us the hall?"

"No it was *not* because you were protestants, I only mentioned that because you don't seem to understand that this is a Hibernian hall, a catholic hall, and I had other plans, other priorities. It had nothing whatever to do with religion."

"But if you will pardon me Father Corrigan ... you denied me the right to feed my family, and if that has nothing to do with religion then I don't know what has."

"I have nothing more to say to you on the subject. Good night."

Father primed and fired a final volley. "The key will be with the caretaker Father

Corrigan. And by dawn we shall have shaken the dust from off our feet. The disciples, I believe, did that when they were driven out of a city! Goodnight."

The door of the parochial house slammed shut.

We were all washed, dressed, had finished our porridge (apart from father who had a boiled egg) and were ready for the road when the landlord came downstairs the next morning. Mrs Maguire had been up earlier still and had presented us with a parcel of soda farls she'd baked on the griddle that morning, half a pound of country butter, and a tin with four eggs so that we should have something to eat when we got to our destination. The poor lady was very distressed as she bustled round her kitchen. Mr Maguire didn't look very cheerful either, and when we tried to settle up for the lodgings he wouldn't let his wife take the money. Mother was nearly in tears herself by this time, and when the young Maguires, unsmiling and in various stages of undress, began to filter into the kitchen, it looked as though we had gathered for a wake. Indeed I've seen more cheerful wakes in my time. However, "Leave them laughing" was the company's motto, and though neither father nor mother could rise to the occasion, Eileen, quite inadvertently, upheld the tradition and shattered the gloom.

It appears she had wakened in the small hours and demanded a drink. Mother heard her, answered, and then went straight back to sleep. Eileen climbed out of her cot, no mean feat, went out of the bedroom and wandered round the house. Exactly how far she got we never found out, but when she returned she was obviously satisfied with the expedition, climbed into bed alongside mother, putting a foot on my face in the process, and went back to sleep. The incident was forgotten. Then as we were hanging about in the kitchen the following morning waiting for the lorry, mother, trying to think of something to occupy the Maguire household who wouldn't move until we had gone, remembered it.

"And what do you think about this wee rip, Mrs Maguire? Woke me up in the middle of the night demanding a drink!"

"Well, I was thirsty."

"You *said* you were thirsty but you weren't really."

"Yes I was," Eileen was adamant. "I was very thirsty indeed."

"But you didn't get a drink and you went back to sleep … in *our* bed."

"I *did* get a drink."

"You did?"

"Yes. I went out and got a drink and *then* I went back to sleep in your bed."

"But you didn't go downstairs into the kitchen did you?"

All eyes were now on Eileen who immediately moved centre stage.

"No, I didn't go downstairs because it was dark."

"So where did you go?"

"I just went outside the door and got a drink there."

"She's making it up," mother laid a hand on Eileen's shoulder, "she's just showing off."

"I am not showing off. I went outside the door and I got a drink of water."

The landlady stopped what she was doing and began to take an interest in what Eileen was saying.

"And where was the water Eileen?" she asked.

"It was in a bottle."

"A *bottle!*" Father also began to take an interest. "What bottle?"

"Wait a minute," the landlady held up her hand, dashed out of the door, thumped up and down stairs, then came back into the kitchen holding a small dark blue medicine bottle. "Is that the bottle Eileen?"

"Yes, that's the bottle."

Mrs Maguire looked at her husband and laughed. Mr Maguire looked round at the children and they laughed.

"What's the joke?" mother enquired.

"What was in the bottle?" father was hot on her heels.

"*Was* it water?" mother looked uneasy.

"Oh yes, it was water alright."

Mrs Maguire was red in the face, Mr Maguire nearly choked, and the Maguire kids fell all over the floor.

"And what was water doing in a medicine bottle?" father demanded.

"It's *holy* water."

"*Holy water!*"

"Holy water from Lourdes."

"My God," father grabbed hold of Eileen, "the child could be poisoned."

"Not a bit," Mrs Maguire reassured him, "it'll do her good."

"Specially as she's a protestant," mother threw in the line and brought down the house.

Father was the only one who didn't think it funny. He had Eileen gargling T.C.P. for the rest of that week. But it didn't do her a bit of harm.

So we prepared to leave that place. Mother gave the landlady a blouse she had admired, slipped the children a few coppers so they could buy sweets, and when the lorry arrived we clambered aboard, waved farewell and moved on ... and on ... Until one day towards the end of that winter we found ourselves in another remote part of the country, only this time the natives who lived there, the people we hoped would be our audience for the week, were not catholic but protestant. And the hall was Orange, not Green.

12

Under Siege

The landscape was dark, the sky leaden, and all that sheltered the cottage from the rain that swept across miles of black, empty bogland was a clump of trees. We nearly walked past the place as it was almost hidden behind a thick uncut hedge of hawthorn and lay back a few feet below the level of the road. The lorryman had called it a road, but really it was only a lane with no other houses anywhere in sight. It looked very lonely and isolated under those conditions, but not desolate. The rough grass at the front and sides of the building had been mowed. The wild fuchsias (originally natives of South America but quite happy in Irish soil) that grew outside the door and almost obscured the two tiny windows had been cut back in recent times. And there was smoke, a thin white wisp of it darting around the top of the chimney. The half door, the top half that is, was open. It was often like that unless the "weather" was on the front of the cottage, as the occupant liked to see out.

We were to have the bedroom and cook for ourselves for the week, that is my parents and us kids; grandma and grandad had got digs in a farm. And as I had been told there were only two rooms in the cottage, the kitchen and the bedroom off, I wondered, as we approached our new lodgings, where whoever lived there would sleep! The answer was obvious the moment we stepped into the kitchen and were confronted by a four-poster bed with full canopy and drapes which occupied most of the room. Our landlady, who incidentally was to play a small part in the drama The Fates were currently writing with us in mind, was crippled, bedridden, and lived on her own.

"Well, we've arrived, Mrs McKee." Mother called her Mrs but I'm not at all certain that this was correct. The lorryman called her Rosie Ann and told us she had no family or relatives in the area and depended entirely on neighbours, most of them living some distance away.

"Aye, I can see that." The old lady eased herself up in the bed.

"I hope we haven't disturbed you, arriving on a Sunday like this, but we couldn't get the lorry for any other day."

"No, you haven't disturbed me. I'm not going anywhere."

"That's good. Well now," mother turned to me, "this is my young son, Jim."

I advanced, held out my hand and said politely, "Pleased to meet you."

"Well brought up, eh?" The old lady took my hand and would have held on to it but I gently withdrew and retreated to where mother was standing. There was a strong, distinctive and not very pleasant smell, one I had come to associate with things and people of great antiquity, which got stronger the nearer you got to the bed.

"Oh yes, they have to behave ... do as they're told." Mother pressed Eileen forward. "And this is young Eileen. Say hello to the lady." Eileen resisted. "Go on."

"How do you do?" My little sister did as she was told but still stood her ground. And I didn't blame her because apart from the smell, a musty, peppery smell, it may have been some sort of medication, the old lady wore a night cap and all you could focus on was a face, a rather fierce-looking face, peering out from among all the ancient draperies. And on top of that there was a blackthorn stick which the lady who had arranged the digs told us Rosie Ann had been known to use on anybody who annoyed her and got within reach.

"Now they'll be no trouble, Mrs McKee," mother couldn't call her Rosie Ann, not at the beginning, "they'll make no noise."

"Oh, I don't mind the noise of childer," the old lady reassured her, and immediately went up in my estimation. "This is a lonely old place, not many folk pass the door. I don't mind the weans. They can have the run of the house, except ... except when I need to have the room to myself ... you understand, Mrs Mateer?"

"Of course I understand," mother said, "of course. And the minute you want a bit of privacy you just shout. And if I'm not here and the children are, you tell them to get out ... and they'll go."

"Of course we will, Mrs McKee." I thought it prudent to back mother's statement, and of course I could quite understand that the old lady would need to have the place to herself at times. Indeed, how she managed, being in bed all day, I had no idea and didn't consider. Maybe as she had a stick she could get out of bed and walk a few steps. Though during our very brief stay I never saw her anywhere other than in bed. A neighbour, a Katie McCarthy, seemed to attend to all her wants.

"You'll have to turn the mattress," Rosie Ann pointed with her stick, "it hasn't been used for a while. And the bedclothes ... you'll find them in the cupboard ... they'll need airing. Though the house isn't damp."

"Oh, far from it," mother looked at the wide hearth and the turf fire glowing cheerfully in the darkness, "it's very dry and warm. I must say I like a turf fire ... the smell." Mother used the term turf because nobody ever called it peat.

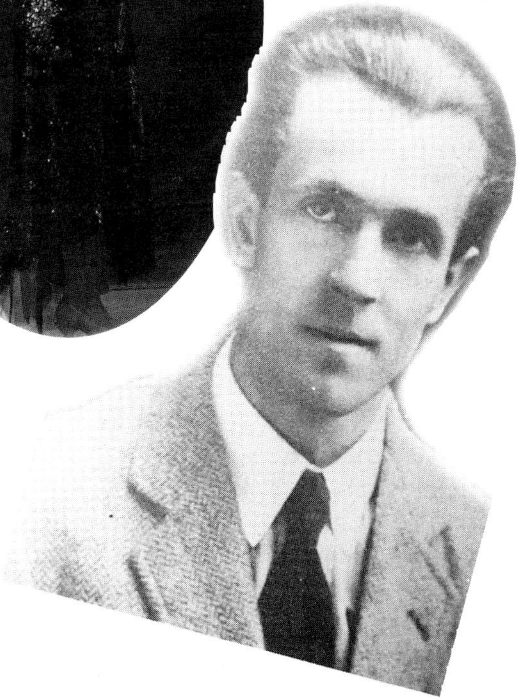

Above left
Father, a dandy round the east end of Belfast in the Roaring Twenties

Above right
Mother, sweet sixteen and a juvenile lead

Centre
Father's leading lady, Lily Wynn

Far right
Bob Mateer 'versatile character actor'

"Oh, you can't beat a turf fire ... it gives out a great heat. And you know the fire in that hearth was lit when I came into this house fifty-three years ago, and it has never been out since."

"Except at night."

"Oh no, not even at night."

"Can you bank it up then?"

"Oh no, it wouldn't last. No, what you do ... what Katie McCarthy does, but you can do it while you're here, save her the trouble ... what you do last thing at night is lift out a nice red turf with the tongs and bury it in the ashpit. Then the next morning all you have to do is lift it out, put a few more turves round it, give it a bit of a blow with the bellows and you're away. The same fire... never goes out ... it would be very bad luck for the house if it did."

"Right then, I'll do that at night, and Jim will bring in the turf. Oh, and then there's the matter of groceries. Katie McCarthy tells me there's no shop in the area."

"No shop, but the grocery van will be round tomorrow. He comes once a week, and you can get all you want from him. The breadserver comes past the house every day, and the butcher twice a week. And of course the well is just up the lane a wee bit, on the opposite side, in the field."

"Oh, you're very well provided for."

"We are. And you can get milk, butter and eggs from the farm where Katie McCarthy works."

"She comes in every day to help you?"

"Twice a day. And there's another neighbour ... her husband looks after the grass and the hedge. I'm well cared for."

"That's good, and of course if there's anything I can do while we're here I'll be only too pleased."

"Thank you."

"No, it's very good of you to take strangers into your home, and at such short notice."

"Not a bit. Katie said you were decent people and I'm glad of the company. You're welcome."

So we moved in with Rosie Ann McKee. The rain eased off, the sky brightened a little, and my parents, taking Eileen along with them, went to the hall to set up the scenery and unpack while I spent the last couple of hours of daylight exploring the terrain. There wasn't much to see at the front of the cottage, only fields, but at the back, right at the end of the garden there was a midden (probably only archaeologists use a term like that now, but it was in everyday use then, in Ireland) where rubbish and what was cleared out of the fire and the dry lavatory was thrown. There was also a peat stack, nearer than the midden, covered with an old tarpaulin to keep it dry. And at the end of the garden stood the trees, ash trees, which were tall and old and had obviously survived many a storm. Behind that there was open, treeless country and bog. It was very lonely, quiet, and peaceful, only the cry of a curlew disturbed the silence. I liked such places. The old lady told me that there were other cottages and farms further along her road but we didn't see any of the inhabitants during our stay there. Either the residents went out at the other end of the road or they didn't go anywhere at all. The only person, apart from Katie McCarthy and her husband, and they came off the main road as we did, who passed the cottage during our stay there was a big, burly man with red hair. This man, though I didn't know it at the time, was to play a leading role in the drama to be enacted later the following week at the Orange Hall.

By the time father had finished work and returned to the cottage where mother, who had left before him, was preparing our evening meal (mashed potatoes and fried sausages which was my favourite dish) I was completely at home in our new quarters. Mind you, it never took me long to adjust. I had been in a few different digs and dealt quite successfully with any number of solitary old landladies in my time. Though one of them, in a place called Dunnamanagh, once insisted on dosing me and Eileen with caster oil because we made a noise while father and mother were working in the hall. But Rosie Ann wasn't like that; she looked fierce at times but she was kindly, though not sentimental, and I quite liked her, at a distance of course. Mother and she, needless to say, got on well from the start. So things looked promising, and after we had finished our meal we were introduced to Katie McCarthy's husband when they both came to visit, as was their habit on Sunday evenings, to have a chat with Rosie Ann.

"Bring the two chairs out of the bedroom, Mrs Mateer," the old lady ordered as the visitors entered, "and the wee lad can have the stool."

"Oh yes, that's my favourite." I collected the three-legged stool and we all, apart from Eileen who had been put to bed, sat in a semi-circle, leaving a gap so that the old lady could see the fire. Outside the night got darker, while inside, with the door shut tight and the firelight casting strange shadows on the whitewashed walls, the conversation got more interesting. At first it was just chat about the countryside, and gossip relating to people who lived in the area. After that there were anecdotes about remarkable characters of the past. Then, as so often happens on dark winter nights and in lonely places where country folk gather together round the fire, the talk turned to the subject of ghosts.

I loved ghost stories and knew all about the signs and portents that precede strange happenings; such as hens that went out pecking after dark; roosters that crowed on the stroke of midnight; and large black dogs that appeared from nowhere and disappeared under the bed of someone who was about to die. Many times I'd heard tales about lonely country roads where solitary travellers returning home late at night turned a corner and came face to face with something sitting on the top of a gatepost, something white ... a shape ... a figure ... a *woman*, who, without warning rent the silent air with a fiendish, bloodcurdling shriek and disappeared ... *the banshee*. Of course, as father pointed out to the small gathering round the fireside, there may have been natural explanations for that sort of phenomenon. Though he had to admit, as Shakespeare said, "There are more things in heaven and earth than are dreamt of in your philosophy." While grandma (on previous occasions that is), who was a Spiritualist, maintained that despite father's disbelief and even mockery at times he had great sensitivity, a positive aura, and would have made an excellent medium. And the fact that on occasions like this father could tell the best, the most hair-raising ghost stories of all, things that had *actually happened to him*, seemed to prove grandma was right.

"No, to be quite honest, there was a time when I would have said I do not believe in ghosts, but then once ..." Father paused and there was silence in the room. Then in the midst of the silence, from somewhere at the back of the fireplace, indeed it seemed somewhere inside the fire itself, came the chirping of a solitary cricket. And when it stopped, the voice of Rosie Ann from the bed behind us.

"And that's a phenomenon as well, because those wee grasshopper creatures who live at the back of my fireplace drive me mad with their chirping in the summer, but I never heard one make a noise like that on a winter's night."

Father continued. "No, I didn't really believe in such things until once I had an experience, an experience I'll never forget." He sat back in his chair. "It was just after we'd got married ... even people like me make mistakes at times!" There was an immediate response but no laughter from his audience, nobody wanted to hold up the story.

"And we'd had an argument," mother joined in, "a row, and I flounced off to bed."

"We were down in the Free State at the time – that was before I got an outfit of my own together – working in a company called The Late Roberto Lena's Company. The boss was Gertie Lena, wife of the late Roberto, and the manager was a man called Frank Donovan. The wife's people, who weren't with us at that time, were working in another company and had just moved up into Scotland taking their youngest child, a little girl, with them."

"That was Ivy," mother explained, "my only sister. She was ten at the time and travelled with my parents playing child parts just like our Jim does now."

Heads turned in my direction, faces smiled, then quickly focused on father again.

"They were working in a Stock company, a big company that could play in one theatre, a real theatre, for months at a time. And they were in the town of Dunoon."

"While we were in a rep, a repertory company out in the wilds" mother threw open her arms, "of the Irish Free State. I'd never been to Ireland before and all my English friends told me wild stories about leprechauns and how the people ate with the pigs. And do you know, I hadn't been down there for more than a couple of weeks when we got digs in a farmhouse where the pig, and the hens, all came in and wandered round the kitchen when we were having breakfast."

"Yes, we travelled through some pretty remote areas in the south, but oddly enough it was in a sizeable town where this occurrence took place, and in a large house, I think it had six bedrooms. The owner was a professional landlady who took in regular boarders, commercial travellers, government inspectors and the like. We moved in fairly late on in the day, and as the wife has just remarked, we had a row."

"He called me a right stupid bitch so I wasn't speaking to him, and when we went up to our room after the evening meal I went straight to bed. A big bed, in a huge room right at the top of this very dark old house."

"Yes, the bed was at one end of the room and the fireplace was at the other end, though there was no fire because it was summer. I sat down by the fireplace, cleaned out, filled up my pipe and had a smoke. It was quite late by then, getting dark, and after sitting for a while I decided, before the light went completely, I would sort out my razors which I'd left in a heap on the washstand earlier on. In those days I was very fussy about my razors (open razors, cut-throats father called them), I had seven, one for each day of the week. They weren't marked and they all looked very much alike but of course I knew the difference, so I picked out the one for the following day, which was Monday. Then I lifted up my strap with the intention of stropping and putting a good edge on the blade, but when I looked round I couldn't see a nail or peg or anything to hang the strap on. So I fiddled about for a minute or two, wrapping the strap round the leg of the washstand, then I decided it was a waste of time so I laid down the razor and the strap and returned to my chair.

"By now the room was quite dark, so dark that I could barely see the wall opposite, so I took out my matches and reached up towards a small oil lamp that was sitting on the mantelpiece, but before I could remove the glass the room suddenly filled with light. The moon had come out. Its pale blue light flooded in through the high window behind me and fell directly on the washstand opposite. And it happened so suddenly and gave such an eerie aspect to the washstand that I didn't move for a moment, I just stared, I was fascinated, so fascinated that I didn't hear the bedroom door open! Though I did feel a presence, I knew someone had entered the room. Slowly I turned my head and then saw the person, a man, standing in the darkness between the washstand and the door.

"My first thought was that this was another lodger and he'd got the wrong room, though the landlady hadn't mentioned she'd any other lodgers besides us. My next thought was that I must speak, announce my presence, but before I could get the words out of my mouth the man moved swiftly out of the darkness and into the light. He was about my own height and build, though unlike me he had thick, dark, wavy hair. What his face looked like I couldn't tell at that point because he had his back to me. He didn't speak, he didn't pay any attention to me at all, he just stopped at the washstand and looked down. I waited to see what he would do. He reached out and picked up the razor I'd set aside a few moments before. Then he turned and looked me full in the face."

A ripple of fear and excitement ran through the listeners clustered round the fireside. Nobody moved, but it seemed, without taking our eyes off father, we had all drawn closer together.

"*I've got a mad man on my hands!*"

Behind us the old lady stirred in the bed.

"I've got a Sweeney Todd! I looked down to see if there was a poker or anything I could use to defend myself, but the man seemed to know what was going through my mind because he smiled … a slow, gentle smile that told me immediately he meant me no harm. Then he turned back to the washstand, lifted up the razors I'd left in a heap and laid them down one by one, in a straight line. I got to my feet, cleared my throat, opened my mouth to speak to him and suddenly realised … he wasn't there, he'd gone! And I never saw the door open. I never heard a sound."

The silence in Rosie Ann's kitchen was like the silence of the grave. Father waited, and then went on with his story.

"I stood by my chair for a moment or two, paralysed, then when the feeling came back into my legs I walked across to the washstand and looked down at the razors, their seven blades gleaming in the light of the moon. And as I looked at them it slowly dawned on me they were laid out in perfect order … Monday, Tuesday, Wednesday, the whole week. And nobody, nobody but myself, could have known how I used them! Then I lost my nerve, hurried across the room, got undressed and jumped into bed."

"Freezing cold," mother took up the story, "and shaking like a leaf. I was half asleep, dreaming, when suddenly I became conscious of this cold corpse-like thing in the bed beside me. I said, what's the matter? What's wrong? Are you ill? But he didn't answer or explain until the morning."

"Yes, well, the next morning when we were having our breakfast I took a quick look at the landlord who put his head round the door while we were eating – he worked in a pub, or maybe he owned the pub, I can't remember now – just to see if he resembled the man I'd seen the previous night. But he was a short, stocky, balding man with hardly any hair at all. Then I sounded out the landlady when she came to clear the dishes away. I asked casually how many other lodgers she had staying with her?"

"None at the moment," she replied. "Why do you ask?" So I told her the whole story and she listened carefully, waited patiently till I'd finished, then inquired, almost in a whisper, "Was he a tall man, well-built but slim … something like yourself, only older with dark curly hair?"

"That's him," I said, "that's him. Black curly hair with sideburns. And my build only older … maybe in his early forties. Do you know him?"

The landlady went pale and her hands shook as she nodded her head. "I *did* know him."

"And where does he live now? And what was he doing in our bedroom?"

"*He died in that bedroom!*"

Mouths fell open. Katie McCarthy took hold of her husband's arm and held on like she thought something might reach down, grab her and carry her off into outer darkness.

"*He died in it!* She said it was two years before they moved in. He had been the doctor in the town and that was his house, and where we were standing had been his surgery. He was very well liked but they were a very unlucky family. His wife died of pneumonia only a year before he did. The house was empty for ages. And of course our landlady heard all the rumours but took no notice and never heard anything or saw anything … until now. It was *him*, it was the doctor I saw and no mistake."

Nobody in the kitchen spoke for what seemed a very long time and then father leaned forward and knocked out his pipe on the firebar.

"So there you have it. Just as it happened."

"Well, that's a very strange story," the old lady remarked.

"Very strange indeed," agreed father.

"And stranger still," added mother, "because that wasn't the end of it."

"It *wasn't*?" Rosie Ann fairly shot up in bed.

"Oh no, because that very day, that is the day after my husband saw this … this ghost – what else could you call it, the man had been dead for years – we got a telegram from my parents in Dunoon telling us my little sister Ivy had died suddenly, of diphtheria … *a disease of the throat*."

"Dear God!" Katie McCarthy took hold of her husband's arm again and held on like grim death. "Did you ever in your whole life hear such a thing?"

"You were forewarned." Rosie Ann's voice came out of the darkness. "It was a warning."

"I believe it was," agreed mother.

"And what do *you* think, Mr Mateer?"

"I never found an answer."

"It was a warning." The old lady punched her pillow and lay back in her bed. "It was a warning."

*

On Monday it rained, blew, and in the evening as we battled our way to the Orange Hall showers of hail bounced off the roadway.

"This is going to be a washout … literally." Father poked around trying to find the keyhole. "Nobody's going to turn out on a night like this."

"And you could hardly blame them," mother mumbled from inside her coat collar. "It's a blizzard. Let's get into the hall, quick."

"I'm trying to open the door but I've got to find the keyhole first." The lock clicked, the door opened, father advanced and the rest of us hurried into the hall after him. All except grandad who stood on the doorstep like "The Stag at Bay" and defied the rain, the darkness and the emptiness beyond.

"Not a soul Louie," he announced, "not a sinner in sight."

"Come in out of the cold you old goat," grandma called out good-naturedly. "And shut the door before we all freeze to death."

"No, it's a washout," repeated father, picking up the oil lamp he'd left inside the doorway. "I had a feeling the moment I set eyes on this place."

"A *cold* feeling," mother remarked, shivering. "It's nearly as cold inside as out." Of course, there was rarely any heating in these small halls and we depended on body heat to warm the place up.

"We'll hang about until a quarter past eight." Father lit the lamp and then, without so much as a thought, walked off with it towards the small room behind the stage, leaving the rest of us in darkness.

"Oh, find your own way, sir, she said," quipped mother, but father never noticed, he just walked into the dressing room repeating, "Eight-fifteen and we pack up." Then at eight-thirty, when not so much as a rat had sniffed round the hall door, he suddenly blew out the lamp in the dressing room. We scrambled for our belongings and scurried after him like a flock of chickens when somebody rattles a tin. He ushered us out, locked the door, we went back to our digs, and I for one was quite pleased. It didn't occur to me that there were no takings that night, no money. I just fancied a quiet sit round the turf fire and maybe the chance to make toast for supper.

"Och, you got terrible weather for your first night," commiserated Rosie Ann. "Nobody would walk the roads or get on their bikes in weather like that. But it'll pass over, it'll blow itself out and you'll have a good day tomorrow, and a good crowd. There's plenty of people round the district you know, enough to fill the Orange Hall three times over, you'll be alright tomorrow." Rosie Ann was right … about the weather. But she was wrong about everything else.

The following evening, about seven, when mother had got Eileen off to sleep, father trimmed and lit the tiny oil lamp he always left in the room where my little sister was sleeping, as a night light. The lamp was almost exactly the same as the ones we found burning in front of pictures of Jesus in catholic houses, except that the globe was pearl and not red, and the bottom was weighted so that it couldn't capsize. Though as an additional security measure father then placed the lighted lamp inside a wash bowl, or in this case it may have been a large basin. Then, satisfied with the arrangements he left the bedroom door ajar and the three of us went out onto the road, collected grandma and grandad and made our way to the hall. The show wasn't due to start until eight and it was quite dark, but as we turned off the road and into the lane that led up to the hall we could hear voices, men's voices, a little further along the road.

"Well that sounds a bit more hopeful Bob," grandma said cheerfully.

"At least there's somebody about," father responded.

"Yes, and it's early," mother added, "and not raining. Maybe we'll get an audience tonight."

Father opened the door and once inside the hall grandad went round and lit all the lamps.

Mother got the primus going so we would have a little heat in the dressing room while we changed. A record was put on, and when we had made-up, changed and put our overcoats back on again we sat, or walked about, waiting for our audience to arrive.

The voices were a lot nearer now, in fact some of them came from outside the small frosted window in the back wall of the dressing room. They were quiet voices, and they were not the voices of men laughing or larking about. We listened in silence for a few minutes.

"Having a look round, I expect ... curiosity," grandma remarked.

"Yes, well, time's getting on." Father took out his pocket watch. "It's just gone half-past-seven. I expect we could open the door and let them in." He made his way to the other end of the hall, turned up the small lamp that was sitting on the upended script box, opened the hall door, and as he did so something (a large sod it turned out to be) came flying through the air, missed him, and spread itself across the hall floor.

"Hey! What's the idea?" He could hear the sound of feet running across the gravel but he couldn't see anyone. "Somebody out there having a little game?" There was no response so he shut the door and came back into the hall.

"What was all that about?" Mother put her head out of the dressing room door.

"Louts!" father replied.

"Anyone else out there?"

"It doesn't look like it."

"Oh." She regarded the mess on the floor. "Well, I'd better see if there's a brush in the dressing room and clear this up."

"Any luck Bob?" Grandad emerged from behind the Actdrop and came bustling along the gangway, unaware of the nature of the incident. "Any sign of an audience?"

"No."

"Well it's nearly twenty ..." grandad took out his own pocket watch and then noticed the sod and the soil on the floor. "Oh! Who did that?" Before anyone could answer someone on the outside gave the door an almighty kick.

"*They* did." Father angrily reached for the door handle.

"Watch out Bob," mother warned.

"Just what's the big ..." Father opened the door, and as he did so a stone, a sizeable stone, hit the post beside his head. He slammed the door and turned the key in the lock. A volley of smaller stones then followed, peppering the front of the hall. "We've got a right bunch of hooligans ... they're trying to kick in the hall door."

"And the window," mother called out in alarm. "Look Bob!"

Father looked up in time to see a hand come through the top part of one of the windows that hadn't been properly closed and drop something.

"*Look out!*" There was a loud bang which brought grandma running out of the dressing room.

"What in heaven's name was that?"

"A firecracker!" Grandad hurried across and stopped her going any further. "A big one. And they're heaving stones. Get back into the dressing room Louie."

"We've got a real bunch of louts out there," remarked mother.

"Oh, I think we've got more than a bunch of louts." Father trailed a chair across to the side of the hall, stood on it and secured the window.

"You think they might be catholics … attacking an Orange Hall?"

"Catholic or protestant that lot mean trouble." Another stone hit the top of a window on the opposite side of the hall, shattering the glass. "Get back in the dressing room. You too, Jim."

We hurriedly retreated. Fortunately there was no outside door to the little room but there was a window and when father looked in he ordered, "Keep away from that window. And put out the light." Mother quickly lowered the wick and blew down the glass, leaving the three of us in darkness.

"What are we going to do Bob?" Grandad was prowling around the end of the hall, scowling and rubbing his hands together.

"I don't know."

"And what's their game?" In answer to his question there were shouts, fists hammered on the side of the hall and a voice yelled out,

"Out … Out … Out ye Fenian bastards."

"Huh!" father snorted, "they're protestants!"

"So why are they attacking *us*, Bob?"

"They obviously think we're catholics."

"Then let's get out there and put them right." Grandad made for the door but father grabbed hold of his arm.

"They'll kill you, you bloody idiot. There's a mob out there."

"But if we explained …" Grandad always had simple, straightforward solutions.

"That lot don't want explanations."

"But we're protestants Bob, Church of England." More stones rattled onto the corrugated iron roof, and another window was hit but not broken.

"Put out all the lights in the hall," father ordered. "If they hit one the whole place'll go up." Grandad moved off at the double.

"They're outside our window now Bob," mother announced from the dressing room. She spoke quietly and showed no fear, but of course she was concerned. "What are we going to do?"

"Well how the hell do I know what we're going to do?" Father was looking for a safe place to store the lamps. "Stay holed up … if they don't break down the door … till they get bored I suppose."

"But we'll freeze in this place."

"Yes, well, outside we'll get *stoned!*"

"We've never had this sort of trouble before." Grandma nervously came up behind mother. "I suppose there's no way somebody could slip out and fetch the police?"

"*The police!*" father echoed derisively. "The police are about ten miles away ... two of them ... probably in bed by this time."

"Ah the scum ... the swine." Grandad clenched and shook his fists. "If we'd had that lot in the army Louie ... if they'd spent a couple of weeks in the trenches with old Gerry blasting ..."

"*Shut up!*" Father put his ear to the back of the hall door. "I want to listen."

We stood in silence, huddled together against the side of the hall, as he listened for a moment then said, "Well, there's at least a dozen of them out there. They're talking ... consulting ... and I'd say ..." a barrage of fists and boots battered the door and the front of the hall, "... that they've no intention of going away. So ... if we want to get out of this place we'll have to make a run for it."

"Oh, but they'll slaughter us." Mother didn't fancy the idea at all.

"Yes, well, we'll have to try and frighten them off first ... do something that will give us a head start."

"Like what?"

"Where's my little blue case?"

"Beside the basket in the dressing room. Shall I get it?"

"No, I'll get it. The rest of you pick up your belongings and get ready to run."

"Oh dear, dear," grandma moaned quietly, "I don't think I'm quite up to running Lily."

"Don't you worry old girl." Grandad put an arm round her shoulder. "I'll look after you. They'll have to get to me first."

"Come on. Hurry up." Father came back out of the dressing room carrying his little blue case. We scrambled for our belongings and then groped our way to where he, lamp in hand, stood behind the hall door.

"What are you going to do Bob?" mother whispered.

Father bent down, listened, then straightened up and said in a loud stage whisper, "*I'm going to use the Colt.*"

Mother twigged immediately and in an equally loud whisper responded, "*Oh no Bob, you might shoot someone!*"

"*Not if I don't have to. But we have a right to defend ourselves. Hold the lamp while I load.*" Mother did as instructed. Father opened the little case which contained his personal effects and anything he considered important – tickets, Excise stamps, beards, moustaches, spirit gum – and took out the revolver.

I always believed it was a real revolver, indeed I think that may well have been the case. It was large, heavy, made of metal, and although I had it in my hands on numerous occasions I was never allowed to use it. Of course, it couldn't have been used, I mean not with bullets, because the barrel and the chambers had been blocked off and it only fired blanks. Father loaded from a small box of cartridges, spun the chambers, snapped the gun shut, then got down on one knee and put his face close to the keyhole.

"Now we'll let that lot outside know what we're doing. *You out there*," he called out. "*Can you hear me?*" Nobody replied. "*Well, I know you're out there so I'm telling you ... we're coming out.*" Cheers, jeers and more abuse aimed at catholics greeted his announcement. "*We're coming out, but I warn you we are not coming out unarmed.*" The noise stopped abruptly. "*I've got a gun, a revolver, it's fully loaded and if anyone so much as lays a finger on the women, children, or any of the company ... I'll blow his head off. You hear? You understand?* BLOW HIS BLOODY HEAD OFF!"

There was movement outside in the darkness ... shuffling, whispering. Father listened and then went on with his act. "*So I'll give you ten seconds to clear off.*" Noisily he unlocked the hall door, opened it a couple of inches and stuck the barrel of the gun into the crack. "*Five seconds. And just throw a stone or lay a finger and I warn you I'll shoot* ... I'LL SHOOT!"

Then, without any warning or indication to those of us inside the hall as to what he intended to do next, father let off two rounds in quick succession. We all jumped, while outside there were shouts, oaths, a mad scrambling across the gravel, and a few moments later the sound of feet running on the roadway.

"*Out!*" Father blew out the lamp. "Quick! And mind how you go."

"I'll lead the way," grandad courageously moved out onto the step, peered into the darkness, listened, then in a hoarse whisper advised us, "All clear. Take your mam's arm Lily. Follow me, and if I ... Aaagh!" He took a step forward, stumbled, groaned again ... "Aaagh!" then fell to the ground.

"Harry," grandma cried out, "Harry!"

"I told you to watch your bloody feet," father wasn't in the least sympathetic.

"Don't move," warned the old man, "don't move ... *barbed wire!*"

"Oh, the sods," mother swore. "Where is it? Where are you dad? I can't see a thing."

"Wait a minute," father struck a match.

"Are you hurt Harry?" Grandma leaned forward, still holding tight to my hand.

"Just my knee Louie," grandad felt his injured leg. "Nothing broken, just a gash where the wire went in."

"Oh, my poor Harry."

"Take his arm," father bent down. "and watch out for the wire."

"The swine!" mother hissed as she got to the other side of grandad.

"Couldn't see it Lil," the old man was helped to his feet. "Didn't expect it."

"They've tied it to the drain pipe," father struck another match and followed the wire along. "The other end's somewhere in the hedge."

"Give me your hanky dad," mother pulled aside the torn trouser leg and placed her own handkerchief where she presumed the wound to be.

"Here you are Lil … bit lower down I think."

"It's quite deep dad … and bleeding."

"Ah it's just a scratch Lil, just a scratch."

"We've got to get out of here," father returned to where mother was administering first aid.

"I know, I know," she responded irritably, "but I've got to get this tied round first. We can't just let him bleed to death."

"Well, hurry up. We'll have that mob round us again. That'll do … that's enough … let's go." Father struck another match and held down the wire with his foot. "Quick!" Cautiously we stepped over the length of barbed wire they'd set to trap anyone leaving the hall. Mother then took grandma on one arm and grandad on the other, while I went on ahead to look out for obstacles or more wire. Father locked the hall door then joined us. Carefully we stole down the narrow, dark lane.

The voices were some way off now, laughing and joking. Fortunately the mob seemed to be heading in the opposite direction to where we were going. Just the same, when we got to the end of the lane father stopped, listened, then gave the "all clear". We headed back, first to grandma's then to our own digs as quickly as age and infirmity would allow. No-one followed or molested us further. Either they were concerned about father's gun, or satisfied that they'd achieved their objective and driven us out.

Rosie Ann was raging mad when she heard what had happened at the hall.

"Oh, the villains," she said, "the scoundrels. To stone decent people. To lay wire across the path like you were beasts of the field. They're heathens … they're savages … I never heard the like of it in all my days. But I'll tell you one thing for sure, Mrs Mateer, I know who's at the back of this devilment. I know who's responsible for this night's work and he'll feel the weight of my tongue, the weight of my stick." She thumped the bed with the blackthorn. "I'll massacre the ejit when I get near him, I'll massacre him."

Nobody fancied toast that night so I didn't even mention the subject. We had supper and went to bed early. The next morning after breakfast, probably porridge for me and Eileen, bread and marmalade for mother and an egg for the boss, father set out to see what damage had been done to the hall, and to discuss the situation with the caretaker. He took his bike, and before leaving warned us not to go anywhere near the hall till he got back. My grandparents, who were lodging in a small farm further along the main road, were given their instructions. And then while Eileen and I played out at the back, mother, who could never sit still (she was exactly like grandad in that respect and actually enjoyed hard, physical work) set-to and cleaned up the cottage. Rosie Ann, though she gave her permission and must have been quite pleased about the "spring cleaning", said very little that morning. She was unusually quiet and just sat up in her bed, her cap over her ears, her eyes fixed on the window, and watched like a cat outside a mousehole. All morning she sat hunched up watching and waiting, then just about twelve o'clock, lunch time, she straightened up, listened, then called out to mother.

"Mrs Mateer, Mrs Mateer. Quick!"

"What's the matter?" mother hurried out of the bedroom.

"Listen!" Rosie Ann held up her hand. Mother couldn't hear anything unusual.

"What am I supposed to …?"

"Listen!"

"Someone coming?"

"Look out … look out, up the lane." Mother opened the top half of the door, leaned out, looked right, then immediately pulled her head back inside.

"Yes you're right, there is somebody coming, a young man."

"Big fella?"

"Big, with red hair."

"That's him, that's him, that's Willie Morrison. Go out and tell him I want to have a word with him. Quick, before he passes."

"Well … he looks a bit fierce Rosie Ann."

"He won't touch you, he won't harm you. Tell him Rosie Ann wants a word with him."

"Alright." Mother unbolted the bottom half of the door, went out onto the step, and when the big fellow drew level she smiled sweetly and spoke very politely. "Excuse me, Mr Morrison, Mrs McKee would like to have a word with you if you can spare the time."

The big fellow didn't answer, didn't stop, he just carried on past the cottage as though she didn't exist. Mother shrugged and came back inside the kitchen. But that wasn't the end of the matter. Rosie Ann had no intention of leaving it at that.

"Don't you run away from me Willie Morrison," she yelled out from among the draperies. "Don't you run away from an old cripple." Silence greeted this outcry. Rosie Ann waited for a moment, took a deep breath, then launched another salvo. "*Willie Morrison!*"

There was the sound of footsteps and the next minute the kitchen darkened as the big man appeared above the half door, bending down so he could see into the room. Mother made a quick exit in the direction of the bedroom and shut the door, while the old lady eased herself up in the bed.

"I want a word with you Willie Morrison."

"So ah believe," growled the big fellow, his face as black and cheerless as the grate when the fire has gone out.

"Come inside the house."

"Ah'm alright where ah am."

"Are ye feared te come inte my house, Willie Morrison?"

"No, ah'm not feared, but ah've no time. What d'ye want?"

"Ye know right well what ah want."

"Ah do, and so ah'll save ye the bother an tell ye straight ..."

"Ye'll tell me nothin'," screeched the old lady from out of the darkness, "because ye know nothin', and ye never knew nothin'. Yer an ejit and ye haven't changed a whit since ye ran through these fields with the backside out o' yer breeks ... since Charlie Adair cuffed ye fer stonin' his cattle ... since ye messed yerself standin' on that very step."

"Aw ..." the big fellow's face went as red as his hair and he took hold of the half door with both hands as though he was about to tear it off its hinges. "Ah'm not goin' te stan' here ..."

"Ye *are* goin' te stan' there," yelled the old woman, "because ah'm goin' te tell ye somethin' about last night's affair you don't know."

"What?" The big fellow stopped, turned and came back to the half door. "What are ye goin' te tell me that ah don't know?"

"Last night you an' a wheen o' other ignorant hallions went te the Orange Hall and tormented as dacent a lot of people as ye're ever likely te meet."

"They're Fenians," the big man said defiantly. "They should never have bin allowed inte the Orange Hall. An' we'll not be content till they're out."

"Ye blattered at the door," the old lady continued, "broke a winda, threw fireworks, and scared the life out of two dacent women and a child."

"They'd no right te go inte our hall ... they're catholics."

"And *that*, Willie Morrison, *is just where yer wrong*."

The big man took hold of the door again, bent down and looked hard at the woman in the bed. "What de ye mean?"

"I mean that they are not catholics, they're protestants, better protestants and christians than you and yer like are ever likely te be."

"What are you ... ah mean ... who told ye that?"

"*They* did. But they had no need to tell me because I can tell the difference between a catholic and a protestant and so could you if ye'd taken the trouble te find out."

"Ah, I don't ... we were told ... are you pullin' my leg?"

"They're protestants I tell you, not a catholic among them. And they were tormented. And you and that fly-be-night gang o' yours will pay ... ye'll answer to The Almighty God for last night's work." She flailed the air with her walking stick.

"Is this the truth ye're tellin' me Rosie Ann?"

"Why would I lie te ye?"

"Well, I don't ..." the big fellow scowled, furrowed his brows, thought for a minute, then came out with, "But they're Playactors, Rosie Ann!"

"An' you think every Playactor's got to be a catholic?"

"An' they went inte the hall on a Sunday."

"And you work in the fields with the beasts on a Sunday. No, they're dacent people Willie Morrison. The head man's from Belfast, his wife's from England, and they're every one a protestant … yer own kind."

The big man wiped his hand across his mouth, scratched his head, then brought down a huge fist on top of the half door. "Right then, if that's the way of it … we made a mistake."

"*You* made a mistake."

"Alright, *I* made a mistake and by God ah'll soon put it right. You tell that woman," he pointed at the bedroom door which was still shut tight, "to tell her man that we made a mistake and if he puts his play on tonight we'll fill that hall, by God we'll fill it te the door." He backed out, hitting his head on the lintel "*Ah'll see te it.*"

But he didn't see to it. Oh, I'm sure he intended to, and it's quite likely if he'd roused the neighbourhood he *could* have filled the hall to the door. But when father returned and heard the story his immediate response to mother's announcement, "They'll pack the hall Bob," was:

"Oh no they won't, oh no they bloody won't. We don't play to bigots and hooligans. We're moving out in the morning."

"You've got another hall?" mother was astounded.

"Couple of miles further on."

"And a lorry?"

"A rickshifter!"

"A *rickshifter*?"

"With a horse."

*

It was still dark the following morning when the entire cast, apart from the boss, moved out of the lane that led from the hall and onto the quiet country road. At least it was quiet before our rickshifter, which had iron wheels, rumbled up behind us with the scenery, skips and all our possessions lashed down with ropes and binder twine. (A rickshifter, by the way, was a long, low-slung, sideless cart designed for loading haystacks in the fields and transporting them to the haysheds for winter feeding.) Progress was slow. And the mood of the Playactors on that cold, grey, featureless morning, after three nights without takings and one night subject to various forms of assault and battery, was one, you might well imagine, of gloom and despondency. But you would have been wrong. When the dustman in Shaw's *Pygmalion* tried to get cash out of Professor Higgins on account of the gentleman's interest in his daughter, and was asked if he'd no morals, he replied, "Can't afford 'em guv'nor." And "despair", considering we couldn't stay put, or go back, and the only way was *on*, was something we couldn't afford either. Father put his unlit pipe in his mouth, mounted his bike, and from the rear concerned himself with the safe transportation of our scenery. While up front, arm in arm or hand in hand, we talked, joked and sang songs. We were moving on we told ourselves. The winter was nearly over. Our luck was bound to take a turn for the better. (And it did.) But before the evil spirits who had been dogging our footsteps drifted off to plague some other hapless group of mortals, and before the new spring came up decking the roadside and the banks with primroses and violets, The Fates had one last fling.

: :PROGRAMME: :

Bob Mateer's - - Broadway Players

DRAMATIC REPERTORY includes :

"HARD TIMES" or The Right to Live
"DESTINY" or The Call of a Child
ROBBIE BURNS Romantic Scottish Drama
"ARSENIC" "SALLY IN OUR ALLEY"
"O'FARRELL SQUARES ACCOUNTS"
"BACK FROM BEYOND"
"THE MAN FROM DARTMOOR"
"TEN NIGHTS IN A BAR ROOM"
"AN EXILE OF ERIN" Romantic Irish Drama

VARIETIES BY

HARRY O'NEILL Vocalist	**LENORD LE ROY** Light Vocalist & Dancer
ANNIE RYAN Comedienne & Dancer	**BOB MATEER** in Monologues

LIL WYNNE Soubrette &

Wee Teddy

Ulster's Own Comedian

E. Baxter, Printer, 9A, Mosley St., Manchester.

13

The Farce

I will now present a very brief production for your entertainment and delight because, although I've already given you an example of the sort of humorous sketches we used at the end of each play, this particular one was unique. *We* didn't write it. Nobody wrote it. It was created by The Fates and was designed to devastate one tiny mortal who drifted in on the tide of misfortune. Originally, of course, it was intended as a tragedy – The Fates have no sense of humour. In this case however they overdid things and the result not only raised the roof of the auditorium (a rather grandiose term for what may well have been a tin hut), but it also got a few strangulated laughs in the dressing room (and that hardly describes the space we occupied at that point either). As a farce it was a thundering if unrepeatable success. Although there were at least two people I can think of who didn't find it funny, and one of them, though I wasn't directly involved, was me.

I could never bear to see a lone individual harassed, tormented or unjustly treated. For instance, once when we were in England and my grandparents took me to a variety show there was a young woman who climbed up onto a trapeze high above our heads and proceeded to take off all her clothes. Now for the life of me I could not understand at that time why any person should have to take off their clothes in public. It upset me, I tried hard not to look, and I never forgot the incident. Of course, the striptease act I've just mentioned had been planned, prepared and was part of the entertainment, I realised that at a later date. The farce, however, that erupted one night in the middle of what was probably a serious play was not planned, was not intended, and was fashioned by those "evil ladies" out of human frailty and the spartan conditions under which we worked. And they *were* spartan.

You had to be tough and determined to survive in our line of business. Having said that I realise that living conditions were very much the same for most of the working population in those days. Things were never very comfortable. Beds were sometimes so damp we had to lay coats or whatever material we could find under the sheets. Houses, particularly in the rural areas, no matter how well looked after, provided shelter not only for humans but for fleas, lice, mice, bugs, earwigs and cockroaches. And working conditions in many of the halls where we played were primitive, particularly as far as toilet facilities were concerned. And when I say toilet facilities I don't mean anything as sophisticated as hot water, cold water, or even a place to wash your hands ... I mean that often there was no lavatory. And even if the hall was owned by a church or some other well-established organisation and a water closet *was* provided, then it was intended for the audience and was situated at the wrong end of the hall. This, you can imagine, was very awkward for us if there was no back door to the dressing room, because you couldn't walk through the audience during a performance, or even get to the little room during the interval. Most of the small halls we were using at that time had either dry lavatories, which were unusable, or no convenience at all. The artistes therefore had the choice of sharing the same facilities as were afforded to the audience ... the fields and the hedges. And for the ladies, the cold black countryside in the wind and the rain was not at all suitable. And even for the men, never knowing where the cows had trod before you wasn't all that pleasant either. So we had to provide our own convenience, and in an emergency resort to *the bucket*. Not very sophisticated I admit, but at least it meant that during a performance when the dressing room was occupied by one sex, or one desperate person in need of a pee, relief was possible. The bucket was galvanised ... not the most suitable material if secrecy was of the essence, but then it was only used when no other facilities were available. Fortunately we were a small family group for the most part and so this arrangement, under normal conditions, worked very well. But normal conditions we didn't always get. Which brings me back to the farce.

We had moved into a sizeable market town though I've no idea what it was called nor where it was situated. It was very late on in the day and father was in a desperate hurry (and when he was desperate he was totally unreasonable) to set up the scenery for a performance that night. It was a very small hall (though there was a much bigger and better-equipped hall in another part of the town), so small that it didn't even have an ante-room at the back of the stage and we had to construct a makeshift dressing room for ourselves. Now the reason why we couldn't book the bigger hall although it was available, and why father had to lay down a large deposit (shillings, but large for us) for the smaller hall, and why mother and grandma had almost to get down on their knees to get digs, was fully explained by an incident which took place quite soon after the company arrived in the town.

We were about to cross the street, mother, Eileen and I, when a lady emerged from a house, caught sight of us, immediately dashed across and with tears of joy running down her cheeks threw her arms around mother's neck.

"Oh, Lillian my dear, Lillian my dear, I have never been so pleased to see anyone in my whole life. Oh, thank God you've come, thank God you're here." The lady was Ethyl. And Ethyl if you remember had been our pianist, until she fell for our comedian Wee Teddy, married him and they both went off to work in another company.

"Well, this *is* a surprise Ethyl," mother disengaged herself, "though I have to admit …"

"And the children … Jimmy … and Eileen."

"… not a complete surprise because there have been stories … signs …"

"Oh, so you've heard all about it?"

"No, we've heard very little about it but … for certain reasons the city fathers wouldn't rent us the main hall and we've had terrible trouble trying to get digs."

"Oh, it has been absolutely *awful* my dear … *ghastly* … you've no idea. The company collapsed."

"Collapsed?"

"Well, no, that's not exactly true, what happened was the manager and his little bird did a moonlight flit, scarpered, didn't pay the rent, the digs, the pubs … *us*."

"That's what we gathered. And when somebody mentioned the comedian and the pianist we had an idea it might be your company."

"Oh, it was our company alright."

"So you're stranded?"

"High and dry Lillian, high and dry. My piano's still in the hall and they won't let it out. The landlady's standing in the hallway watching our suitcases. And we've been here since Friday with no money, nowhere to go and nothing to do but wait for mamma to reply to my wire. I told her immediately of our plight of course, and asked for a loan – a Money Order to be payable at this post office – and when it comes we'll put the piano on the train, head for Belfast and stay with Teddy's people until something turns up. In the meantime we're like two lost, desolate souls."

"What's happened to the rest of the company then? Where are they?"

"Well, the drummer and his wife … she was a singer … it was variety and not legit as I'm sure you've guessed … cleared out two days before Reginald, the swine," she smiled sweetly at Eileen and me, "the unmitigated swine, did his flit. They saw it coming, well of course we all did, business was terrible and Reg was drunk all the time, but we didn't think it would happen here, and like this. Then the morning after the disaster our tenor – a beautiful voice he had, and a lovely personality – Terence and his little dancer just packed up and went off on the train. She was a crafty little madam was Sylvia, and *mean*, she had money tucked away under her tutu but when I tried to touch her for a couple of pounds … to stop the landlady throwing us out on the street, she smiled sweetly and said, 'Sorry my dear but we need every penny ourselves'."

"So you're the only two left?"

"The only two my dear, the only two poor, starving, shipwrecked … nothing but the clothes we stand up in."

"And where's Teddy at the moment?"

"Ah now Teddy, my dear," Ethyl's shipwrecked expression dissolved in a flash and she laid a hand on the lapel of mother's coat, "Teddy has gone round to have a few words with the caretaker. You see the moment we heard there was another company moving in and guessed it was you ... well, we nearly wept for joy. It's a miracle I told Teddy, the answer to all our prayers."

"Well, I don't know that we could be considered the answer to anybody's prayers Ethyl." Mother began to look uneasy. "I mean what have *we* got? And why has Teddy gone round to the caretaker? What does he expect to get?"

"My piano my dear, my piano. You see the hall rent is not our responsibility and the caretaker knows that. The people who are holding it have no right ... and of course we were not in a position ... but now that you're here, now that Bobbie ... Oh, and how *is* my dear Bobbie?"

"Oh, he's alright, his usual self, but what exactly do you expect us...?"

"Teddy's just dying to see him again ... and so am I. Oh, you have no idea of the anguish Lillian, and then the relief. When we saw your bill outside the post office this morning – we practically sleep on the post office doorstep – we rushed straight back to the landlady and told her to expect her money any time now because we had landed another job."

"Oh, now wait a minute Ethyl," mother's worst fears were confirmed, "you can't count ... I mean ..."

"It'll only be for a couple of nights my dear," nothing could stop Ethyl now, "mamma won't let us down, the Money Order will be in that post office tomorrow morning ... or the day after."

"But business has been awful ... just as bad for us as everyone else."

"Oh, I know, I know, but Bobbie won't let us down, Bobbie won't see us starve. And when I get my piano back ... I'll play for you."

Play for us! That was the last thing we needed, especially when it meant wages, two extra mouths to feed. And out of what? Father never had any money to spare. And grandma had long since gone through their savings. We had nothing at that point except the hire of a tin hut and the ill-will and resentment created by another company who had left a trail of debts in their wake. And to add insult ... Ethyl and Teddy had left our company without notice and without a comedian, to say nothing of a pianist. Father would slaughter someone. And as he always turned to the family first mother was convinced it would be *her*. After all, Ethyl was *her* cousin.

But father didn't slaughter anybody, he didn't even blame anybody apart from Reginald. And he seemed genuinely pleased to see Teddy, who incidentally had been unable to locate the caretaker at that point. Yes, of course they could join the company for a couple of nights, and as they were broke ... father put his hand into his pocket and advanced Ethyl a little something so she could pacify the landlady, and Teddy a little something so he could ...

"Go round to the pub and booze the lot." Mother was incensed.

"He's not going round to the pub to booze," father protested, "he's going to try and find the caretaker and get their piano back."

"And to do that he'll treat the caretaker and anybody else in sight, with your money, with *my* money!"

"It's not your money."

"It is, I work and I earn and I need money, money to buy food. You haven't given me a penny since last Friday and yet Teddy turns up, tells you a hard-luck story and you give him your all."

"Because they're stranded woman, can't you see? They're broke, no money, no work, and their landlady is about to chuck them into the street."

"Even if you'd given the money to Ethyl I could understand it, but to Teddy!"

"Him, her, what does it matter?" Father was reasonable and charitable. "They're actors and they're stranded, they need help. What sort of a Christian are you?"

"A bloody hungry Christian," mother shouted back, "I haven't had anything to eat since yesterday."

"Alright, so what do you need?" Father was on the defensive, so mother immediately went onto the attack.

"A pound," she replied.

"A pound?" That was probably a farm labourer's wages, or what was doled out to two old age pensioners for a week at that time.

"A pound," mother insisted, though she knew she wouldn't get it.

"But I haven't got a pound. And what happened to the five shillings I gave you before we left the last place?"

"I had to give it to our new landlady because she didn't trust us on account of the *boozy* company you keep." Teddy had spread it all round that they used to work in our company and that he and father were friends.

"Look, all I can manage is ten bob," father took a note out of his wallet.

"Not enough," mother thought she saw another note in there.

"But I haven't got any more. I had to put down a deposit on the hall … and pay the lorryman … I haven't got any more."

"Alright then," mother reckoned she wasn't doing too badly, "if you can't manage a pound I'll try and make do with fifteen shillings."

"Here's twelve," father dug out a two shilling piece.

"Fifteen," mother insisted.

"Fourteen," he added two more shillings. "And now I haven't even got the price of an ounce of tobacco."

"Too bad," mother took the money and quickly tucked it away in her pocket before father changed his mind. "And if you hadn't acted the big fellow and given so generously to Teddy … who is probably round at the pub this minute laughing his head off!"

"Aaagh!" Father angrily turned away and walked off. Mother was right.

Teddy was indeed round at the pub, drinking and buying porter all round. But Teddy expected to get something in return for this generosity. He'd eventually got hold of the caretaker, joined up with two other men already in the pub, stood them a round, and while they were imbibing he regaled them with such a wild account of recent events, and such a colourful description (Teddy's language would have set your ears on fire at times) of the life, history and origin of his late boss Reginald, that when he had finished and the audience had picked themselves up off the floor, he had three pals for life. So they all left the pub together, the two men procured a handcart, the caretaker let them in at the back of the hall, they retrieved the piano and then delivered it to where we were setting up shop. Ethyl, who had looked in to see if there was anything she could do, and had no idea that the piano would materialise in front of her very eyes, was ecstatic.

"Oh, my piano, my piano, you've got it, you've saved it. Oh, my darling Teddy." She rushed across and threw her arms round the little man who made such horrible faces over her shoulder that the men with the handcart were convulsed. "You are an angel Teddy," she withdrew and laid hands on the piano, "an absolute saint."

"Och sure I know that but it just comes naturally. And now lads," Teddy turned to his helpers, "let's get this instrument into the hall before yon ould get (he referred to the gentleman who had impounded the piano) comes round the corner and catches sight of it." The piano was lifted quickly off the cart and set on the ground.

"Where de ye want it Teddy?"

"Inside the hall, and take it easy ... easy ... mind the door, the old girl doesn't like her wires jangled. That's it. Front of the stage Robert?" Teddy looked up to where father was working.

"No, leave it inside the door for the minute ... we're short of space."

"Right boss. Just here lads ... that's it ... that's right ... that's great. Yer a dacent lota lads an' ah'll be round te the pub te see yis all on Friday." Teddy hoped to be in Belfast, piano and all by Friday. "And now I'll have to get down to some work." He whipped off his coat. "Right boss, where do you want me?"

"See you Friday then Teddy."

"No, tonight. Come and see the show."

"Right Teddy, right."

The men filed out, laughing, and very pleased with themselves. Teddy could do that to people. Father, grandad and their new helper then went on with the race to get the hall ready for the performance that night. And remember, as well as the usual routine they had also to rig up a dressing room. Not that that required a lot of extra effort because what father had already done was move the set out about six feet from the back wall of the hall, intending to make use of the Backcloth as a partition. You may recall that although we had another backscene, our *Backcloth* was the only scene without a roller, and so it couldn't be raised or lowered during the performance; it was either up or down. To mask the spaces at each end of the Backcloth he would eventually hang heavy curtains, leaving one lot loose so that we could have access to the rather cramped and rather dark area (we would have to use candles in order to make-up) that would serve as our communal dressing room behind the set. Work continued at breakneck speed, and when it was finished and the hall seated, the ladies who had been hanging around moved into the dressing room to sort out costumes and props, while the men, sweat still glistening on their foreheads, quickly pulled on their coats and dashed off to the pub for a well-earned pint. And that pint – mother swears – was their undoing. Or rather it was *Ethyl's* undoing.

The hall was full on our first night; there was no standing at the back when we started, but all the seats were taken. Father was unusually cheerful. "Good start for a first night," he said.

"Ah you'll be alright here Robert." Teddy, standing in the wings, stubbed out and carefully stowed away in a tin box what remained of the cigarette he'd been smoking. "You'll be alright." Teddy was back as our comedian for a couple of nights, and although I never wanted the job, indeed when he left the company and it was suggested, because father was stuck and couldn't afford another salary anyhow, that I was quite capable of taking on the role, I protested. I dug in my heels and would have held out forever, had it not been for grandma who actually *made* the suggestion and then smooth-talked me into changing my mind. Just the same I was a little put out at being pushed offstage and out of the limelight, but father said Teddy and Ethyl were stranded and needed the money so I didn't complain.

Out front amid the noise and the laughter, head up, eyes closed, oblivious to everything around her, Ethyl played her piano. That was all she did. She didn't act, didn't sing, didn't stand on the door, and wasn't asked to sell programmes. She was a pianist and play the piano was all she considered she had to do. And dead on time the curtain went up, father made a brief announcement, welcomed the audience, promised them a night's, indeed a whole week's entertainment, and then we went on with the show. Grandma sang "Lily of Laguna" (and had piano accompaniment for a change) with all the clever trills and yodelling her musician father had taught her; Teddy followed on with one of his comic songs, getting a wonderful introduction on the piano; and father came last with a short dramatic monologue. The curtain came down, and there was a brief pause during which father sent Teddy, who wasn't in the play, to sit at the back of the hall. There were late-comers, men who had been to the pub first, and they kept turning up and rattling the door. Once inside they were quiet enough, and of course paid their admission, so apart from the disturbance, and they hadn't actually disturbed *him*, father didn't get too upset. Then the curtain went up a second time, the audience settled down in their seats, and the play began.

Once again I don't remember what the play was, but I know it wasn't a comedy, and it had a great many scene-changes. And scene-changes were father's responsibility; that is, although he got help to set the stage, he personally either hauled up, or let down each painted scene at precisely the right moment, and in precisely the right fashion. And considering he was always in the play himself, and we were usually restricted for space at the side of the stage, that wasn't always easy. He had to move very quickly at times. And so had everybody else because he would have knocked you flat. He was a stickler for precision, and although there were times when he could have given the scene-shifting to someone else, *he* insisted on doing it because he said *they* never did it right. And *right* meant not jerking it as you hauled it up hand over hand (and as the fifteen foot roller was heavy, jerking it came naturally), and not letting it hit the boards with a thump. And another difficulty for a one-man-operator was that, depending on which side of the painted canvas faced the audience, the ropes controlling it would be either on the left or the right of the stage.

Now the play we were doing that night was particularly tricky because not only were there several quick scene-changes, and the controlling ropes were on *both* sides, but apart from Teddy who had been sent to the back of the hall, and Ethyl who wasn't involved anyhow, everyone else would be on stage at the same time. Father, of course, had worked out a system, though that meant getting grandad to help.

Ethyl therefore was the only person who wasn't on stage and had nothing to do, so she retired to the dressing room, put a cigarette into the holder she always used, snuffed out the candle burning on the card table (there was sufficient light coming in over the top of the set from the stage), sat down, put her feet up on the prop basket and, as she inhaled the smoke from her Gallaher's Blue, contemplated with satisfaction the pleasant and unexpected change in their fortunes. She was happy. But she was not comfortable, and for a very natural reason. And there was no lavatory in the hall, and she couldn't get out of the building before the end of the act. And where would she go even if she did get out because her digs were miles away. But she was very uncomfortable, indeed so uncomfortable that something would have to be done ... and soon ... it was urgent ... in fact it was an emergency! So she got up and listened at the back of the canvas to the talk and the action for a few moments, then, knowing the act wouldn't end for at least another ten minutes, and being privy, if I may use the word, to the arrangements we had for such emergencies, she looked round and finally unearthed the bucket.

On the other side of the scene, on stage, at that particular moment everything was going very nicely. The audience was attentive, listening to every word and watching every gesture ... and we were due for a very quick scene-change. Father and grandad were on stage together at that point, out in front of a *street* scene, which came down about four feet back from the footlights. Behind that scene the rest of us, having set out the furniture and taken up our positions, were waiting patiently for the front scene to end so that grandad could exit Left and pull up the *drawing room* scene behind us (this hadn't been changed because neither of the men had been able to get to it), and in doing so reveal the Backcloth on which was painted the interior of a kitchen, which is where we were supposed to be. Grandad made *his* exit without falling over anything, and at the same time father made *his* exit in the opposite direction, had a quick look back to make sure we were in position and that grandad had started to haul up the unwanted scene – we were … and he had – then proceeded to raise the *street* scene and in doing so reveal a full stage, a kitchen interior, and us. Everything was going according to plan. Or so we thought.

The first inkling that Ethyl – who at that juncture had lowered her nether garment, raised her skirts and presented herself to the Backcloth and the bucket – the first hint she had that something was amiss, came when the light round her feet began to increase. The next thing that struck her as extraordinary was the deathly silence, not just from the house but out on the stage. And the *next* thing, as she turned her head, still poised above the bucket, to assess the situation, was the blinding glare of the footlights and an almost deafening roar from the house … followed by a howl from father, "DOWN … DOWN … DOWN!" aimed at grandad, who stopped dead, the rope in his hands, the scene poised between heaven and earth, and a series of expressions registering confusion, consternation and bewilderment racing across his face. What had he done wrong? Then he looked down and saw the bucket … Ethyl … and the empty space. "Oh my God!" *There was no Backcloth behind the scene he was raising*. It was still rolled up and tied securely to the frame above his head. In their haste they had fitted up the drawing room scene, but had forgotten to untie and lower the Backcloth which was behind it.

The drawing room scene hit the boards with a thump that rocked all the furniture on the stage. The audience laughed themselves sick. Father went as white as a sheet, let down the street scene in order to put a barrier between them and us, then charged across the set and came crashing through the curtain like something on wheels. We all flew in different directions trying to get out of his way, not knowing what on earth he intended to do. And what he intended to do was … *untie and lower the Backcloth!* Never mind the difficulty, the confusion, the poor woman cowering against the wall trying to cover her shame, and probably her person, the only thing that mattered was that the scene was put right.

"*The steps! The steps!*" he yelled, hauling the drawing room scene up out of the way. "*Get the bloody steps*." Grandad started to clear the basket and props out of the way but was immediately shouldered to one side.

"Get a chair … put it this end … *this* end you bloody idiot." Father dashed up the steps, untied one end of the Backcloth and lowered it to grandad who stood on a chair and supported it until father dragged the steps across and untied the other end. Then between them they unrolled and lowered the canvas onto the stage. Seconds later we had taken up our positions again, this time with the kitchen scene *behind* us, and father raised the front scene. The audience craned expectantly, hoping no doubt for further signs of the catastrophe, but all was as it should be. Mother delivered the lines which opened the scene, the noise out in the house died down, and we carried on with the play as though nothing had happened.

Well, naturally, Ethyl wouldn't go out into the hall at the interval to play the piano! And nothing that could be said alleviated her distress. Everyone did their best. Though it seemed to me there was the ghost of a smile at the edge of mother's mouth as she poured words of comfort and sympathy into Ethyl's ear. And father, as you might expect, only mentioned the subject in order to say that some idiot, looking at grandad, had forgotten to untie the Backcloth. While Teddy, who had a grandstand view of the incident, and came back into the dressing room at the interval, summed up the situation and offered a piece of philosophy which unfortunately made matters worse. And he did it in such a thoroughly confident manner that I had grave doubts about his sincerity. I mean, I knew he and Ethyl had been married for some time and that all married people fought and rarely showed a lot of affection for each other (though grandma didn't fight, and grandad was always calling her his "dear old Dutch"). And I also knew that it was Ethyl who had done all the chasing when they were courting, because Teddy wasn't the sentimental type. Just the same I think he liked her, or at least I think he cared about her, and so I couldn't see why he should deliberately add to her sorrow and shame. Yet that is what he did. I can only suppose it was because he was what mother called "a natural" comedian and always said funny things no matter what the situation happened to be. Anyhow, when *he* came into the dressing room and saw that neither mother nor grandma had been successful in calming Ethyl, he put his arm round her shoulder and said in a very kindly way,

"Now come on old girl, come on … it was an accident … forget it."

"Forget it! Forget it!" wailed Ethyl. "Oh, I'd be pleased to forget it, but what about *them*?" She pointed at the Backcloth.

"It's over … it's over … put it out of your mind."

"But I'm ruined Teddy, ruined, as a professional, as a pianist … I daren't go out there again. And how can I face the man in the post office tomorrow morning?"

"Ah never mind the man in the post office, I'll deal with him. You just stop crying and listen to me because," Teddy paused, "I have something particular to say to you."

"What?" Ethyl didn't sound very hopeful. "What have you got to say to me that is particular Teddy?"

"Well now," Teddy looked very wise and very serious. "I know everyone in here has been saying all sorts of things to calm you down, but I'll guarantee there's one thing they *haven't* said."

"And what's that Teddy?" Ethyl took hold of his hands and looked beseechingly into his face. "What is that Teddy darling?"

"Well you stop crying and I'll tell you. And when I tell you you're going to feel a whole lot better."

"Am I Teddy, oh am I Teddy my darling?" She drew his hands against her cheek. "So what is it you're going to tell me?"

"Well now, before I say another word there's one thing you have to face up to."

"What?"

"It happened."

"*It happened?*" Ethyl let go of his hands and looked up in amazement.

"Yes. You see you must never try to kid yourself about things like this … it happened Ethyl."

"Well of course it happened," Ethyl said impatiently, "of course it happened, everybody *knows* it happened. But what is this thing you're going to tell me that's going to make me feel better?"

"Just this." Teddy moved away, took up his position and wagged a finger at the sufferer in the chair. "When that scene went up out there … and the Backcloth wasn't behind it … and there was no furniture … and nobody standing in the way (he was going too far, making too much out of it and that's when I began to have doubts), when that scene went up and you were … exposed, there's one thing you haven't considered, one thing I know … one thing I'd swear on the grave of my dear departed mother."

"What Teddy, what, for God's sake tell me, what?"

"From the minute that scene went up, until the minute Harry let it down again, nobody … nobody … not a single, solitary soul out there in that hall tonight *caught a glimpse of your face.*"

"Oooh …" Ethyl clenched and shook her fists in agony and desperation. "*But that was about the only thing they didn't catch a glimpse of.*"

Teddy gave up, which was probably a good thing. And eventually Ethyl gave up too, though when the show was over she refused to leave the hall until she was assured that the audience had dispersed and the street was clear. She also refused, the following morning, to put a foot outside the door of their digs. Though in the afternoon she had a quick change of heart because the letter they had both been waiting for, praying for, the letter from Ethyl's mamma, arrived, and inside was what Teddy joyously referred to as, "A lovely big Post Lorder". Of course it wasn't a Post Lorder it was a Money Order, there's no such thing as a Post Lorder, but that's what Teddy called it, and for years so did I. Indeed when I found out one day that the correct term was Postal Order I was rather disappointed, it didn't sound nearly as exciting as the document Teddy and Ethyl had received.

Anyhow the Money Order arrived and as it was made out to Ethyl she had to go down to the post office and sign for the cash. In order to do this she wore a wig and made-up in such a grotesque fashion that everybody in the street stared at her. But she didn't care any more, she just collected her money and paid the landlady while Teddy got the piano transported to the station and loaded it into the guard's van. Mother, grandma, Eileen and I stood on the platform as they climbed aboard the train for Belfast, and waved them goodbye.

We never saw the pair of them together again. Though oddly enough mother told me that years later, when I had gone to work in England, Ethyl and her two daughters turned up in the village where my parents had finally settled. They came with a tent and a variety act but Teddy wasn't with them. I suppose he had died.

After the departure of our pianist and comedian from that place of ill-fortune, we played to packed houses for the rest of the week. It would have been nice to think that our show was good, that word had got round and people just couldn't stay away, but I think we had Ethyl to thank for our popularity. Although our luck, like the weather, had certainly taken a turn for the better as we left the boglands and headed north through the counties of Tyrone and Londonderry and into Antrim, playing at Ballinderry, Bellaghy, Gulladuff, Upperlands, Magherafelt, Swatragh, Claudy, Tamlaght O'Crilly, Grace Hill, Aghadowey, Ballyrashane ... And then one beautiful fresh morning with a blue sky, a blue-green sea, and a caravan of small white clouds lined up along the horizon, we stood on the small harbour at Ballycastle (not far from the famous Giant's Causeway) and looked out across six miles of the North Atlantic at the distant outline of *Rathlin*.

14

Marooned on Rathlin

"Maybe we should have waited for a calmer day," grandma looked apprehensively out into the bay and then up at the heavens.

"Ach no, it's only a wee bit of a breeze," the boatman who squatted down on his hunkers in order to steady the boat reassured her.

"I'm not very good in boats I'm afraid."

"Ah there's nothing to worry about," the second boatman reached up and took hold of her arm as she stepped down off what they called the boatslip and into the small craft that bobbed about below.

"I'm not a very good sailor either."

"You'll be alright ... just another wee step."

"Another wee step? Right." Grandma came down heavily off the narrow seat and onto the bottom of the boat. "There ... I'm down ... I've arrived."

"And it's only a wee bit of a sail." The boatman turned away and reached up to help mother.

"Yes but even a wee bit of a sail, as you call it, is a wee bit too much for me," grandma quipped as she sat down and pulled her coat round her shoulders for added protection. She hated the sea. More than once I had heard her telling people that when the steamer had moved away from the harbour at Heysham, on her first voyage to Ireland, and headed out into the open sea, she had prayed and commended her soul to God. And those were *big* boats! Big, uncomfortable boats. Of course we never had berths – I think they cost half-a-crown each – therefore we spent the night sitting or lying on hard slatted seats in draughty lounges that smelt of chips, beer and sea-sickness. You couldn't even get relief by going up on deck because if you did you were either frozen, or suffocated by the smoke from the funnels. But they were big boats and this was a small boat; about twenty-five feet from stem to stern, open, and sitting so low in the water at the back you could reach down and put a hand in the sea. I thought it quite an exciting way to travel, at the beginning, but then I hadn't grasped the fact that we would be sailing out into the Atlantic. Grandma hadn't considered that either, not that it would have made any difference because she just didn't like the idea and was very unhappy. And before that journey was over so were a few other people ... including the boatmen.

Just how much of our scenery we loaded into that boat I can't honestly remember, not all of it certainly, because father had been informed by people who knew the island that the hall was very small. And of course so was the boat. The music-making equipment was naturally included, father saw to that himself, stowing it away with great care under a tarpaulin that must have covered our props and the rest of our belongings. Several lengths of the frame and a couple of scenes must also have been shipped aboard because I seem to remember them lying along the bottom of the boat on either side of the engine which was housed in a large wooden box. And beyond the box, which stood about half way along the length of the boat, there were several large parcels and packages that had nothing to do with us. These, I realised afterwards, were supplies and mail for the islanders.

Despite it being a long time ago I have a very clear picture in my mind's eye – like one of those Victorian portraits that fade into nothing at the edges – of our boat and us setting out on our journey that morning. And from two black and white photographs, one of Church Bay on Rathlin, and the other a view of the ferry arriving at the island loaded with cargo and passengers, I have been able to fill in a few of the details that were missing. The photographs must have been taken some time in the late twenties, and were made into postcards which were sent by my grandma to her sister in England, from where, after the deaths of both grandma and her sister, they found their way back to mother and then to me. The lady passengers on one of the photographs wore cloche hats and looked out of place sitting among the cargo, but then I think we must have presented a rather unusual sight when *we* sailed, with our belongings, into the bay. Had they ever had a company of Playactors on the island before? I don't know. And would they ever see us again? Grandma had very positive views regarding that possibility.

"Alright Andy?" With everything aboard the boatman on the slipway nodded to his companion who seemed to be the senior, and was to be our helmsman on the journey.

"Aye, right," Andy replied, climbing over our feet to get at the engine. The mate, with the mooring rope in one hand, then stepped in at the bow and held the boat from banging against the slipway. It took quite a few minutes poking, fiddling and cranking the engine, but eventually the motor spluttered and then roared into life.

"Right ye are," the mate flicked the rope off the bollard and sat down by the engine. The helmsman came back and took charge of the tiller. We were all seated at the back of the boat; grandad and grandma on the helmsman's right, mother and I on his left, while father, further along the seat but still on our side, had positioned himself where he would be close to his equipment. Slowly the ferry moved away from the slipway, increased speed, chugged across the bay for a few minutes then turned and headed out towards the open sea.

Exactly what time of the year it was I had great difficulty in remembering at first. Oh that I had then the little knowledge I have since acquired regarding the wild flowers that grow, and the sea birds that come to these islands to winter or to breed. What a terrible waste it is to be surrounded by so many interesting and beautiful things and be unable to appreciate them because one has never been trained to observe. However, by piecing together events before and after I now feel certain it must have been spring, or more likely early summer, "the turn of the year", a time in those northern parts when the winter is likely to have a last fling. Not that there was any sign of it, not to us anyhow, when we started off. The water was a little lively in the bay, and choppy close to the coast, but as we ploughed out into the channel things changed dramatically. It got colder. And we got wetter, as more than one wave slapped the side of the boat and sent over a cloud of fine spray. The swell increased, and as it did so our small craft began to rise up and then dip down so steeply into the wall of green water above us that it seemed certain, sooner or later, we would be swamped.

Ballycastle and the mainland looked a long way behind now, as the misty greyness crept out to where we were. And the island of Rathlin which had looked quite near when we started out seemed to be disappearing into the distance. We felt we were out in the middle of the ocean and a hundred miles away from the nearest land. The weather was changing. There'd be a storm! AND AT THAT POINT THE ENGINE FAILED. It spluttered, changed key, picked up again, then went out like a light. The mate immediately got down, opened the box, fiddled and cranked the engine for all he was worth. But it wouldn't start.

"A wee drop of sea-water Andy!" he shouted back at his companion who got to his feet.

"Aye, likely." The helmsman paused for a moment then took a short length of rope, lashed the tiller to the seat and stumbled forward to help. Both men got down on their knees and vigorously applied skill and the experience of a lifetime but to no avail, the engine would not start. The boat began to drift. The waves began to ease us round into a position where one decent broadside would finish us off. We were without an engine … virtually without a crew … and completely at the mercy of the sea.

Grandma, who had stopped praying, buried her head in her coat and began to rock back and forth, moaning quietly. Grandad, one hand holding onto the side of the boat and the other arm round grandma's shoulder, did his best to comfort her, and when that didn't work brought down the curtain by declaring, "Ah well Louie, there's one consolation, if we go down we go down together!" Father lay his full length along the seat and with both arms outstretched tried to pull the tarpaulin, which was breaking loose, back over his precious apparatus. The boatmen withdrew their heads from the engine box simultaneously and looked at each other, and at that point mother said she felt certain they had no idea what to do next, and was terrified. There was only one soul aboard that stricken craft who wasn't afraid. There was only one sinner who didn't care, indeed who wasn't even the slightest concerned ... and that was *me*. With both feet I vigorously pounded the floorboards, coughed up the last of my breakfast, looked out into the emptiness and yelled at the sea, the heavens and The Almighty Himself, "*Let me outa here! Let me outa here!*"

Fortunately, or my story would have ended abruptly at that point, the boatmen got the engine going again. So I didn't get out, though I think that was mainly because mother, desperately clinging to the boat with one hand reached out with the other and took hold of me by the scruff of the neck. Hanging on to me, she said afterwards, at least took her mind off our predicament, though she didn't enjoy the experience, none of us did. Mind you, looking back, we may not have been in as dangerous a situation as we imagined, and the engine may not have been out of action for as long as I recall. Just the same, when it started again and the helmsman returned to take charge of the steering we were all very much relieved.

There were no more breakdowns on the journey, and our little craft in a slow but doggedly determined fashion climbed the waves, ploughed the waters and headed for Rathlin, with the helmsman taking our minds off our near catastrophe by pointing out to certain areas (and in one case I believe to the actual remains ... the tip of a mast), where there had been famous shipwrecks in the past. Going on from there to heighten our interest still further by informing us that, as the Atlantic Ocean poured round the north coast and channelled itself into the Irish Sea between Rathlin and Ballycastle, it made this one of the most treacherous stretches of water anywhere in the British Isles. We were not only relieved, you can imagine, after that piece of information, but quite surprised when the eastern arm of the island began to curve round on our right, the rocky heights of the west coast rose up on our left, and in the quiet, sheltered waters ahead we could make out the harbour, a few white houses, and the little church and tower which gave the bay its name.

"Welcome to Rathlin!" A little old man with a grizzly beard and lots of wiry hair poking out from under an engine driver's cap, greeted mother as she climbed out of the ferry and onto the narrow quay.

"Oh ... thank you," mother replied breathlessly. "I'm very pleased to be here. In fact I'm very *surprised* to be here."

"A wee bit bumpy out there was it?" the old man grinned, showing that half his teeth were missing and the rest were as black as the pot.

"You could say that." Grandma, being assisted onto the quay, and already making a remarkable recovery from her ordeal, joined in the conversation. "Thank you," she smiled at the boatmen who had helped her, "thank you very much indeed gentlemen. I'm ashore now." Then she advanced towards the old man. "Yes, you could say that. And when the engine stopped somewhere out there," she waved an arm but did not look back, "I can't even bear to look, there was one old lady in that boat who thought her end had come."

The boatmen grinned and the old man chuckled. "Oh, they wouldn't have let you go down, they've never lost a man yet … nor a woman. Where's yer bags?"

"My bags?" Grandma looked puzzled but mother knew what he meant.

"Oh, all the luggage is under there," she pointed at the tarpaulin.

"Don't worry about the bags grandad," one of several men who had come down to see the ferry in called out. "I'll bring the ladies' things up to the post office."

"Well, that's very kind of you," mother gave him a smile.

"Not at all."

"Right then ladies!" The old man about-turned and headed for the houses.

"Very good sir!" Grandma responded in similar military fashion as she, mother and I fell in behind our leader.

"See you at the post office, Bob," mother called out as we left.

"Right." Father had the gramophone under his arm.

"You too dad."

"Right Lil, right." Grandad was down in the bottom of the boat grappling with the scenery. "As soon as we get our stuff into the hall we'll be with you."

Getting our stuff into the hall wasn't as difficult as father had imagined because the hall was quite near and there were many hands, people who were used to manhandling their belongings (there were no lorries and not a single car on the island at that time), only too willing to help. Of course, we were visitors, guests, and must be looked after. We were also something of a novelty and there were quite a few curious but discreet glances directed at us and our equipment.

"Pleased to see you. And welcome to Rathlin." The postmistress, a quiet, sombre and I thought very tired-looking lady, though she couldn't have been any older than mother, came out to the doorstep to greet us.

"Thank you, and we're pleased to see you … Mrs McCreedy isn't it?" Mother stepped forward.

"That's right." The postmistress, who was also to be our landlady (full bed and board for all of us for the week), took mother's hand.

"I'm Mrs Mateer and this is my mother Mrs Wynn."

"Pleased to meet you, Mrs Wynn."

"How do you do," grandma held Mrs McCreedy's hand for a moment. "I'm very pleased to be here. And I would add, very grateful."

"It was a wee bit bumpy in the channel was it?"

"It was a whole lot bumpy," grandma said. "And when the engine broke down half way across I thought we'd all end up at the bottom of the sea."

"But the boatman soon got it going again," mother came in quickly, thinking no doubt that this was a slur on the boatman's reputation, and anyhow we'd had enough of that topic. "Let me introduce you to the rest of the family," she looked down at me. "Well, some of it. My husband and father are still down at the harbour, and I have a little girl, Eileen, who's not with us, she's been left with an aunt in Co. Down. But this is my son, Jim."

"Pleased to meet you, Jim," the lady smiled. "I have a wee boy just about your age," then she looked sad again. "But he's not very well at the moment I'm afraid."

"Oh dear, I'm very sorry to hear that," mother commiserated.

"Not very well at all," the lady looked very sad indeed. "But come into the house."

"I'll away to see them getting the things up to the hall." The old man who had taken no part in the introductions, and was standing silently a few yards to our rear, suddenly called out.

"Alright grandad," Mrs McCreedy replied. "Then come back with the rest for your dinner."

"Right, right." The old man turned about and trotted back in the direction of the quay.

"Come into the house and warm yourselves, you must be foundered."

"Foundered?" grandma queried, but mother translated.

"Frozen."

"Oh, what a wonderful way with words the Irish have ... *to be sure*," grandma chuckled. "Foundered ... frozen and nearly drowned. It's lovely."

"It's always cold out in the channel no matter what time of the day or year. You'll feel better after a warm. I've got your rooms ready."

"Lovely. I expect my husband and father won't take too long sorting out the scenery ... there were lots of willing hands."

"Oh yes, my Tom's down there."

"Ah, he must have been the man who said he'd bring our bags up to the post office."

"That would be him."

"And the hall's not very far away I believe?"

"Oh, no distance at all, they'll not be long. In the meantime I'll make you a cup of tea."

"A cup of tea!" grandma raised her hands and looked towards the ceiling.

"Take that chair in the corner, Mrs Wynn."

"I'm beginning to feel quite human again."

"And here's one for you, Mrs Mateer. Jimmy can have Danny's stool. I'll just put some water in this pot ... in the scullery ... I won't be a minute." Mrs McCreedy did everything she could to make us comfortable. And she tried very hard to be cheerful while she was about it, but clearly her mind and her thoughts were elsewhere ... with the little boy upstairs. We didn't really have to inquire what was wrong with him because only minutes after our arrival we could hear, in the room above us, the coughing, the retching, the terrible gasping as young Danny tried to get breath.

"That's your little boy upstairs is it?" mother inquired as our landlady hurried back into the kitchen.

"It is indeed." Mrs McCreedy stood in the middle of the floor and looked up at the ceiling. "And I think I'll have to go up to him again."

"Oh yes do," mother agreed. "Go to him, don't mind us, we'll be alright."

"Is it asthma?" grandma looked very serious.

"It is. He's had a terrible bout, and the doctor's been with him but he's going back now on the ferry to Ballycastle."

"Poor little soul."

"He's having a terrible time ... the doctor can do nothing more for him. The next few hours will be critical. He'll either get over it ... or ..."

"Please God he'll get over it," grandma said in a quiet voice. "I know exactly how you must feel, what you're going through at this minute, because I had a little boy once."

"You go up to him now," mother cut in. She didn't want grandma to get on to the subject of Tommy, not then anyway. "You go up and then I think *you* should have a cup of tea too. It's a great strain being a mother at times like this."

"Oh, it is. You know I haven't had a decent night's sleep the whole week ... just the odd wee doze by the fire now and again. And I don't mind not getting my sleep, or running upstairs a hundred times a day, it's just having to stand here and listen and not be able to do anything that beats me."

"Off you go now," mother got to her feet. "You tell me where the things are and I'll make the tea."

"Oh, that would be good of you, Mrs Mateer. The caddy's on the dresser, the sugar's in the cupboard and the milk's in the scullery."

"I'll have it ready when you come down."

"I'll not be long ... I'll just settle him down. The teapot's on the hob ... and use any cups you can find."

By the time Mrs McCreedy had settled little Danny down and we had finished our tea-drinking the men had returned from their work. We had dinner. After dinner we went to the hall to put up the scenery and get things ready for the show that night. Then when our work in the hall was completed we came back to the post office, had tea, and while the men smoked and talked by the fireside the women washed the dishes and talked in the scullery. And it was during the talking in the scullery that grandma, as soon as she thought our landlady was amenable, asked to see the sick boy.

"So you were quite looking forward to seeing the play tonight, Mrs McCreedy?"

"Oh yes, Mrs Wynn, I was really excited about it, like everybody else on the island. People have talked about nothing else the whole week. I'm very disappointed. Mind you, I've told Tom he must go. Though I wouldn't leave the house, not with Danny the way he is."

"Of course not," grandma agreed. "But maybe, if it's God's will little Danny will get over this bad spell. And we'll be here the whole week." (We would be there for longer than the week, though nobody realised that at the time.)

"Yes, well, we'll just have to pray, Mrs Wynn, we'll just have to pray."

"And prayer is a very powerful thing … and so is faith. I'm a great believer in faith, Mrs McCreedy."

"Oh, so am I."

"And though I don't profess to be a healer myself, I like to help in my own little way whenever I can." She paused for a moment, then asked, "Do you think I could see little Danny before I go off to the show tonight?"

"Oh yes, certainly," the lady was surprised but also pleased. "Though he's not in much of a state for talking."

"Oh, I wouldn't dream of talking and tiring the poor child out. No, I'd just like to say hello and wish him better."

"Well, that would be very nice of you indeed. He knows you're here, I've told him. And when he heard about your coming to the island he was every bit as keen as the rest of us to see the plays. He'd be very pleased to see you."

"Can we go up there now?"

"Oh yes, he's not asleep. I wish he was."

"Lead the way then." Grandma and Mrs McCreedy climbed the stairs up to the boy's bedroom which was directly above our heads. It was a small room (I was invited up to see it the following day) with a low ceiling which, like the walls, was sheeted with dark, tongue and grooved timber. It was daytime when I saw it but when grandma entered that evening it was dark and a small oil lamp burned by the bed. The boy was lying on his back, pale-faced, his eyes closed and his chest still labouring after the recent attack.

"Mrs Wynn has come up to see you Danny," the woman brushed the hair away from her son's eyes and straightened the bedclothes. "She's with the Playactors, and she has a wee grandson downstairs exactly the same age as you. You'll be able to meet him when you're a bit better … tomorrow maybe." The boy opened his eyes and gave a weak smile. "He's very tired, Mrs Wynn."

"Of course he is," grandma spoke in a very low voice. "I've just come to say hello Danny." She touched his hand. "You don't have to keep your eyes open, or try to speak. We all want you to rest and get better. That's it." The boy closed his eyes again. "Can I sit with him for a few minutes, Mrs McCreedy?"

"Yes, of course."

"Good." Grandma reached out and gently took hold of the boy's hand, and still holding it sat down on the chair beside the bed. "I'll just stay for a minute or two Danny. I won't talk, I'll just sit and think … and hope." She looked up at the boy's mother. "I'm a great believer in hope, Mrs McCreedy."

"Oh indeed."

"And faith."

"What else is there?"

"And I never ask a man or a woman what their religion is, as long as their God is a God of love that's all I need to know."

"That's a good way to be, Mrs Wynn."

"Is there anything you want to do downstairs at the moment? I'll be alright here for a little while."

"Well, yes, there's always something to do."

"You go down then. I can call out if Danny wants you."

"I'll be in the kitchen." Mrs McCreedy withdrew and quietly closed the door behind her. The boy lay very still for a few moments, his eyes closed, then he sighed. Grandma reached across with her free hand and laid it gently on his forehead. He smiled and after a little while grandma turned away, and still holding his hand she closed her eyes, lowered her head and, I suppose, prayed.

Grandma, as I've already mentioned, was a Spiritualist and not only believed in prayer but was convinced that you could contact the spirits of people who had died, or "passed over" as she termed it. If help was needed by someone, a sick person like Danny for instance, then what you had to do was contact the spirit of a doctor in the next world and he would offer assistance. How it actually worked I never found out, but on more than one occasion when I had come running in with a bashed knee or a sore head she had cured me by touching the ailing part and then sitting quietly, holding my hand just as she was doing with Danny. I believed in her powers. And I think, though they hadn't actually discussed "faith healing", Mrs McCreedy did as well.

Grandma was up there for nearly an hour. Father said she'd gone to sleep, but during that time the boy didn't cough once. And he was still silent when the entire company, plus *Mr* McCreedy and the old man who had been invited to see the show, went off to the hall. I was the last person to leave the post office because, as usual, I'd made a last-minute dash out to the back. Our landlady was sitting by the fire, her head down over her sewing, when I carefully closed the front door behind me. In the distance I could hear the roaring of the sea. Ahead of me, some way along the narrow winding road, the cheerful voices of our party disturbed the silence of the lonely landscape. But close to, and in the house, everything was silent and as quiet as the grave. Up in the little hall, however, things were different.

*

"*Full house.*" Father picked his way through to the corner of the dressing room where he'd set up his gramophone. "You ready, Wee Jim?"

"I'm ready." I picked up my blackthorn stick and pulled on my old paddy hat.

"And when you're getting up on the stage mind your back … if a late-comer opens the door you could get bashed."

"I'll watch."

"I'll raise the curtain and announce your number, then let me get off before you go on."

The hall had a very low ceiling and our scenery had to be built around the stage rather than on it. And another problem was the door which was situated in the side of the hall near the back. There was no other way into the building, so when the audience entered they were immediately confronted by the side of the stage (they could see right across it), and had to turn sharp left to get into the hall. While we, facing the same obstacle, turned sharp right to get into the dressing room. The position of the door and the size of the hall made moving on and off stage very difficult indeed because you couldn't cross behind the scenery to get to the opposite side, and you couldn't stand in the wings. All our exits, therefore, had to be made by the prompt side (that is, by the door). To make an entrance you had to wait for your cue standing in the doorway of the dressing room, then hurry up the steps (grandad fell up them on several occasions) in order to get on the stage. This inconvenience, however, had an advantage as far as I was concerned, because by sheer chance it enabled me, and me alone, to witness a mysterious little incident that occurred right at the beginning of the show.

"One minute to go," father stood by the gramophone with his watch in his hand.

"*We're* ready," mother responded cheerfully. We were all in very good spirits that evening because we had survived the crossing, were settled in warm, clean, homely lodgings, and on our opening night we had a hall packed to the walls with cheerful and excited people waiting to be entertained. The little building reverberated with animated talk and laughter. And above the clamour of the audience father's loud-speaker sprayed out a thin, tinny medley of airs ancient and modern: *The Whistler And His Dog*; *The Bard Of Armagh*; *Singing In The Bathtub*; *Sucking Cider Through A Straw*; *Painting The Clouds With Sunshine*; *Tiptoe Through The Tulips* ... And after the homely fare, the islanders on that remote shelf of black basalt were treated to the latest (though as father always bought second-hand they weren't all that modern) dreamy sophisticated numbers like *Dancing With Tears In My Eyes*; *That's You Baby*; *Big City Blues*; *My Dear*; and a special favourite of mine, a duet sung by a very proper English lady and gentleman:

> "There is so little I can do for you,
> All that I can do I'll do dear.
> Dreams are my treasure ... though I have but few,
> And they can come true, for you dear."

Chorus:

> "There's nothing in the world I wouldn't do, for you ... for you.
> I would gather stars out of the blue, for you ... for you.
> Over the highway and over the street
> A carpet of clover I'd lay at your feet ..."

I don't suppose the audience heard a lot of the words, but each time the music stopped they stopped, and when, finally, it became obvious that father had taken off the last record and there was a slight movement on stage behind the curtain, the hall went silent.

"Right!" Father hurried from the dressing room, climbed the steps, crossed the stage and raised the curtain to the delight and admiration of our audience. Then he made an entrance, delivered his usual first-night speech, and announced my song:

"And now, ladies and gentlemen, our first number tonight will be a song ... one of your own old comeallyes, about a farmer called Dan Murphy. And it will be sung by *our* own ... WEE JIM!"

Applause as he came off and I went on, dressed as a farmer. The air was a traditional one, and like most airs that had been around for a long time it had several different sets of lyrics. The one I was about to do was always a great favourite. Which wasn't surprising in a country where bachelors were plentiful, no longer young, and had great difficulty in coming to terms with the idea of matrimony, or even the opposite sex. Poverty and tradition had decreed that men in rural areas didn't marry early. For a start their mothers were none too keen on the idea of bringing another woman into the kitchen. So single girls had to work hard to interest a man in marriage. The audience before me waited patiently and sympathetically, as they usually did at the sight of a small boy standing up there on the stage all on his own. Without accompaniment, and getting off in the right key (a great fear of mine), I began.

"My name is Dan Murphy a farmer am I.
I courted a lassie and felt very shy.
She bad me come in for a moment or two,
Well bedad and says I, I don't mind if I do.
Touralay ... touraloo.
Well bedad and says I, I don't mind if I do.

I entered the kitchen 'twas cosy and bright
And a nice hearty supper I put out of sight.
She says have a drop of the old mountain dew,
Well bedad and says I, I don't mind if I do.
Touralay ... touraloo ... I don't mind if I do.

And when I had finished I picked up my hat.
Says Peggy the darlin' don't lave me like that.
She asked me to kiss her like true lovers do,
Well bedad and says I, I don't mind if I do.
Touralay ... touraloo ... I don't mind if I do.

We kissed and we squeezed I'd the court o' me life.
She asked me to wed her and make her me wife.
She said I've a cow and an acre or two,
Well bedad and says I, I don't mind if I do.
Touralay … touraloo … I don't mind if I do.

'twas early next Sunday in the church we did stand.
The priest stood fornenst us the book in his hand.
Now do you take Peggy and Peggy take you?
WELL BEDAD AND SAYS SHE HE DON'T MIND IF HE DO."

The audience clapped and cheered and father standing down on the floor by the stage nodded so I went back and took another bow. Then I made my exit off right, opposite the door. This wasn't a mistake on my part; I'd made arrangements beforehand and got father's permission because it was clear to me there was no space in the dressing room, and I wasn't on stage again until the curtain came down and went up for the play, so I reckoned I'd be comfortably out of everyone's way if I sat behind the proscenium curtain down right. Father wasn't too keen on the idea at first but then he said it would be alright providing I couldn't be seen by the audience. Father never wanted you to be seen by the audience when you were off stage during a performance. And something else that upset him even more – though I never did it – was to see an actor going out among the public after the show without removing his make-up. On stage or behind the proscenium was the place for an actor. Anywhere else you were a member of the public and should dress and behave as such. Anyhow I told him I wouldn't be seen, and to make sure this was the case, when I made my exit I immediately sat down with my back against the wall, tucked myself in close to the curtain, and pulled my knees up to my chin. I couldn't be seen by anyone out in the hall.

Grandma came on after me, did a little patter in a broad Lancashire accent, just like Gracie Fields, then charmed the house by singing Gracie's famous song, "Sally". Grandma had a beautiful voice, it was so true, and it soared and filled, yet didn't over-fill that little hall on Rathlin. There were no mikes for us in those days, and if you couldn't be heard at the back of the largest theatre or hall without shouting, then you weren't an actor and that was that. Grandma could sing in your ear, or throw her voice so that you could hear her half a mile away. And of course it was a lovely song, so she got a hearty round of applause. Father was due on next to do one of his monologues. And it was during his monologue that the mysterious happening occurred.

I can't recall the title now, indeed I can only remember the first and the last couple of lines, but the story was a favourite of mine so I settled down that evening to listen, and when he came to the last line and the unexpected twist …! Well, let's wait and see. Father introduced himself, announced the title, and when there was absolute silence in the hall, began.

"Now Sam Magee was from Tennessee where the cotton blooms and grows ..." The story was about Sam and his partner, the person telling the tale, setting out and heading for the Klondyke in search of gold. (It must have been a very popular pastime and topic in those days because there were lots of poems, plays, and even a silent film about prospecting and the Gold Rush.) They cross the Canadian border, find the Klondyke, settle in an old wooden shack and begin to dig. And they dig, and they dig, and they dig, but they don't find any gold. The winter sets in. The wind blows from the north. And no matter how many furs Sam lays on his bed, and no matter how hard he works out in the snow, first thing in the morning and last thing at night his partner hears the same phrase again and again ... "*I'm cold*".

And the cold eventually gets to him because one morning he won't get out of bed, saying not only is he cold, but he's ill. His partner builds up the fire, makes him as comfortable as he can, then goes off to dig on his own. When he returns at the end of the day, however, he finds Sam still in bed, and when he inquires how he feels his friend doesn't speak, doesn't move ... *he's dead.*

The ground was frozen hard. A shallow grave would be desecrated by wolves. His partner doesn't know what to do about a burial, then he remembers the wreck of an old steamer lying jammed against the bank of the frozen river some distance away. So he loads the body onto the sledge, and when he gets to the riverside he builds a pyre inside the old steamer's boiler, lays the body on top, and sets it alight. Then, closing the great iron doors behind him he retires to the river bank to say a little prayer for the soul of poor Sam.

It was at this point, from a position where I could look past father and across the stage, that I noticed the handle of the door begin to move. It turned gently, the door opened a few inches and then stopped. But no-one looked in. No-one tried to enter. Had I been on the other side I would have investigated, assuming it was some curious boy, but of course I couldn't cross until the curtain came down. So I just fixed my eye on the door and peered at the narrow opening until, gradually, I began to make out a shape, a face, but it wasn't the face of a boy because it was much too high up, it was the face of a man. And he seemed to be wearing a hat, which was unusual because most of the men on the island wore caps, if they wore anything at all on their heads. I kept watching, and after a few moments the door began to move again. Slowly it swung in towards the stage, but before it got wide enough for me to get a clear view a hand came round and pulled it back though not the whole way. Somebody out there was listening. Father, who wasn't aware of the incident, went on with his story.

On the river bank Sam's partner offers up a prayer, then sits on the sledge and quietly watches the funeral smoke pouring out of the ship's funnel. And when the smoke dies down, thinking he will scrape up the ashes and sprinkle them over the snow, he again approaches the steamer. But just as he reaches out to open the doors of the boiler he hears a strange noise coming from inside. He pauses. Is it the heat expanding the metal? Is it the ice that entombs the ship beginning to crack? He waits, but the noise stops, so he takes hold of the heavy iron doors, pulls them open, and there, to his astonishment, on the floor of the boiler and warming his hands at the embers, sits Sam.

> "Who turned and looked and smiled at me.
> That's the first time I've been warm, he said
> Since I left Tennessee."

Applause! The audience were just as pleasantly surprised by the twist at the end as I always was. Father took his bow, made his exit Right and came alongside me in order to let down the curtain. And as he did so the door on the opposite side of the stage was quietly closed. I hurried across the moment the roller came to rest on the boards, opened the door again and looked out ... but there was no-one to be seen. I told father about the mysterious incident but he didn't think it very significant. I thought it significant, however, and I was right.

After the variety came the play, *The Smugglers*. And although the islanders were miles away from the border they knew all about smuggling. Whether there was any going on there at that particular time I don't know, but in the past, certainly during the lengthy trade wars that went on between Britain, France and America, some 1,400 articles, including tea, soap, tobacco, leather, brandy and silk had heavy duties imposed on them. Smuggling was a lot more profitable than fishing or working a farm! Besides, poor people found beating the system, the tax system, a challenge. They loved the play, and the farce, and when the curtain came down at the end they cheered and then noisily and cheerfully stumbled out into the night. And how dark the darkness is on an island, when there is no moon, no street lamps, and not even the light from a cottage to guide you on your way.

Minutes later we too left the hall and returned to the post office where the table was laid and a great iron pot of porridge bubbled on the hob. It wasn't quick, instant porridge, this stuff had taken hours to boil and would last us for nearly a week. The old man was the first to get to the table where he had his cap removed (he often forgot about his cap), and a bib tied round his neck. Half his food and drink ended up in his tough, wiry beard, and if there was no bib it could be shaken all round the place and over everybody. As well as the porridge (and we were all hungry, we were always hungry at that time of night) there was tea, cheese, country butter that had been made in a barrel churn with a little window so you could see when the butter was ready, and bread. Barley bread that was dark grey and rather indigestible, and yellow meal bread that was sharp, crisp, yellow (made from maize), and became a great favourite with father. Everything was laid out on a big, well-scrubbed table, and served up cheerfully by a tired but happy mother who announced the moment we went in.

"Mrs Wynn, Danny hasn't coughed, he hasn't moved, he's sound asleep. The first decent sleep he's had the whole week. Your prayers have been answered."

"Thank God," grandma said softly.

"And thank *you*."

15

Rathlin *continued*

There was no mail from Ballycastle during our first week on the island. There was no ferryboat either. The swell increased, the wind blew harder, and as Mrs McCreedy accurately prophesied as we headed towards our first weekend, "Oh, at this time of the year and with the wind in that quarter it could blow for a fortnight." No boat put out from Ballycastle that week or the next. Indeed, we were into our third week before the weather improved and we were able to leave. On a Wednesday I believe; not that I remember the day, but I have one of grandma's postcards (a picture of the shore road on Rathlin), obviously written on the island and probably posted a day or so later when the ferry started running again. It had been sent to her sister and nephew in England.

"Dear Bella and Joe. I'll write you by Tuesday's mail. This is to give you an idea where we have drifted. I shall know better what we are doing by Tuesday, our last night here. Best love, Louie. P.S. X marks where we live."

I don't believe there was even a telephone on the island at that time. I think they had to wait another twenty years, until the fifties, before the line was laid down on the sea-bed. Father, resourceful as ever, must have made all his arrangements with the ferrymen the week before we left Ballycastle, and would arrange our next venue as soon as we got back there again. In the meantime the gale-force winds and the angry seas threatened, encircled and pinned us down on those few square miles of treeless, volcanic rock. Not that it seemed to worry the islanders a great deal, they were used to it. And of course they were self-contained, buying all the provisions they needed in hundredweight sacks ... though I don't remember seeing a shop on Rathlin. Nor do I remember that we were all that concerned either about being cut off and confined. We were comfortable, well looked after, and the islanders cheerfully filled the little hall every night of the week, apart from Sunday. It was fortunate that our repertoire was equal to the occasion. Although as this was the longest stay in one place I can ever remember, and we had to provide twelve different plays in two weeks, rehearsals were necessary; that is, we had a run-through in the afternoon before the show at night.

It must have been a unique experience for the inhabitants of Rathlin. I mean, when you consider modern methods of travel, the radio, and all the canned entertainment people get on television these days, and set that against the fact that at that time the islanders, most of whom didn't possess a wireless and had never even been to Belfast, depended on one small ferryboat (and the mail, newspapers and gossip it carried) to connect them with the outside world. Yet despite that isolation, for nearly three weeks the people of Rathlin had live actors – artists with considerable skills and a great variety of professional experience – to entertain them. And plays, some of which would only have been produced in theatres in cities on mainland Britain. I can't remember every play we presented to our island audiences, but leaving out the regulars mentioned earlier, they must have seen some, if not all, of the following.

The Life of an Actress — Set in the greenroom of a west-end theatre, this is the story of a famous actress and a wealthy patron who takes a flower-girl off the street with the intention of making her a star (Pygmalion?). However, before he gets very far his financial empire crashes and he is left penniless (well, almost penniless), and humbled (the famous actress ditches him). So he devotes the rest of his life to the flower-girl, making her a shining light in the theatre, and eventually marrying her into the aristocracy.

Pete's Baby — The eternal triangle ... a fisherman, his beautiful but restless young wife, and an upper-class scoundrel with a yacht. There is also a baby. And although on Rathlin the baby would have been a fake, on an earlier tour of Scotland my little sister Eileen, then about three months old (according to mother), was introduced to the stage and rose magnificently to the occasion. Because, when her fisherman daddy returns from the sea and can't find her mother, the small babe-in-arms reaches out and picks up a sparkling necklace (to pay for the child's upkeep) attached to which is a note that tells the terrible truth. A very sad play indeed, and Eileen played her part so well that two members of the audience came to the stage door after the show in order to settle a wager: Was it a real baby or a mechanical doll? The winnings were deposited on the baby's cot. Eileen was dead lucky with money. And of course her mammy came back, singing, "There's a little grey home in the west."

The Romance of a Prince — Set in Bavaria and all about a tyrant prince, an actress, and a young trooper whose origin is unknown because he has been brought up by the gypsies! I'll let you consider the possibilities of that plot for yourself.

Caste — "... and the colonel's lady and Judy O'Grady are sisters under the skin." Everybody knows that one.

Old Bill — The trenches in the first World War. Lots of loud explosions, one of which, a couple of years earlier, singed grandad's hair, burnt off his eyebrows and blinded him for nearly a week. There was also a thundersheet which father tried to keep out of my reach. It was all very exciting and a bit like … in fact a *lot* like *Journey's End.*

The O'Donnels of Donneybrook — Southern Ireland. Rackrenting and the suffering of the peasant farmers with no security of tenure. Not as miserable as it sounds, in fact quite a humorous, rumbustious affair with dirty tricks, attempted house-burnings, and the villain, Capt. Danville, sent to prison thanks to the sterling work of Father Rafferty the local priest.

Father O'Flynn — Somewhere in the western states of North America. The priest has two brothers, one a saint and the other an outlaw. The battle is for the soul of the outlaw and the love of a good woman.

There was also *Lady Audley's Secret, Jane Corder, Deception*, and a play that might have been specially dedicated to the island itself: *Midnight Wireless S.O.S.* This was about the infamous murderer Dr. Crippen and his capture on board ship while trying to escape to America; something he would have succeeded in doing had it not been for a wonderful new invention … the wireless. And the connection with Rathlin? Well, by the strangest coincidence Marconi, some twenty-five years before we arrived on the scene, set up a wireless installation there and to the amazement of the locals, transmitted a message across the Sound to a house in Ballycastle.

And finally, despite our long sojourn there, we provided the islanders with a great variety of songs, double-acts and sketches. Old Victorian ballads like *Tears for Souvenirs, Only a Bird in a Gilded Cage, When Other Lips and Other Hearts*, and *I Haven't Any Gold to Leave When I Grow Old.* Double-acts like *The Burroo* (the Employment Bureau), which was a dialogue between an overbearing representative of the system (played by father) and an unemployed veteran (me) who opens the act by asking, "Is there any fear of a start mister?" And of course, at the end of the night there was the farce.

Simple Simon was one of those short sketches, which our audience (mostly farmers or people connected in some way with the land) always enjoyed. It goes like this: A country yokel and his widowed mother have brought their cow to the market. While the mother goes into a chemist's shop (or is it a pub?) the lad gets conned by a city-slicker who worms out of him the fact that the cow is a pedigree animal worth ten pounds, but as they always get cheated at the market they'll be lucky to get five. The conman, out of the kindness of his heart, offers to sell the beast on their behalf and gives the boy six. He then trots off to the market to off-load what is in fact an *unsaleable* cow, while the boy and his mother laugh all the way home.

The Burglar — An old gag. A burglar picks the lock of a safe, gathers up the contents and is then apprehended by a gent in a dressing-gown. After a long sob-story the burglar is allowed to go free, without the loot, and the gent then whips off the dressing-gown to reveal the traditional black and white striped jersey of another burglar.

Fanny — A mix-up on a farm where the farmer's daughter, Fanny, is about to be wed. The farmer's mare, also called Fanny, is up for sale. And an undertaker has arrived (at the wrong address) to make arrangements for a funeral.

The islanders loved everything we offered and came back to fill the little hall night after night. I believe the population today is about a hundred, although way back before the famine it was nearer a thousand. In our time it was probably a good three hundred, and mixed, with the protestant community shepherded by a Church of Ireland clergyman, and the larger catholic community by a priest; a man who, we soon discovered, held the key to many secrets, *including the identity of the mystery man at the door!* But to get to that we have to return to our first week, in fact to the day after our arrival.

Danny had survived the crisis, indeed when I went up to see him the following morning he was cheerful, talked a bit, and we became friends. Our first show had been a resounding success. Though despite a thorough inquiry nobody in the McCreedy household had the faintest idea who the mystery man could be. "I mean, who would wander round the island in the dark at that time of night? And if they wanted to see the play why wouldn't they go, or be taken?" They had no idea who the stranger might be. But the priest knew … who he was, why he didn't go into the hall, why he *couldn't* go into the hall. And later on that afternoon so did the rest of us.

We had finished our lunch (a light one because now our landlady realised we preferred our main meal after the show), father had filled up his pipe, got it going, and announced he was going out for a walk, on his own. He headed straight for the sea but got no further than the little harbour when he came face to face with the parish priest, a man about his own age, who hailed him.

"Ah, good afternoon to you sir."

"Good afternoon to you too … er …"

"Neeson … the parish priest. And you must be the boss of the Playactors."

"That's right … name's Mateer, Bob Mateer."

"Delighted to meet you, Bob." The priest held out his hand. "You don't mind my calling you Bob?"

"I've been called a lot worse than that in my time."

"So have I," Father Neeson laughed as they shook hands, "so have I. Well Bob, they tell me you gave them a marvellous play last night."

"They certainly seemed to enjoy it."

"Oh, they thought it was great, great … all that smuggling. Where did you get your information … I mean, who wrote the play?"

"I did."

"Did you now! And wrote it well from all accounts. Have you lived near the border … or worked there? Where are you from?"

"Oh, I'm from Belfast."

"I'm a Down man myself, from a wee place called Kilcoo, near Rathfriland."

"Oh, we've played in Rathfriland."

"Isn't it a small world! And now you're up here … and so am I. But all the ideas, the information … have you been down in the south?"

"Oh, I started my professional career in the south, in Dublin."

"In Dublin?"

"I was only nineteen at the time, and the company I joined had a very short run in the Abbey. Then I came back north and a while later I was down in Dublin again, for a much longer run this time, in the old Queen's Theatre."

"On the other side of the river?"

"That's right. I also played at the Gate … right at the top of what was then Sackville Street."

"O'Connell Street now."

"That's right. And after Dublin we moved out and did a tour of the south."

"With what sort of plays?"

"Well, some you probably wouldn't know, but there were Irish ones like *The Colleen Bawn, The Shaughraun, Tir-na-nOg …*"

"Oh yes, I know them all … great plays."

"And they were great days … the days of Sara Allgood, Lennox Robinson, Louis D'Alton, and a fine repertory company run by an actor who called himself Brefni O'Rourke … he had a boy working with him who is now making a name for himself in the theatre."

"Cyril Cusack!"

"Ah, you're well-informed."

"Well, I'm interested in these things."

"Yes, the theatre was booming then. They were good days."

"Ah but they were also bad days Bob … The Troubles!"

"Ah yes, The Troubles, I saw some of those. In fact, when I was down in the south in 1920 I got caught up in one incident that nearly cost me my life."

"Do you tell me that!"

"We had moved into a hall somewhere near where the border is today. The women had gone in to the town – though I wasn't married or even thinking about it at the time – and we were fitting up the scenery. It was all very quiet, then we heard a commotion outside and the next minute the door was kicked in and a bunch of what turned out to be republicans, armed with revolvers, burst in, ordered us out, lined us up against the wall and said we were going to be shot."

"Dear God. What for? Why?"

"They didn't say. Just swore and pointed their guns and we stood there with our hands in the air."

"But they didn't … I mean it's obvious they didn't *shoot* you."

"Only because their officer came wandering in and after some consultation they lowered their guns and just went off."

"Without an explanation … or an apology?"

"Nothing at all. We learnt afterwards that some independent gang had moved into the area and these fellows thought we had something to do with them."

"And they were going to sort the matter out, quick."

"That's the way things were at the time. And you know on the same tour we had another experience which I was certain would turn out to be my last."

"What was that?"

"We had loaded up the lorry and were on the way to another hall when the driver … a big fellow from Limerick …"

"Ah they have some big fellows down there."

"… suddenly swung out into a main road, drew up, and informed us that there was talk the road had been mined."

"*Mined?*"

"That's right."

"So you didn't go down it."

"Oh yes we did, because the big fellow assured us there was no real danger as he would drive like hell and if a mine went off it would go off behind us."

"You didn't believe that did you?"

"No; but before we could argue he'd started up again and with our behinds bouncing off the seat and our heads banging against the roof we went down that road like the wind."

"And did you hit anything?"

"We did."

"A *mine?*"

"No, a hen."

"A *hen!*"

"Yes. And the minute we hit it the driver slammed on the brakes, leapt out of the cab, lifted the bird, threw it in among our feet and drove off shouting above the roar of the engine, 'It's alright, it's alright'."

"*It's dead,*" I yelled in his ear, "what do you mean, it's alright?"

"It is," he said, "but I only ran over its head. It'll make a nice little item for the pot."

"Ah, this is great stuff Bob, great stuff." Father Neeson was genuinely excited. "I never see anybody, I never hear anybody who's been anywhere … and I'm going to miss all the plays. And I only caught the tail end of your recitation about the man who was cremated in the … "

Before he could finish father opened his mouth wide and said, "*AH!*" Then raised his hand and pointed his pipe at the priest. "The mystery's solved."

"What mystery?" Father Neeson looked puzzled.

"Why, the mystery of the stranger who silently opened the door, listened, then disappeared into the night."

"Oh, that … well yes … you see I was curious to hear what was going on inside so I opened the door, quietly, so as not to disturb anybody, listened, then got so caught up in your story I just had to hear it out to the end."

"But why didn't you come in? Why didn't you come in? Come tonight, tomorrow night, any night you like. Be our guest."

"Ah well, you see Bob, there's a wee bit of a problem. It's a protestant hall." (Mother said it was an Orange hall, but she always dramatised. I presume it was attached to the protestant church.)

"Yes, but it was probably half-filled, maybe three-quarters filled with catholics!"

"True, true, but it's different for them. You see I have to get permission from my bishop and by the time that happens, you could be away in Donegal. So I can't go, and I'll miss the plays and the poems … Listen Bob, would you care to come up to the house some afternoon and I'll find a wee glass of something and we can have a bit of a yarn?"

"Certainly. I'd be delighted."

"Tomorrow then … about three?"

"I'll be there." And he was. The priest and father became good friends after that. And because of that friendship (a friendship that extended beyond Rathlin. Indeed as the days of both men drew to a close their lives touched on one more occasion) father made an arrangement to recite a special monologue for the benefit of the priest. But before we get to the actual performance, I would like to say something about those monologues.

Father usually wrote any new material he required, with the help of other members of the company from time to time; plays, sketches, songs and monologues. Writers' names, therefore, were hardly ever mentioned. And if they were, well it was nearly sixty years ago and I can find little trace of them now. There were, of course, poems by famous writers like Kipling, and father couldn't have written every poem he recited. Indeed shortly after his death when I was going through the very few papers that had miraculously survived his early nomadic life, I found a fascinating document that shed some light on the subject, though it still didn't do anything for writers. It was a highly decorative, florally-inscribed receipt – brick-red coloured script on a pale cream background – dated 16th January 1918.

THE HERBERT GEORGE COMPANY
The Home of PART—RIGHT Successes
All acts named below can be performed by … Robert Mateer
at any Music Hall or Theatre.
Upton Park, London, E13

It then listed the title of a particular monologue (no clue at all as to the author) and gave father permission to perform it … forever as far as I could see. Whether the special monologue to be presented on Father Neeson's behalf had been obtained in a similar fashion (because father didn't write it) I don't know. I hope so, and I accept in good faith that this was the case. Anyway, wherever it came from it was a very exciting poem, one of the most exciting father ever did. At least I thought that, and so did he. And as it was about a famous battle between the Irish and the English every Irishman, north and south, catholic or protestant, was of the same opinion. In fact, in one northern hall a huge fellow sitting right in the front row got so worked up when the Irish troops charged that he leapt to his feet, yelled, and ran up to the stage. Father thought he was about to be attacked, backed off, and completely forgot his lines. He couldn't go on. Like the true professional he was, however, he blamed everything on the ill-mannered behaviour of the enthusiast who nearly wept, apologised and begged him to finish the poem. But father was adamant (he had no idea what the next lines were). The audience, however, began to hurl abuse at the big fellow so in order to defuse the situation father gave them a humorous recitation instead.

The hall on Rathlin was filled, as usual, on the evening that father had arranged to do his special recitation. About two minutes before he was due on he slipped outside to where the priest was already in position, had a few quiet words, then returned, leaving the door ajar so that his friend could hear and see all that was happening on stage. Mother finished her number and came off, father straightened his tie, nipped up the steps, announced his monologue, *The Battle of Fontenoy*, and began.

> "Thrice at the huts of Fontenoy the English column failed.
> And twice the lines of St. Antoine the Dutch in vain assailed."

Only fragments of the work are available so I will tell you something about the history and the plot. Fontenoy is in Belgium, near the French border, and it was the scene of a famous battle fought in the year 1745. The English, with Hungarian and Dutch troops, were lined up against the French, who had employed a large contingent of Irish mercenaries. These mercenaries had not volunteered simply for the fight, but for revenge. Though at the beginning it didn't look as though they were about to get much satisfaction because their enemy relentlessly advanced and all but carried the day.

> "Six thousand English veterans in stately column tread
> The cannons blaze at front and flank, Lord Hay is at their head.
> Steady they step down the slope … steady they climb the hill
> Through rampart, trench and palisade, though thinner grow their ranks
> They charge … and *break*, as broke the Zuider Zee through Holland's ocean
> banks."

The French are shattered, devastated, about to flee the field, but their Marshall cries out to Louis, "Not yet my liege, the Irish troops remain." So the mercenaries move up.

"How fierce the look those exiles wear, who're wont to be so gay.
The treasured wrongs of fifty years are in their hearts today.
O'Brien's voice is hoarse with joy as halting he commands
Fix bayonets ... *Charge* ... like mountain storm rush on those fiery bands.

Like lions leaping at a fold when mad with hunger's pang
Right up against the English line the Irish exiles sprang.
Bright was their steel, 'tis bloody now, their guns are filled with gore
Through shattered ranks and severed files and trampled flags they tore.

The English strove with desperate strength, paused, rallied, shattered, fled.
The green hillside is matted close with dying and with dead.
On Fontenoy, on Fontenoy, like *eagles* in the sun
With bloody plumes the Irish stand ... the field is fought ... and won."

The house roared, the priest hurrahed, poked a fist through, shook it, then withdrew and closed the door behind him. The play followed. The curtain came down. The hall emptied, and the island settled quietly into the night. Only the long bright shaft of light from the lighthouse swept across the dark headlands and shone out over the desolate sea. A light that was to bring hope and solace to more than the travellers on the deep ... if we are to believe the tale father and grandad had to tell!

*

By the end of the second week the wind had abated, the white horses disappeared, and the ferry with provisions, mail, and the latest news from the mainland was again nosing into the harbour. For some reason – I suppose father had made arrangements with the ferryman concerning our next move – the following Tuesday was to be our last night and we were to return to Ballycastle on Wednesday morning. By now we were very much a part of the island scene, and at home in the post office. The ladies worked together, the men smoked, and on Sunday morning Danny, quite recovered, took me along the coast to a high point from where we could look down at the gulls in their thousands screaming across the cliff face and diving into the sea far below. And in the afternoon the entire company was invited to inspect the lighthouse. I think there was only one lighthouse on the island in those days, on the east side, facing the north channel ... there are three now.

We arrived as a very jolly party, were given tea and cakes, and afterwards while mother and grandma stayed down below to talk to the keeper's wife, father, grandad and I climbed to the top of the lighthouse to see the views and find out how everything worked. I have only the vaguest idea now as to how the lights were constructed, but the energy must have been derived from paraffin, vaporised … the burners were probably like giant tilley lamps. There was also some sort of frame fitted with metal and glass panels which revolved so that the light from the lamps was either shut off or left to shine out over the sea. It was all very interesting and enjoyable and when we were leaving the keeper issued a special invitation to father and grandad: "Come back again this evening and we'll continue the conversation over something a wee bit stronger than tea."

Now I have only father's word for what happened during their visit, so if anyone remotely connected with Trinity House, The Northern Lights or the Inland Revenue is following our adventures … I can vouch for nothing. Certainly father and grandad did return to the lighthouse that evening, or rather to the home of the keeper which was nearby, where they said they were generously supplied with glasses of liquid which, it was suggested, might well have been distilled not far from where they were sitting! And as Mountain Dew (poteen) is apparently a rather potent drink, when they finally took their leave and attempted to return to the post office along a very ill-defined track, and on a very dark night, they ran into difficulties. In fact they got lost, with father somewhere out in the wilderness on one side of the track, and grandad deep in a bog on the other.

"Where are you Bob?"

"I've no idea."

"I think I must be in a bog."

"Oh … well, the ground's hard enough where I am, but I can't see a thing."

"Where's the road?"

"I don't know, but it can't be that far away … I mean, we only … Ah! The lighthouse!"

"What about the lighthouse?"

"I can see it."

"So can I but what good's that … we're trying to get away from it."

"Yes, but can't you see the light swings round in a circle, and it's moving in our direction."

"Ah!"

"So if we watch … and wait … and the minute it comes round …"

"We make a dash for it!"

"Here it comes … steady … GO!" They both got up off their knees and stumbled towards the spot where the light swept across the track they should have been following. Unfortunately it only took a couple of seconds to pass and after it had gone the darkness was deeper still.

"I think we're off the road again Bob."

"It's a good job we're not at the edge of the cliff."

"If it had stayed there about two minutes longer."

"We'll have to wait till it comes round again." So they waited, as the light swept the sea, touched the island coast, and then,

"It's coming Harry … get ready … steady … *Run!*" They ran, got back on the path and staggered along for a dozen yards or so.

"Keep going," gasped grandad.

"I think we're getting a bit longer this time," father called back as he zig-zagged in front of his companion.

"Keep going Bob, I'm right behind you."

"I'm sure we're getting a bit longer, it's still there."

"Keep going, keep going."

"I'm *certain* … in fact, I think it's stopped."

"Stopped?" Grandad came to an abrupt halt, turned and looked back in the direction of the lighthouse.

"It *has* stopped." The powerful beam picked out, illuminated the two figures swaying gently in the middle of the path, and didn't move.

"Do you think Bob …?"

"Yes. He can see us … from the lighthouse. He's stopped the machinery. *He's lighting the way home!*"

Well, that was father's story. And our story, or rather the end of it as far as Rathlin was concerned, began the following day when the priest, after a cheerful greeting, placed a hand on father's shoulder and said,

"Robert, you're great playactors, and you're great people, but would you get away te hell outa this before you bankrupt the island!"

To which father replied, "Have no fear. The wind is set fair. Our departure is emminent your imminence." And on Wednesday morning we were standing on Rathlin's little harbour watching our scenery and belongings being loaded back on the ferry. The sun was shining, there was no wind, and the water in the bay was like a millpond. While out in the channel, when we got there, the ocean rocked our small craft so gently that it sent grandma to sleep.

"How's your cough this morning, Jimmy?" Mrs McCreedy had left the post office in order to see us off.

"Oh, it's much better thank you, nearly gone." I settled myself at the back of the boat.

"I told you carragheen would do the trick." Mrs McCreedy had heard me coughing one night and the next morning she had gone down to the shore and collected a handful of what she called carragheen. It grew on the rocks and could only be gathered when the tide was low. She also called it Irish Moss, but I found out later it wasn't moss, it was seaweed. She boiled it and added flavour … something similar, I imagine, to what the keeper gave father and grandad at the lighthouse, because I can't remember what it did for my cough but it made *me* feel great.

"I've brought you a wee present, Jimmy." Danny, who had been hiding something behind his back, stepped forward and held out a small boat. It was carved out of wood, painted blue, and rigged like a real yacht.

"Oh, that's great Danny." I stood up and reached out as my friend got down on his knees and leaned over the jetty.

"Mind how you go Danny," his mother took hold of his jersey, "we don't want you to fall in."

"That's really great. Thank you very much." I carefully examined the gift.

"A very nice present Danny." Mother smiled at my friend and looked at his mother.

"He wanted to give Jimmy a keepsake ... something to remember him by."

"A nice thought," added grandma.

"And look," I held the little boat aloft, "it's rigged like a real yacht! I'll just try it." I leaned over the back of the ferry and carefully set the boat down on the water. "And it doesn't fall over."

"Oh, it'll not fall over," Danny reassured me, "the keel keeps her straight. And she'll sail ... you can set the sails."

"His father made it for him," explained Mrs McCreedy. "It's a real model."

"And here's a piece of string," Danny again got down on his knees. "There's a wee screw on the stern and if you tie the string to it she'll not get away from you."

"That's a good idea, I'll do it right away."

"Right then, Mr Mateer!" The boatman called out to father who was the last of the passengers to get into the ferry. He'd just tipped the two men who had helped to bring the scenery from the hall.

"Yes, that's the lot," father answered.

"And we're all aboard captain," grandad joined in.

"Start her up then." The second boatman, already in the ferry and down on his knees, switched on, cranked, and the engine started first go.

"Ah well, that's a good beginning Louie," grandad turned to grandma.

"A very good beginning Harry. Things look much more promising this time. There's no wind."

"And the water's as smooth as a baby's bottom."

"*Harry!*"

The ferry was pushed clear of the quay and the engine revved up.

"Goodbye." Mrs McCreedy, Danny and the old man in his engineer's cap waved to us.

"Goodbye." We waved back.

"And thanks for everything," mother shouted.

"Safe journey."

"Goodbye Danny."

"Goodbye."

"Come back soon."

"We will."

But we never did. Many times I've studied the map, and on at least two occasions I've actually stood on the mainland and looked across at the island, but I didn't go back, and I never saw Danny again. Years later, however, long after the company had ceased to exist and father was earning a steady income and a respectable reputation as the village postmaster, a customer came into his office one day with a message from a priest who had taken up duty in another village only a few miles away. And that priest was Father Neeson. Whether my father and he ever got together again I don't know because by then I had moved on, but certainly greetings and good wishes were exchanged via customers and parishioners from both villages. And years after that, when my father died, he was buried in a little Presbyterian churchyard that looked across the lough to the Mountains of Mourne. And when Father Neeson died – though he did so before my father – he was laid to rest in a small *Catholic* churchyard that also looked across at the Mournes ... but from the opposite side!

PROGRAMME.

THE BROADWAY PLAYERS

MR. X. DOPE.

JANE CORDER.

DAWN. LITTLE PAL.

OLD BILL.

Orphans of The Storm.

The Romance of a Prince.

POWER OF GOLD.

DESTINY.

END OF THE ROAD

BURKE AND HARE.

C. H. Bowcott & Sons, Printers, Wednesbury and London—10604

16

An Act from the New World

We headed south to Cushendall, Cushendun, Carnlough, Culleybackey, Doagh, Dunadry, Templepatrick, Brown's Bay, Hyde Park, Holywood, Bangor and Donaghadee. Then west to Lisburn, Lurgan, Portadown, Loughgall, Armagh City, Caledon and into the Clogher Valley ... where catastrophe struck. And I think I can legitimately use that phrase despite the fact that I personally recall no feelings of anxiety or distress. Though I still remember (and as the event took place a long time ago that would seem to suggest some emotion), I still carry the picture of myself standing in the middle of a large open space awaiting the arrival of a train. I had seen many trains coming and going in my time, and I had, unlike many of the people I encountered on my wanderings, also travelled in them on more than one occasion. But this train was special and this experience was unique, because after it, for me as for all the other members of the company, life would be different.

We were in County Tyrone, the Clogher Valley, which rests between hills that lie to the south of the county. And in our time, through this little valley ran a single track railway which connected three of the villages or small towns, Augher, Clogher and Fivemiletown, which were marked on father's travelling map. Exactly which of the three we were playing in on that occasion I can't remember, but as I turn my mind back to that morning I can see the entire company, apart from Eileen who must have stayed behind with the landlady's children, standing in the middle of this large empty square waiting for the train. And a rather sorry, dejected group we must have looked, with nobody talking. And as to what anyone was thinking, well I don't know, but what was uppermost in *my* mind was the idea that from my position I would be the first to catch a glimpse of the train as it entered the town. I had already discovered the track because it ran past the hall a little way outside the town, and along the roadside with nothing to separate it from pedestrians, cyclists, horses or anything else that came along. Now I was looking forward to an unobscured view of the engine with its attendant carriages as it entered the town, crossed the square, and puffed its way out into the countryside beyond.

The prospect was exciting. Although I remember being a bit fed-up with all the waiting. Indeed, as time went by and we hung about or walked up and down I began to think the train wasn't going to come at all. Then I heard it, close to, and so did grandad.

"Here she comes, Louie." He tucked his violin case under his arm (he'd taught himself to play though father wouldn't let him anywhere near the stage with the instrument), and although the train was still out of sight, picked up his old suitcase whose bulging sides were held together by a leather strap, and got ready to board.

"Stand away from the line Harry," grandma glanced in his direction.

"Oh, I'm alright Louie."

"You're not alright ... you're too near ... stand back a bit ... *Harry!*"

"Ah!" grandad growled, retreated a couple of steps then turned and squinted along the track in the direction of the oncoming train. I also moved back from the lines and away from the rest of the company, not because I felt unsafe but in order to distance myself from the proceedings. What exactly had happened, what had brought about this crisis I didn't know, no-one had explained, and anyhow I didn't want to be involved so I withdrew and concentrated, like grandad, on the space between the houses at the far end of the street. And my vigilance was soon rewarded because moments later I caught sight of the engine's smoke above the rooftops and was first to hail it, "Here it is!", as it appeared puffing and whistling at the edge of the town. I think it had only three coaches, one of those was probably the guard's van, and when it came to a stop it drew up, wheels clanging and squealing on the rails, right alongside where we stood. A couple of doors opened and about three people, including the guard with an armful of parcels, got out. We were the only passengers waiting to embark.

"Goodbye dad," mother, tears running down her cheeks (a rare occurrence offstage) went over and kissed grandad.

"Goodbye Lil, goodbye." The old man set down his suitcase and put his free arm round mother's shoulder. "And keep your chin up old girl, keep your chin up." Then he quickly removed his arm, picked up his suitcase and headed for the train. "We'll be in touch."

"Goodbye mam," mother then advanced on grandma who was also weeping.

"Goodbye my love." Grandma set her parcels on the ground, put both her arms round mother, and they kissed. "Keep in touch. Let us know where you are."

"I will, I will."

"And be a good girl ... support Bob." Grandma looked round but father had also distanced himself. "Help him all you can."

"I will, though he doesn't deserve it," mother sobbed.

"All you can," grandma insisted, "because things won't be easy ... for any of us."

"Goodbye, Jimmy." Grandad had opened one of the carriage doors, pushed his case inside, then turned and shouted in my direction.

"Goodbye grandad," I called back, and walked across to where he was standing.

"Goodbye." He shook my hand and ruffled my hair. "We'll see you again soon ... we'll be in touch ... get together and do a spot of fishing ... for tiddlers ... eh? Now go and say goodbye to your grandma." Grandma was standing with her arms outstretched so I màde my way towards her, quickly without actually running.

"Goodbye, Jimmy," she bent down and kissed me. "You'll come and see your old grandma sometime won't you?"

"Oh yes," I replied.

"And grandad will take you fishing again. Goodbye. And be a good boy while we're away. Look after your mother."

"I will."

"That's grandma's boy. And now," she turned to mother who had gathered up her parcels, "we'd better get aboard or the train will leave without us. Where's ...?" she looked across to where father was standing, and as he didn't move called out, "Goodbye Bob."

"Oh ..." father responded as though he'd only just become aware of what was going on. "Cheerio."

"And good luck."

"Come on Louie, come on." Grandad was getting impatient. "There's plenty of room ... a whole carriage to ourselves. In you get." Grandma was helped into the train and as grandad followed her the guard, who had delivered his parcels to a nearby shop, returned, slammed an open door, blew a whistle, waved his flag and climbed up into the guard's van.

"Safe journey." Mother looked up at the open window.

"Ah we'll be alright Lil, we'll be alright." Grandad squeezed his head alongside grandma's.

"And let me know when you arrive mam."

"Soon as we get to Jacksdale." (Where grandma's sister Bella lived.)

"I'll make sure your basket is sent off tomorrow."

"Good girl."

"Goodbye."

"Goodbye and good ... Oooh!" The engine spat out jets of steam, clouds of black smoke, and with buffers and couplings clanking began to move. My grandparents waved from behind the window. Mother and I waved back and watched as the train slowly edged across the square and headed out into the open country leaving the town quiet and the square deserted, apart from father, mother and me, each holding their own ground as though we didn't belong to each other. Which I suppose at that particular moment was the case.

The company had collapsed. Or it would be more accurate to say, ceased to exist. An irreplaceable half had gone never to return. No other actors with my grandparents' talents would be found to work with father (indeed no actors of any sort would have been able to exist on the wages he had to offer). There had been a terrible row I learnt afterwards; father had been impossible, grandad had threatened physical violence, and grandma, the peacemaker had reached the end of her patience. What mother's contribution had been wasn't related, but as she was every bit as short-sighted as grandad and never missed an opportunity of getting back at father, I can't imagine it was very constructive. Some trivial incident I suppose had sparked off the row, and for once grandma had stood her ground, delivered home truths, and said it would be better if she and grandad left. To which father replied "Good idea and the sooner the better". Of course, business had been bad for a very long time, and there was always friction in the family circle, so grandma must have known this would happen one day and had made plans. This was obvious the morning after the row when she sent a wire to her sister Bella (who had also been on the stage, had buried her third husband, and was now running a small café not far from the city of Nottingham) which brought an immediate reply and the offer of a home and a job in the café until grandma found another company … in England. So my grandparents left.

The Broadway Players were no more. We were destitute, father, mother, Eileen and me, with no company, no money and nowhere to go. What could we do? Or more to the point, what could *father* do? He wasn't a countryman or a farmer, and even if he got a job in a shop – which was highly unlikely despite the fact that he'd been a furniture salesman in his youth – how long would it be before he told the owner how to run things and got the sack? We were well and truly stranded, and whether I actually considered the depth of the problem at the time I don't know. I'm sure no-one discussed the matter with me, apart from mother, and she would have dramatised and had us all begging and starving in the street. But one thing was clear, one thing I am certain I did believe, and that was that for us as actors, and a company, this was the final curtain. But I was wrong.

*

Ballinamallard is only a few miles away from the Clogher Valley, and very close to the Lakes. How we got there or why we went there I have no idea. We had no company, we had stopped being Strolling Players and were about to become travelling tinkers … less, because at least tinkers had tents and could fix kettles and sell clothes pegs. We had nothing, and the prospect must have been frightening; no work, no money, and no help from friends, relatives or The State. Yet I don't remember any of us crying or bemoaning our fate. Indeed I can still see father, after he had stowed the scenery somewhere and had a drink with the lorryman, walking down the main street of that town with his hat on the back of his head and his pipe in the air, perfectly contented. And as for me! Well, the sun was shining, there were banks along a wide clear fast-running river to explore, and I remember Ballinamallard as being the place from where we started out on the hottest, sunniest, happiest summer in all my travelling days.

Of course, father must have had ideas; he was a great man for ideas, inventions, or anything like that. And he had a wife and two small children to provide for, so he must have been thinking and planning ahead. Though I don't recollect him even hinting at what he intended to do. It came as a great surprise, one of several very pleasant surprises that I associate with that town. The first, a trivial affair, occurred on the day of our arrival. Eileen and I had been given a penny apiece to spend on sweets. Which in itself was not just a pleasant but a very unusual occurrence, because there was no such thing as pocket money for us in those days, and although sometimes we coaxed a ha'penny out of father, and of course grandma was generous whenever she could afford it, as a rule we depended on the generosity of strangers ... someone in the digs or the audience. Some benevolent soul therefore had given us a penny each as a leaving present, and I remember Eileen and I standing out in the street, the sun pouring down all round us, discussing how we were going to dispose of the bounty that had come our way. Mind you, it couldn't have been a very long or serious discussion because if I got a penny my policy was to save half and spend half, whereas if anything in the shape of money came Eileen's way she was off to the sweet shop as fast as her legs would carry her. This time, however, I had decided to be indulgent, so we had located the local emporium and approached with the intention of blowing the lot.

"But I can't see any sweets in the window," Eileen, her face pressed against the glass, anxiously remarked. "It doesn't look like a sweet shop to me."

"Well they do sell sweets," I reassured her, though I quite understood her having doubts because what stood in front of us was a very large redbrick building which may have been a dairy, or maybe a Co-Operative Store. There was very little on display in the window, and I suppose they sold other things, groceries and the like, but they also sold sweets because through the glass in the door I could see a line of jars standing at the far end of the counter.

"Where are the sweets?" Eileen persisted.

"Inside, inside. Come on." I held open the door and my little sister cautiously advanced, looked round, then made a beeline for the end of the counter. Before she could get to the jars however, a large man with a red face and wearing a white coat came in from a back room and said in a very loud voice,

"Good afternoon young lady."

"Good afternoon." Eileen looked up then back at the jars of sweets.

"And what can I do for you?"

"I'd like some sweets please." She reached up and placed her penny on the counter.

"Well now we've got plenty of sweets, any amount." He leaned over and looked down at the small figure. "What sort of sweets would you like?"

Eileen quickly ran her eyes along the line of jars, hesitated, then very seriously and deliberately answered his question.

"Well, I'd like a pennyworth of what you get a lot of."

The man laughed, he straightened up, opened his mouth wide and he laughed. I frowned at Eileen's grammar and open display of greed.

"And I would like a pennyworth of those please." I pointed to the jar of my choice.

"Right you are sir." The man, still chuckling, lifted the jar I had indicated and set it on a shelf behind him. Then he picked up another jar and held it up so Eileen could see. "How about a pennyworth of these? You get a lot of these."

"Yes please," Eileen agreed.

"Right you are then." He set the second jar alongside the first, took two squares of white paper, twisted them into cornets, or pokes as we called them, filled them with sweets, tucked in the tops and handed them over the counter. "There you are."

"Thank you." Eileen carefully took hold of her purchase.

"And yours young man."

"Thank you very much." Then as I followed Eileen towards the door I turned and politely added, "Good afternoon."

"Good afternoon. Come back again."

"We will." I held open the door, and as Eileen passed through opening her poke in what I considered undue haste, I hissed at her, "Not now. Wait!" She closed the top again, hurried outside and waited for me by the window.

"Alright." I proceeded to open my own poke but before I caught a glimpse of the sweets themselves Eileen cried out.

"My penny!"

"You gave it to the man for your sweets!" I looked at her in astonishment.

"Yes but it's inside my poke!" I looked, opened by own packet, and there on the top of the sweets was a penny.

"So is mine. It must be a mistake. We must go back ... quick."

I re-entered the shop, Eileen reluctantly following on behind. The man was still there, standing by the window.

"That was a quick turn round," he said, coming up to the counter.

"Well you see," I held out my poke so he could look into it, "my penny's inside." He leaned over, looked, then expressed surprise.

"So it is." Eileen held hers up for inspection. "Yours too? Well, I wonder how that happened."

"I don't know," Eileen replied mournfully. She obviously expected both the sweets and her penny to be taken from her.

"They must have fallen in." I picked out and offered my coin but the shopkeeper held up his hands.

"Oh no, if they're in your sweets then they're your pennies." Eileen and I looked at each other. "They're yours." Eileen's face lit up.

"Well that's very nice." I lowered my offering.

"Isn't it now!" The man winked, and immediately I understood the situation. It was a present.

"Very nice indeed. Thank you very much."

"Not at all. It's your lucky day."

"Thank the gentleman Eileen." My little sister gave one of her big smiles and did as instructed, then turned and made for the door before anybody changed their mind.

"See you again Eileen!" the shopkeeper called after her.

"Goodbye." I opened the door, we went out into the street with our sweets and our pennies intact, and that man will never know – well of course he'd be dead and buried by now – would *never* have known the happiness his generosity brought to two children.

Slowly we wandered back sucking our sweets, discussing our good fortune, and about to encounter our second surprise of the day.

I don't remember exactly where our digs were on that occasion, but they seemed to be at the edge of the town because I recall the house was on its own and there was a wooden gate leading into the front garden. We were just about to enter that gate when we noticed a man, loaded down with luggage, coming along the street in our direction. We paused, the man caught sight of us and smiled, or rather grinned, as though he knew who we were. Eileen looked at me and I shrugged because I didn't instantly recognise who it was, although there was something familiar about him. He wasn't anybody from the town because he wore a felt hat, like father's only in better condition, carried a suitcase, a cardboard box, and a very large bag like a sailor's kitbag slung over his shoulder. We stood our ground and the more I looked the more I felt sure I knew who it was. In fact, an idea was just beginning to take shape in my mind when, within a few yards of us, the man set down his case and his bag but held onto the cardboard box, pushed his hat to the back of his head and greeted us with a hearty, "Hello Jimmy … and Eileen."

"*It's Uncle Joe!*" Suddenly I knew him, I remembered, although it must have been nearly four years since I stood on the quay in Belfast and watched the tender carry him and his friend out to the big ship that was to take them to Canada.

"That's right. You've remembered." He advanced and took hold of my hand. "And how are you, Jimmy?"

"Very well thank you." I took a good look at my uncle whose travels and adventures had been the subject of conversation, quite recently it occurred to me. He had a definite look of my father, was about the same height and brushed his hair back in the same fashion. Though father had finer features and was better-looking, despite being ten years his brother's senior. Of course, I thought Uncle Joe also quite old at the time, but he could only have been in his mid-twenties, the youngest member of the family. He had been born about five years after everybody else, maybe to compensate his mother for the loss of her first child, a girl, who had died when she was sixteen. My grandmother, that is my father's mother, also died early in her late forties, so Joe had been brought up by the girls, mostly

Aunt Agnes. We were all together in Belfast, quite by chance, when Uncle Joe was setting out for Canada. We stayed in the family home for a little while and I remember my uncle told stories and played games. So I was genuinely pleased to see him. And he seemed very pleased to see us.

"And this is our Eileen." Uncle Joe squatted down in front of my sister. "You were only a baby when I left the country. I have a picture of you in my case ... I'll show it to you later on ... I'm holding you up in my arms and Jimmy is standing by my side. Oh, but you've grown since then. You're a real big girl now."

"I'm four," Eileen announced with satisfaction, then turned her attention to the cardboard box.

"Four!" Uncle Joe straightened up. "So Jimmy must be about ..."

"I'll be nine in February."

"And you've put on about three feet."

"I expect I have." As I spoke I caught a glimpse of Eileen whose eyes were boring a hole in the mysterious box, and knew she was going to ask a direct question. I'd have to stop her. But she was already closing in.

"Have you come to see us Uncle Joe?" she enquired.

"All the way from Canada."

"It's a very long way Eileen." I tried to distract her.

"Nearly three thousand miles."

"Did you see any Mounties when you were in Canada?" Father, in one of his storytelling moods had told me about the redcoats and how they always got their man.

"Oh, scores of times, on foot and on horseback. Yes I've seen the redcoats, in fact I nearly got arrested by one of them once when I was ... what they call out there ... riding a freight train. You jump on the train when it's moving and hitch a ride without buying a ticket."

"You rode on a train without buying a ticket!" The full impact of Uncle Joe and his visit drove the cardboard box right out of my mind.

"On the roof ... went hundreds of miles like that ... saw all sorts of things ... grizzly bears."

"Grizzly bears!"

"And rattlesnakes."

"*Rattlesnakes!*" I was enthralled. Eileen however wasn't a bit interested in Canada.

"What's in the box, Uncle Joe?" She raised her hand and pointed.

"Food," he replied curtly and went on talking to me. "Yes sometimes you only knew the rattlers were there when they lifted a tail out of the grass and started to rattle."

"Food?" Eileen balefully regarded the cardboard box.

"Food," Uncle Joe repeated without attempting to do anything about my sister's obvious disappointment.

"And would rattlesnakes kill you?"

"Oh, their bites are poisonous."

"Haven't you come to visit us then?" A note of righteous indignation had crept into Eileen's voice. People who visited always brought presents.

"No Eileen," Uncle Joe looked very serious, "I haven't come to visit you." Then he squatted down in front of her again and added, "I've come to *stay* with you."

"To *stay* with us?" I was shocked.

"Travel with you … work with your dad."

"Doing *what*?" It must have sounded a very rude question indeed but I was totally unprepared for this revelation.

"Acting." Uncle Joe wasn't in the least offended. "Anything that's needed."

"But I didn't know …" I began, then gave up, not knowing what to say next. I mean never mind the fact that we didn't have a company any more, Uncle Joe wasn't an actor, he'd never been on the stage, he knew nothing at all about the business as far as I was aware. He was interested in games, swimming, sport … so what did he mean, he was coming to work with father? *And did father know? Had he been told?* Someone must have said something otherwise how did Uncle Joe know where we were? Maybe it was mother … she wrote all the letters in the family. Perhaps she'd written and told Uncle Joe my grandparents had left and he'd just come along. And if that was the case then there was going to be trouble. While all this was going through my mind Eileen, whose world was a lot less complicated than mine, continued her quest.

"Are you going to live with us then Uncle Joe?" she piped up.

"No Eileen," again our visitor looked grave, "I'm not going to live with you." (Well at least the landlady wouldn't get a shock.) "I'm going to live in my tent." He indicated the kitbag.

"Is that a *tent*?" Again he had all my attention.

"It is."

"And are you going to sleep in it?"

"I am. In Canada I slept in a tent all through the summer. And now the weather's warming up …"

"Is it a big tent?" I wouldn't mind sleeping in a tent myself.

"No, not really."

"Will you sleep on the ground?"

"On a groundsheet, in a sleeping bag. Though in this country if the weather turns wet I may need to get a camp bed."

"I've never slept in a tent … never even *been* in a tent."

"Well, if the pair of you behave maybe one day I'll invite you and Eileen into my tent for a picnic."

"A picnic!" Eileen furrowed her brow and seriously considered this prospect.

"And talking about picnics," Uncle Joe put his hand in his jacket pocket and pulled out a brown paper bag, "I've got something here … if it's not melted." He opened the bag and took out two of the largest chocolate bars I had ever seen outside a shop window. "One for you Eileen …"

"Oh, thank you Uncle Joe." Eileen took a firm grip of the bar with her free hand.

"And one for you."

"Thank you very much indeed. This *is* our lucky day. We just bought sweets in a shop back there …"

"And the man put our pennies in our pokes and we went back in the shop and … Here's Daddy!" Eileen spotted him first, walking back from the town followed by mother who was a few yards behind carrying the shopping. "Daddy! Daddy!" She ran to meet him "Uncle Joe's here and he gave us chocolate and the man in the shop put our pennies back in our pokes and we're going to have a picnic."

"Good heavens!" Father gathered my little sister up in his arms. "Aren't you the lucky girl! Chocolate!" He kissed her. "Sweets!" He kissed her again. "And Uncle Joe's come to see you all the way from Canada."

"Hello Bob." My uncle went up to father and the two men shook hands.

"No trouble in finding us, Joe?"

"No, I just followed the yellow bills in the shop windows."

"Well … glad to see you. You look fit."

"Oh, there's nothing like wandering across the prairie to give you a tan. Hello Lily."

"Hello Joe." Mother also shook hands. She didn't kiss Uncle Joe. When she had first met father's family she had kissed everybody and father had remarked, out loud, that the English were great kissers. So she never did it again. "You've brought the good weather."

"All the way from Belfast. The sun's shining there too. It's going to be a long hot summer."

"But not too long," mother laughed, "or too hot, it's bad for business."

"Well, maybe an odd shower now and again."

"So have you had anything to eat, Joe?" Father set Eileen down on the ground but held on to her hand.

"I had a sandwich on the train."

"A sandwich! Oh, the man needs something more substantial than a sandwich."

"We all need something more substantial than a sandwich," mother agreed.

"So let's get him into the digs."

"I've brought my rations with me Lily." Uncle Joe held out, and mother took charge of, the cardboard box.

"My … it's heavy!"

"Everything Agnes could think of is in there."

"I'll take this." Father lifted the suitcase and shepherded Eileen in through the wooden gate. "In you go."

I brought up the rear volunteering, "Uncle Joe's brought his tent. He's going to live in it."

"Good," father remarked without turning his head. "If it's big enough maybe we can *all* live in it." Everybody laughed. Everybody was happy. And instead of dinner, which never interested me very much unless there were chips and sausages, we had a high tea. What mother supplied as the main course that evening I don't remember, probably corned beef, but along with it there was potato bread, scones, buns, tarts and a huge cake, all freshly baked by Aunt Agnes and produced with a flourish from the cardboard box.

"This is better than Christmas," I said, as the tea and the talk flowed freely. We were all great tea drinkers and talkers.

"Oh *yes*." Eileen, her face and hands smeared with jam, heartily agreed.

"They had a very poor Christmas last year," mother removed some of the jam with her apron. "The old lady we were lodging with didn't have any decorations or a Christmas tree … and of course we couldn't afford one. And the chicken my mam bought was about the size of a pigeon … for six of us! It was a pretty lean year."

"Which is why …" father grabbed everyone's attention by pointing in my direction, "he's making up for it now."

"There's no need to eat everything on the table, Jim," mother remonstrated.

"But I'm only having one of each," I protested. "And I *asked*."

"Oh yes," mother laughed, "he always *asks*. Like the time we were in Scotland. Remember Bob?"

"Inverary, the Duke of Argyll's place."

"And the Duke came in to see the show."

"You had a duke in to see the show Lily!" Uncle Joe stopped eating.

"Oh yes," father added, "and he brought all his fine London friends with their jewels and posh accents."

"And after the show," mother continued, "on our last night His Grace announced that his steward, or laird, or whatever they call such people, had prepared a supper and we were all invited to attend. The Duke himself wasn't going to be there, of course."

"No, he went off to pheasant, venison and bottles of red wine with the toffs."

"And we were ushered into this great vault of a room, in the middle of which was an enormous table coming down with food. And we were all hungry."

"Was I there?" Eileen entered the conversation.

"No … and don't talk with your mouth full. You were a baby and stayed with the landlady. But our Jim was there – he was probably about the age Eileen is now – and before we sat down I warned him: be polite and always say 'yes please' and 'no thank you'." Father took up the story.

"So we all tucked in and talked and it was some time before I cast a glance in this young fellow's direction, and when I did … his cheeks were blown out like this … his face had gone purple … and his plate was so full he could hardly see over the top."

"He said 'yes please' alright, but he never *once* said 'no thank you'!"

Everybody laughed and father lit his pipe. Mother offered Uncle Joe a Park Drive but he didn't smoke, took one herself, and we all settled down to listen to Uncle Joe's adventures on the other side of the world.

"So where did you go in Canada?"

"From the east to the west."

"And what did you do?" Mother leaned both elbows on the table.

"Oh, everything … from washing bottles in the backyard of a pub to dishing out dollars across the counter of a bank."

"You got a job in a bank, Joe?" Father was impressed.

"For a while. Things got so difficult out there I couldn't even get casual work on the land, there were thousands going on relief. I had clerical experience, was good at maths, and anyhow the harvest was finished, so I got a temporary job in this bank. And they would have kept me on but by then I was aching to get back to the old country. But most of the time I worked on the land."

"A real farmer's boy," mother said, then followed up with, "But tell me, Joe, on your travels did you ever get anywhere near your sister Mary?"

Now this was just typical of mother. There we were waiting to hear about bears, snakes and freight trains, and she starts off about relatives. And in this case one I had never met, though I had heard about her and knew exactly why mother raised the subject. In father's family they didn't talk a lot about Aunty Mary. Certainly nobody had ever explained, or even hinted at why a young woman not long out of her teens, had been sent off (on her own as far as I could gather) to the other side of the world. Mother knew of course.

"Yes, I saw Mary. I stayed with her on my way back from Vancouver."

"You got as far as Vancouver!" Father had taken his pipe apart and was prodding the stem to unblock it. "That's on the west, isn't it?"

"Yes. I started off at Toronto in the east, travelled the lakes, the wheatlands, the prairies, over the Rocky Mountains and then on to Vancouver. I stayed there for a while, then made my way back east and ended up in Winnipeg."

"That's where Mary's living now, isn't it?" Mother got the subject back in focus.

"That's right, she's in Winnipeg. I stayed with her for a while and we went on trips and sightseeing together, then I travelled up to Saskatoon and the harvest."

"And is she alright?" Father, though he rarely mentioned the subject either, was naturally concerned about his younger sister.

"Oh yes, she's keeping pretty well. She was ill for a while but she seems to have got over that. She's got a regular job now, in a hospital. Not much of a job … cleaning … but it's steady and work is just as hard to find out there as it is here. She seems happy enough."

"And didn't she get married?" Mother knew perfectly well that Aunty Mary got married.

"Oh yes, just after I left Canada. Didn't you know that?"

"Well, I think we did hear something about it from Agnes. Did she marry a Canadian?"

"No, she married a man from Armagh ... nice chap ... I met him and we all went round together. I thought she might end up getting hitched. Jack's a decent sort."

"Good." Father put his pipe together again and sat back in his chair, indicating that that was the end of the topic. But mother persisted.

"So she has no desire to return to the old country and her ... old friends?"

"And why should she do that?" Father glared across the table and the tone of his voice made it quite clear that he knew what mother was getting at and she had better desist.

"Oh, I just wondered," mother remarked innocently, backing off, "I just wondered." And in case you are also wondering I will tell you, very briefly, the story of Aunty Mary.

There had been a scandal in the family. Nobody talked about it but mother got a whiff and once when we were residing in the family home in Belfast, en route for somewhere else, she got to the bottom of the mystery. By then of course Mary had gone to Canada and the old man, my father's father, had had a stroke and was very ill. He was also, he told mother, very lonely because he was living in a house full of women (in fact, only Agnes and Elizabeth were there by that time) who didn't like him. The reasons he gave for this were that he smoked a pipe and they couldn't stand the smell of the smoke; and before his stroke, on his way home from work on Friday nights he used to pop in and have a glass of stout and they couldn't stand the smell of that either. In fact, the minute he came in the front door on a Friday night Agnes set his dinner on the table and she and Elizabeth went off to another part of the house. No-one cared for him, he said, and he had no-one to talk to. So when mother arrived and talked and made him laugh they became friends. And when, one day before we moved on, she actually smuggled a bottle of beer up to his bedroom she earned the undying gratitude of the sick, lonely old man. Though had this indiscretion come to light, had it been known that not only was alcohol brought into, but was actually *consumed* in the house! Well, I don't know what would have happened. And the thing was, mother said she didn't think my grandfather ever got drunk. He was a very respectable man, a Mason, and Treasurer of his branch. Also, because of his craft (he was a cabinet maker, though as he worked on ships in The Yard that may not have been the term they used) he was a senior member of the Ancient Order of Foresters. But he drank, and that the smell of beer offended little Agnes who loved pretty, dainty, genteel customs and things I could understand ... but Elizabeth!

Elizabeth too loved gentility, but she was a truly independent soul, a capable secretary and an excellent sportswoman. She played tennis and badminton, and although she never married she preferred the company of men and cheerfully competed with them in darts and card games (but no gambling) as well as in sport. She was also, I thought, a very courageous woman because she refused to leave Belfast when the bombing started (I mean German bombs); she joined the Fire Service and walked the blacked-out streets alone at night, despite being followed on occasions by strange men; and even in her eighties when left alone and burgled on two occasions, she refused to leave the house, saying she would not allow such things to deprive her of sleeping in her own bed. But *drink!* Well! If there was a man on the bus even smelling of alcohol she got as far away from him as she could. If there was a man, obviously the worse for liquor, weaving about the pavement in front of her she crossed to the other side of the road. What exactly she was afraid of – that he might speak to her … brush against her … touch her – I don't know. But she was afraid. And mother said this fear had been generated by my grandmother (though mother never met her) who was deeply religious and like most respectable women of her day couldn't tolerate even the idea of alcohol. The girls inherited this fear; to such an extent that the first-born actually received a certificate, First Class, from the Hibernian Band of Hope Union for writing an essay entitled "Alcohol and the Circulation of the Blood" … and she was only twelve at the time! This, then, was why the old man lay in isolation in the back room with nobody to talk to until mother arrived. And got the story about Aunty Mary.

My grandmother, that is my father's mother, had been dead for some time. Father had left home and gone on the stage: out of consideration for his mother he waited till after her death before becoming a professional actor (she wanted him to be a clergyman). Three of the girls were out at work, while the fourth, Aunt Agnes, had been left to look after the home and Uncle Joe, who was still at school. Aunty Mary must have been in her early twenties when she informed her sisters she was going to have an illegitimate child. The girls were horrified. Their father, with no wife and no mature or experienced woman in the house to advise him, was stunned. While *my* father (who must have been working near home), when *he* heard the news, rushed up to the attic, loaded his shot-gun and demanded the name of the scoundrel who had done this terrible thing. Fortunately, the name wasn't given. But the family were disgraced; they would never be able to face their neighbours … talk to their friends … or even go to church on Sunday mornings. It was infinitely worse than having a death in the family.

Now who came up with the solution, I don't know (I doubt if it was one of the girls), but there was a close friend, indeed she may have been related to my grandmother though I never found proof, and I suspect she advised the family in this crisis. This lady, who I remember from my boyhood days as a kindly, cheerful (eyes twinkling behind gold-rimmed spectacles) old lady in black, never married and devoted her whole life to stray girls and fallen women. She would have known exactly what had to be done in such circumstances. So Mary was kept out of sight (probably sent into the country to live with cousins) until the baby was born and given over to foster parents, then she was shipped overseas. And although I believe she travelled alone I cannot believe, even considering the terrible disgrace that faced the family, they sent her out into the unknown. She must have gone to one of the many relatives whose forebears had emigrated to the New World in the previous century. Certainly I found several ancient but very stylish portraits of whole families (dressed in their Sunday-best) which had been taken by travelling photographers (who couldn't spell), and these were definitely members of the clan who had left the old country to farm in Canada and the Mid-West. I also found a much more recent portrait of my Aunty Mary taken before her downfall, and a very attractive young woman she was, as were all the girls in the family. Only Mary looked different from the others, more relaxed and more sensuous. So that is the story as I got it. And if mother expected to add to what she already knew she was out of luck because Uncle Joe soon went on to his adventures which so engrossed me that I ceased to worry, indeed ceased even to think about what he was doing in our midst.

"The summers were hot, Bob, and during the harvest we either slept in the barns or out in the open. And when we were out in the open we would sometimes take turns to sit up at night and shoot at prairie dogs – squirrel-like creatures that popped out of the ground and barked at you – because the farmers said they ate the corn."

"And you rode on freight trains," I prompted. I was determined to follow this subject to the end of the line.

"Oh yes, and there was an art in that, one I learnt from the old hands. You see, you had to pick the right spot, usually near the water tank. You had to hide. And you had to hit the train at exactly the right moment. Too soon and they'd stop the train and turf you off. Too late and with the speed of the train you could get thrown off before you got on the roof and down into the recess. Once in there you were safe and could enjoy the free ride and the sunshine. Oh, and there was lots of sunshine ... the summers were great. Though the Depression was hitting the farmers so hard they couldn't take on all the casual hands at my last harvest. I only got a job because the farmer was German and I'd studied the language at nights in the tech. It was hard work but I enjoyed it. And sleeping out in the open ... under the stars ...!"

"But weren't you afraid of wild animals?" asked mother.

"Grizzly bears!" I added.

"Oh no, though once when we were camping not far from the woods I got a nasty scare. I woke up in the small hours, it was still dark, and heard this strange snuffling noise. I turned my head in the direction of the noise and there, not ten feet away from me was a grizzly, a big one with his nose right in my pack."

"Good heavens!" mother appeared suitably alarmed. "So what did you do? Get up and run?"

"Not on your life. A grizzly can run nearly as fast as a horse. I just shut my eyes, lay very still and thought about the Belmont Road."

"And he went away?" Father raised his eyebrows.

"Having eaten the last of my grub. But apart from that I was never in any real danger, though of course in certain areas you had to watch out you didn't lie down on a rattler."

"What a thought!"

"No, it was good. The open air suited me fine. And at night after work we would all sit round the camp fire telling stories and singing songs."

"What sort of songs?" father asked, and immediately I switched my attention away from Uncle Joe.

"Oh, songs about the prairies, riding freight trains and generally bumming around."

"Do you remember any of the songs?"

"Oh yes. There were a couple we used to sing all the time. One was about a lonely tramp waiting to hitch a lift back to his old homestead. Another was about a hobo heading west in search of the mythical Big Rock Candy Mountain … they were all about bums and hobos."

"Sounds good." Father looked meaningfully across the table at mother.

"Sounds *very* good."

"And new." Something was stirring in father's mind. Uncle Joe realised it too.

"Do you think you could make use of the songs then, Bob?"

"Oh yes."

"Well, I'm not much of a singer, and though I'm willing to do anything you want, I've had no experience at all on the stage."

"Oh, that's no problem," father reassured him. "We'll tell you what to do."

"I mean the only time I ever did anything like that was when I was in the Boys' Brigade and three of us got up and did that Gilbert & Sullivan number … you know the one." He sang: "We run them in, we run them in, we run them in, we run them in, to show them we're the bold gendarmes."

"Well at least he can sing in tune."

"Yes, and if we used one of his songs and some jokes … a double act (father looked in my direction) with Wee Jim here."

"Me!" I sat bolt upright in my chair.

"Yes, you and your Uncle Joe. You could sing a song together and we'll put in some patter and some jokes about tramps and hobos. *That's* it!" Father painted a picture in the air. "Straight from the wheatlands, the lonely prairies and the Rocky Mountains … *The Hobos*."

"Go down well," mother agreed. "Can you play an instrument, Joe … a banjo or anything like that?"

"No, the only thing I can play is the mouth-organ."

"Have you got it with you?"

"As a matter of fact I have."

"There you are then," father concluded. And everything became clear as day. Uncle Joe was to become part of the show. But what show? That question father answered as he continued, "Write out the words, Joe, or better still, you and Jim get together and practise … Jim'll soon pick it up. I'll think of some jokes."

"Well I know a few jokes myself," Uncle Joe offered, "about bums and hobos."

"Let's have a look at them."

"And I think I'm up to singing a song, telling a few jokes and … the farmhands never threw anything at me when I played the harmonica! But what about acting?"

"Oh, don't trouble yourself about acting. I've drawn up a list of plays we can put on … Lily and me can take the main parts and we can use our Jim. You can have small parts to begin with."

"I'll still need a bit of coaching and rehearsing."

"Don't worry, don't worry, you'll soon get the hang of it. Look at Agnes! We put *her* on the stage once."

"Yes," Uncle Joe put on a grim, knowing expression. "She *told* me about that." We all laughed. Agnes and her role in *Bluebeard* was one of father's favourite stories.

So everything was arranged. And I suppose during the meal, the talk and all the good-humour I already sensed that something was in the air; that Life, and The Show would go on. Father had it all planned. He would introduce new songs, stories and gags as part of the Variety. He had already drawn up a new repertoire, a list of plays that required only two leading actors, and where the plot demanded it he would write in supporting roles for me and Uncle Joe (as my uncle got more experienced he would get bigger parts). We were in business again. New posters were printed, a new cast (of three and three-quarters as Eileen was to get one-line, walk-on parts) went into rehearsal. And I don't know how soon, but probably only days after, a New Company took to the road.

1925. Bob Mateer and Lily Wynn starting a partnership that was to last for over sixty years

1931. Wee Jim waiting for the ship with Grandad's name on it to come in

Uncle Joe says farewell to Eileen, Jim and Ireland before heading for the New World in the Depressing Twenties

17

The French Farthing Legion

BOB MATEER'S
POPULAR PLAYERS
will visit Irvinestown on Monday, April 23rd for six nights

Monday ... SWEENEY TODD
– with father as the barber, mother as Mrs Lovatt, me as Tobias, and Uncle Joe doubling as the sailor who gets "polished off" and a policeman.

Tuesday ... MARIA MARTEN AND THE RED BARN
– mother as Maria, father as her murderous lover, and Uncle Joe as a policeman again.

Wednesday ... THE BELLS
– mostly father.

Thursday ... FRANKENSTEIN
– Uncle Joe wearing a put-together face stalks across the stage, comes up behind me and Eileen (gasps and at least one cry of "Look behind you!" from the audience) and hurls the pair of us into the river. Father played the mad scientist.

Friday ... AMATEUR NIGHT
– local talent: songs, dances, comedians (with terrible jokes) and prizes all round. The night rounded off with a short play *The Monkey's Paw* (original story by W.W. Jacobs)
– father and mother played the old couple who have an only son. Uncle Joe doubled again,

first as the old salt who gives them the paw which has the power to grant three wishes, then as the mangled body of their son hammering on the door demanding admittance. You see, the father wishes for money and this comes as compensation for the death of their son killed at work. The grieving old man then wishes to see his son again, and as the hammering begins the old lady, realising what her son will look like, wishes that her boy be left in peace.

Saturday Afternoon ... CHILDREN'S MATINEE

– with free gifts and a pantomime version of *Tarzan of the Apes.* Uncle Joe played Tarzan, mother played Jane and father, I presume, was the villain of the piece.

And that reminds me of an event that happened long before Uncle Joe got the role when I was very young indeed. Again it was *Tarzan* and I was dressed up as a cowboy (what a cowboy would have been doing in darkest Africa I can't imagine). I was told to walk on, Tarzan would leap down from the trees, menace me, I would fire two shots from my toy gun and he would run away. I walked on. And immediately the kids in the hall caught sight of me they began to yell, hurl abuse and small missiles in my direction. My presence seemed to inflame them. Or maybe in their ignorance they thought my function was to stand there and be abused. I tried hard at first to ignore the rolled-up papers and assorted toffees that fell round me, but when coins (halfpennies) began to rain down on the stage all restraint dissolved and I bent down ... but collected no more than two before I was hissed, yanked off and reprimanded for unprofessional behaviour.

Uncle Joe was a great success as Tarzan. The kids screamed their heads off and were thrilled to bits when they were handed gifts by the great ape as they left the hall after the show. The gifts, fake watches, brooches and other trivia, father bought by the crate. The cost must have been infinitesimal. Though I still treasure a small buddha made out of some hard, pre-plastic material that looked like soap.

Saturday Night ... RASPUTIN

– mostly father who, having gone out to the back for a pee before the premier performance of the play (with our new company) emerged from the darkness, long black beard, flowing robes, grotesque make-up, and confronted three elderly ladies who had hysterics.

DON'T MISS THE SHOW
DOORS OPEN 7.30 COMMENCE 8pm
CHILDREN'S MATINEE at 2.30 SATURDAY
VARIETY AND A FARCE EVERY NIGHT. ADMISSION 6d, Children 3d
(The Depression was deepening)

*

The plays father now intended to present not only required fewer actors but were shorter. To make up for this he extended our Variety, adding new items.

"And now ladies and gentlemen to open the show tonight we have two characters who know all about hard times, going hungry and sleeping rough. Not in this country mind you, not even across the water in England, but away at the other side of the world on the prairies and the backwoods of Canada. Ladies and gentlemen let me introduce Jim and Joe ... *The Hobos*."

We trudged on dressed as tramps, carrying the traditional stick and bundle over our shoulders, and started off with a little patter.

Joe: I'm hungry, Jim.
Jim: So am I, Joe.
Joe: And I was hungry yesterday.
Jim: Me too.
Joe: You know I was so hungry yesterday I went up to this big house, knocked on the door and when the lady of the house herself came out I said to her, sad and soulful like, Lady could you give a poor bum a handout? I'm starving. I haven't eaten for a week. I'm so hungry I could get down on my knees and eat the grass growing round your front door. "Oh, don't do that my poor man," she said – and I thought, I've struck lucky, a square meal at least – "don't do that. You come round to the back door, the grass is much longer there."
Jim: No heart.
Joe: No soul.
Jim: So what are we going to do, Joe?
Joe: Sit here and wait for a train. There's nothing doing round this place ... they're too well off.
Jim: And when will the train come?
Joe: Oh, there won't be a freight till after midnight.
Jim: It's a long wait.
Joe: Yes and it's starting to rain. Oh, a hobo's life is hard, Jim. People think, you're out in the fresh air ... you've no work ... no worries ... *you're free*.
Jim: You're also hungry.
Joe: And all you can hope for is a train so you can move on. You've got to move on ... like all the other bums along the track. And in the meantime you've got to wait ... and wait ...

We go into our song.

"All around the watertank, waiting for a train
I'm a thousand miles away from home just sleeping in the rain.
I went up to the brakie [brakesman] to give him a line of talk
He says if you've got money then I'll see that you don't walk.
I haven't got a nickel, not a penny can I show.
Get out, get out you railroad bum, he slammed the boxcar [guard's wagon] door.

He put me off in Texas, a state I dearly love
With the wide open space all round me
And the moon and the stars up above.
When your pocketbook is empty, and your heart is full of pain,
You're a thousand miles away from home just sleeping in the rain."

*

Another less doleful number (a copy of which in Uncle Joe's own hand I still possess) we called *The Hobo's Dream*. It was also a duet.

"One evening as the sun went down
And the camp fires they were burning,
A hobo came along the track
And he said boys I'm not turning.
For I'm heading for the land that's far away
Beside the crystal fountain.
So come with me and you shall see
The Big Rock Candy Mountains.

In the Big Rock Candy Mountains
Where you never change your socks
And the little streams of alcohol come a' trickling down the rocks,
There are no short-handled shovels,
No axes, saws or picks,
For they hanged the Turk that invented work
In the Big Rock Candy Mountains."

*

Uncle Joe and I did a few other acts together, and to give you some idea of these and other items of a cultural nature that were introduced, I've listed the following:

Monologues — Though father continued to do his regular monologues, he passed one of them over to me. Dressed as an old soldier I went on and recited that old favourite:

"There's a one-eyed yellow idol to the north of Katmandu
There's a little marble cross beneath the town.
There's a broken-hearted woman tends the grave of mad Karew
And the little god forever gazes down."

He also dug up a short Victorian sonnet which I delivered dressed in velvet trousers and a white blouse. I can't be sure of the title but the lines went like this:

"The little toy dog is covered with dust yet sturdy and staunch he stands.
The little toy soldiers are covered with rust and their muskets mould in their hands.
Time was when the little toy dog was new and the soldiers were passing fair,
That was the time that Little Boy Blue kissed them and put them there.
Now don't you go till I come he said, and don't you make any noise,
And toddling off to his trundle bed he dreamt of his pretty toys.
But while he was dreaming an angel came and wakened Little Boy Blue.
And the years are many, the years are long but the little toy friends are true.
Faithful to Little Boy Blue they stand each in the same old place
Waiting the touch of a little hand and the smile on a pretty face.
And they wonder as through the long, long years in the dust of that old armchair
What has become of their Little Boy Blue since he kissed them and put them there."

Double Acts — Mother did another weepy number using Eileen as a prop. She's supposed to be a well-off lady who has lost her only child, sees this ragged urchin (Eileen) playing in the street and sings to her:

"... when just o'er the way sits a baby at play,
All alone and with none to care.
And close to her breast this poor baby she pressed
And unto the child she did say,
Won't you come over to my house?
Won't you come over and play?
I've lots of play things, a dolly or two,
And I live in that house 'cross the way
I'll give you candies and sweet things,
I'll put your hair in a curl.
Won't you come over to my house
And play that you're my little girl?"

Eileen and I enacted another of these little tragedies that audiences were so fond of in those days. Hand in hand we walked on stage, confronted a policeman (father), told him our mother had gone to heaven and we wanted to visit her but didn't know the way. We sang this. Well *I* sang it because Eileen was nearly as tone-deaf as my father. Though after that mother coached and rehearsed her – as my grandmother had done with me – and in later years Eileen not only joined the church choir but on one occasion actually played the organ at a service. It seems all children have the potential but it has to be developed. So I sang and Eileen droned on behind.

"Which is the way to heaven sir?
Please will you show us the way?
Mother has gone to live there sir
And father's so ill today.

We have no money to pay sir
So we cannot go by train
Mollie and I are walking there
To bring mother back again."

After that Uncle Joe and I came together in a modern number, one he had heard on the wireless – another culture breaking in on our traditions. We didn't have a wireless at the time, nor did many of the people in the audience, but my uncle had had access and picked up the tune, father provided the words, and then, dressed up in shabby frockcoats and top hats we went on as Gallagher and Sheen. I was Mr Gallagher, and as in the original we sang at each other.

Sheen: Oh, Mr Gallagher, oh, Mr Gallagher, I went down to the race the other day / And the winner of each race I backed to win a place / I won so much the bookie couldn't pay.
Gallagher: Oh, Mr Sheen, oh, Mr Sheen, you backed the winner of each race you mean?
Sheen: That's exactly what I did, I won twenty thousand quid. I'm a marvel, Mr Gallagher.
Gallagher: You're a liar, Mr Sheen.

Songs — I added a new number to my own repertoire. Well it wasn't really new, it was an old one I got from an actor and light comedian who had worked with us at one time. I don't remember much about the man except that his name was Adams, he came from The Shankill, and by one of those incredible quirks of fate I found myself, years later, working alongside three female members of his family (nieces maybe) when I was pursuing a career in the linen industry. The song was one I've since heard on an old 78 record, called *Connie in the Cornfield.*

"My Connie would look bonny with her head in a sack.
Her beauty went off duty and forgot to come back.
I met her accidentally when her and all her family
Were in the cornfield digging for gold ...
There was her sister Sue and several others too
When I met Connie in the cornfield.
There was her brother John and several hangers-on
When I met Connie in the cornfield.
But we didn't know we were resting, right where the wasps were nesting.
Connie sat on the nest then began to get undressed
So I left Connie in the cornfield."

Uncle Joe also sang a few songs on his own. One was about a Canadian lad who was having trouble with his family at home.

"I cursed and I swore at my father/And told him his words were a lie.
I packed up my clothes in a bundle/And went to bid mother goodbye.
My poor mother broke down a'crying, / My son, oh my son, do not leave.
Your poor mother's heart will be broken / And all my life long I will grieve."

Another one he did, straight from the old music hall this time, told the sad tale of an old couple about to depart for the workhouse. Before they go they send a desperate plea for help to their grandson, just returned from America, who replies in song:

"Wait for me, only wait another day or two.
Your loving grandson Tony's coming home on shanks's pony.
Don't despair, I'll be with you in a day or two.
Don't go to the workhouse till I get home
Then we'll all go in together."

There were also renditions on the harmonica (a chromatic one which changed key), and these intrigued me so much that Uncle Joe bought a cheap instrument so I could practise. Again my uncle drew on the latest popular numbers which he had got from the wireless, numbers like *Old Faithful We Roamed The Range Together*, *Roll Along Covered Wagon Roll Along*, and *The Wheel of the Wagon is Broken and It Ain't Gonna Turn No More.* The bulk of the songs Uncle Joe and I sang, however, either together or as solos, came from the pen and the imagination of father, cheerfully assisted by his younger brother, Joe. For hours they'd sit together mercilessly attacking the sentiments of all the old "comeallyes" they could lay hands on. In consequence lovely old ballads like *Mother Macree*, which started off with …

"There are colleens with eyes just as blue as the skies
There are colleens the world thinks are winsome and wise …"

became

"There are colleens with legs just as thin as clothes pegs …"

While *The Rose of Tralee* "… When I strayed with my love to the pure crystal fountain …" had some very uncharitable lines about a woman with a cork leg being courted by a lad who:

"Sat on the joint of her skinny cork knee.
Though the leg was of cork the joint was all ragged
And oh I can tell you it did puncture me."

Let Him Go Let Him Tarry was a humorous and jaunty number enough as it stood, but by the time the two songwriters had finished and passed it across to me to sing it had become the lament of a compulsive gambler:

"I'm brokenhearted, the horse I backed has lost.
Knowledge have I gained but good money I have lost.
I went up to the bookie to get my money back
But oh how he abused me, he nearly broke my neck.
He smacked me on the boko, I did the same for him
He knocked some chips off me, I knocked the nose off him.
He can go and get another which I hope won't be so red,
And I think that he'll be spending a month or two in bed.

My wife has got a mother and I've sold her old crutch.
She lives a mile or two away so we won't see her so much.
I've sold the cows and chickens, the insurance on her life,
The only thing I haven't sold is my great big ugly wife.
She will stay and she will tarry, she will rage and she will grouse
You'll hear her voice vibrating throughout our empty house.
And though I've lost the money that I know she wed me for,
I'll have to kick the bucket before I'm rid of her."

*

The Popular Players were on their way and very little had changed. Uncle Joe's Canadian material was new, but the plays and sketches were old, and father's parodies were anything but modern, or subtle. Not that anybody seemed to worry about that. Though mother didn't think much of the parodies. She was much closer to the music hall and knew instinctively what made people laugh. Father was a straight actor, a tragedian, and mother insisted he had no idea about comedy and imagined that if you painted on a red nose and loped round the stage audiences would laugh. Well they did laugh, they had come out to laugh ... at hard times, domestic problems, human frailties ... Maybe crude laughter is as good a way as any of relegating things that have had their day. Anyhow, father did nothing to the melodies which are timeless.

The summer, a long hot glorious summer, and our last in the business, steadily advanced. It must have been the year 1934, and by the end of it Uncle Joe had got himself a salesman's job, our audience had dwindled to a mere handful, and one evening father stood up on the platform of an empty hall in a remote part of his home-county, Down, raised the Actdrop for the last time, and it was all over. He closed and locked the hall door on our props, our scenery and our past, while mother and I stood by a little stone bridge that crossed a burn called the Blackstaff and gazed out over the empty fields at our future. But before that day came, before the final curtain, the sun shone, Ireland looked her most beautiful, and father came up with his final, and to me as a nine year old boy, *his greatest surprise*.

We were still among the lakes and there seemed to be cool, sparkling water wherever you looked. We had whole afternoons, sometimes whole days, to ourselves. Mother usually stayed in the cottage or farm with the landlady on those occasions, washing, cooking or just talking, but the rest of us set out on expeditions.

"Legionnaires in line," ordered Uncle Joe from the rear. "And by the left," father joined in, "*quick march!*" Off we went, barefoot through green fields, rushy meadows, across shallow fords, and in one particular instance along a grassy bank to a bend in the river where the waters lay deep. As we marched swinging towels or socks, we chanted the incidental music from *The Bold Gendarmes*.

> "Rhum ... pa ... pah. Rhum ... pa ... pah. Rhum ... pa ... pah. Rhum ... pa ... pah. Rhum ... pa ... pum ... pa ... pum ... pa ... pum ... pum ... paaah."

I don't know who invented the name of our little band, certainly it was Uncle Joe who introduced the subject, but father came in on the act. Uncle Joe was a fan of the writer P.C. Wren and had a host of stories about the Foreign Legion which I never tired of hearing. Indeed years later (I was 15 and had just started work in a quarry) I remember travelling up to Belfast with an empty suitcase in order to visit my uncle who was then married, and when I returned the case was crammed with all the P.C. Wren books he and his wife, who was also a fan, had in the house. They were all there: *Beau Geste*, *Beau Ideal*, *Beau Sabreur*, *Good Gestes* etc. I don't think father had ever read the stories, but his contribution had followed on from Uncle Joe's information that the Legionnaires of the time were only paid two sous a day. This, father reckoned, equalled a farthing in our money and so ... we were called *The French Farthing Legion*.

"So who's going to be the first to be thrown into the river?" Uncle Joe assumed his monster role and looked directly at Eileen who screamed with excitement and took off across the field. Father ran after her.

"I wish I could swim Uncle Joe." I looked longingly at the dark brown water. "Could you teach me?"

"Oh yes, but not here." Uncle Joe had removed his shirt and trousers and was wearing a proper pair of bathing trunks underneath. "Is it very deep?" He turned to one of the local lads who had come down for a swim (it must have been a Sunday).

"Oh yes. I only touched the bottom once ... and there's mud."

The river was quite wide at that point, and deep, having worked away at the banks and gouged a hole in its bed before sweeping round and hurrying on to ... Lough Erne I suppose. A springboard had been stuck out from the bank but there was no easy way of getting in or out of the water and you couldn't see the bottom. But oh it looked so inviting on that hot Sunday morning.

"Looks alright, Joe." Father had also disrobed and was wearing a pair of khaki shorts that had been hurriedly adapted for bathing.

"It looks very good." Uncle Joe walked along the board. "We'll try it."

"Don't go too near the far side," warned the local lad, "there's weeds. And don't go too far down the river ... the current's strong there."

"I'll take care." Uncle Joe went in off the end of the board and came up shaking his head and calling out, "It's lovely, *lovely*."

"Oh, I wish I could go in," I moaned, "I'm roasted."

"It's too deep," father said.

"But I'm roasted."

"Maybe we could lower him down from the board," Uncle Joe suggested and I took hold of this idea with both hands.

"Oh yes, yes, that's a good idea."

"If he hung onto a towel he'd just about reach it," Uncle Joe calculated the distance.

"I could, I could, I could easily reach it. Can I go in?"

"We'll see when I come out. Keep an eye on Eileen in the meantime. Don't let her get anywhere near the water. We'll see." Father poised, did a little bounce on the end of the board then cut down into the water with hardly a splash. They were both good swimmers and dived and splashed about like a couple of seals. When they came out I had already removed my shirt, and still wearing my short summer trousers which I reckoned would dry quickly in the sun, I got into position on the springboard. Father and Uncle Joe joined me and while I held onto a towel with each hand they slowly lowered me down.

"Oooooh!" My feet touched the cold water, my legs, and then down I went until only my head was above the surface. It was delicious. Of course, Eileen then wanted the same treatment but father said it was too deep for a little girl and she could have a bathe when we got back to the ford. This she did, splashing and screaming like a waterbaby in the shallow water that flowed over smooth sun-warmed stones. Then it was back to the farm with its cows, chickens, home-baked bread and new-laid eggs. But before we ate I had a long cool drink of spring water out of an iron bucket. Though when I first went with the farmer's son to draw water from the well I was rather taken aback at the sight of all the strange creatures that came up in the bucket.

"They live here," the boy reassured me, scooping them out with his hand. "They won't harm you."

Those were halcyon days, and how long they lasted I have no idea, but they were happy days not just because of the weather but because of Uncle Joe. Uncle Joe was very different from my father. Father was a man on his own, difficult to get near, unpredictable and irascible at times. Uncle Joe was just the opposite, out-going, accessible, cheerful, nothing seemed to unsettle or make him bad-tempered. In all the time he was with us I never once saw him angry or out of sorts. And of course he loved children. Not that my father didn't love children, or care for us, he did, but although he could easily show affection for Eileen he didn't show any towards my mother, and he was uneasy and difficult at times with me. But you could always depend on Uncle Joe. No matter when we approached him he grinned that lopsided smirk of his, laughed, something my father rarely did in those days, and was ready for a game. His arrival had a wonderful effect on father who now had a companion, one who was easy-going, agreeable, did what was required and took life as it came. We were much happier as a family, much more relaxed with my uncle around.

Life, however, despite the atmosphere in the family circle, was getting harder, audiences were shrinking, and scraping together enough money for digs and the hall at the end of the week became a serious problem. I don't suppose I gave a great deal of thought to the matter at the time, but my parents, facing poverty daily as they did, had clearly reached the point where they knew something would have to be done. But what? They couldn't drag people into the show, people who were no better off than themselves, and they had nothing more they could sell. They must have talked and racked their brains week after week for a solution, some way out, then father came up with a brilliant idea. Naturally I wasn't in at the birth of this revelation, but mother was, or soon after, and so was Uncle Joe. Indeed when father's idea took shape and finally became a reality, even the farm labourer in whose cottage we lodged was drawn into the conspiracy. But nobody told us, me and Eileen, it was to be a big surprise. Though I sensed something was afoot on the day the event was planned to take place because at breakfast father was in good humour, he and Uncle Joe cracked jokes, and then they went off together without saying where they were going. When I asked mother she told me, rather too casually I thought, that they were off to see a man on some business. She didn't elaborate and I couldn't think of anything they might be up to that could affect me directly, so I left it at that and went out to explore. We were lodging in an isolated cottage, the hall was not far away, but beyond that I remember very little about the place except that there were moors and it seemed to be at the back of beyond. But the sun was shining, everybody was cheerful, and events on that memorable day started off with an incident that has since been recorded in the annals of the family history as *The Tale (!) of Uncle Joe's Shirt.*

Now with regard to shirts, and other articles of clothing, I must tell you that the "family wash" was something that ranked high on mother's long list of grievances. Even higher now that Uncle Joe was in the company and she had extra to do. Despite the fact that my uncle usually bought her a packet of cigarettes as a reward for her efforts, mother still made a point of complaining because she was convinced that neither father nor my uncle realised the enormous difficulty this domestic chore presented. Certainly travelling and living in other people's houses didn't make washing a straightforward affair. Mother had to fit in with the landlady's routine, facilities were often limited, and even getting enough hot water could be a problem at times. And all this with a personal linen supply that was meagre to say the least of it. So mother complained on principle about the problem of keeping the family clean and decently covered. In the case of Uncle Joe's shirt, however, his best Sunday shirt as it happened, there were no complaints from mother that morning, no problems, and washing conditions couldn't have been better.

"It's just marvellous," she started off in high spirits, sleeves rolled up and rushing all over the place. "Just perfect." There was a small stove in the hall, plenty of wood, some coal, and the landlady had lent her a large wash boiler. The sun was splitting the trees and by the afternoon everything (things mother had been longing to wash for ages) was washed and draped over the hedge in the fresh, sweet, Fermanagh air to dry. Well pleased with the morning's work she then placed a chair on the shady side of the hall, had a quiet smoke and then a nap. When she awoke some twenty minutes later she yawned, stretched and looked out at the world with an air of great contentment (a rare thing for mother). Then she got up, wandered off in the direction of her washing … and the first thing she noticed as she approached was that although there was only the gentlest of zephyrs, Uncle Joe's shirt had all but disappeared over the other side of the hedge. And what was more, even as she stood there she could see that it was slowly but steadily being pulled by unseen hands.

"Let go!" She took hold of the tail but whoever had the other end held fast. "Let go, you'll rip the thing." Not an inch did the thieving scoundrel give way. In desperation mother gave up the tug-of-war and, despite thick vegetation and thorns, with her bare hands and arms worked her head and shoulders through until suddenly … *she caught sight of the culprit.*

And the shirt was half-way down its throat! IT WAS A GOAT. It was eating Uncle Joe's shirt. It had swallowed most of it, what was left couldn't be retrieved, was probably partly digested by then … it was a write-off. For a long time after that there were jokes on-stage and off about the shirt-eating goat. But all this happened earlier on in the day and the big event took place about tea time.

There had been some talk in the morning about where we would move next, about where we *could* move next because there wasn't another town or village for miles in any direction. I wasn't surprised therefore that by late afternoon father and my uncle had still not returned; though again I inquired of mother where they had gone and she, with that sly smile she wore when she knew something you didn't, just said it was a long way off and they'd gone on a bus. My curiosity was increased but as she went on with her ironing and wouldn't discuss the matter further I returned to the field at the back of the cottage (Eileen was playing near the front door) and joined up with the landlady's son, a boy about my own age who, like me, had not gone to school that morning. Why he hadn't gone to school I don't know, but why *I* hadn't gone was because I flatly refused to present myself to one more teacher or class until I was cured … I had ringworm, a complaint I got from some old cow. Well, not directly, I think the animal must have scratched itself against a gate and I got it from there. It's not a worm of course, it's a fungus that grows in a ring and hence the name. But it looks horrible, and I was so conscious of the scabs on the side of my head and in my hair that I took to wearing a cap … even in bed. Though at last it was beginning to clear up thanks to an old fellow in a pub who told father he was wasting his money on ointments and what he should do was this: Paint a ring of iodine round the worm; every three days paint another ring closer in; do this seven times and on the twenty-first day the worm will die. And it was working. In the meantime I was quite glad of the excuse to stay away from school, and my companion was also relieved to be left to his own devices. So he and I spent the day building a fort in the field behind the cottage. We'd been there most of the day and it was late on in the afternoon when mother, tired of waiting for father's return and, I suspected, of keeping her secret, drifted round and called out to me,

"No sign of them yet!"

"Well, where have they gone?" I sensed now was the moment to demand an explanation and walked over to where she was standing.

"I don't know the name of the place, they didn't say."

"*Why* have they gone?"

"To meet a man and do business."

"What sort of business?"

"Just business."

"But what sort of business? Is it about a hall, or digs?"

"No, it's not about a hall," mother hesitated, "and it's not about digs … not really."

"Well, what *is* it about then? *You* know … why can't you tell me?"

"Because it's a secret," mother admitted.

"What sort of secret?"

"That's a stupid question to ask. If I told you it wouldn't be a secret."

"And if everybody knows why am I left out? Why can't you tell me?"

"Because it's to be a surprise and your father has sworn me to silence." That intrigued me even more, so I tried another line.

"Alright then, give me a clue."

"I can't think of a clue."

"You *can*. Is it anything to do with Belfast or Aunty Agnes?"

"No," she hesitated again, "not really. Though it has to do with somebody who is connected with the family but you wouldn't know him and I've never met him either."

"Is he coming back with father?"

"No."

"Is *anybody*, apart from Uncle Joe, coming back with father?"

"Oh, look, I'm tired of this game. I can't tell you any more and the truth is I'm not certain what's going to happen myself. You'll just have to be patient. You'll just have to …" At this point my companion abruptly stopped what he was doing, raised his head, listened and then called out,

"Ye hear that, Jimmy?"

"Hear what?"

"A lorry."

"A *lorry!*" mother exclaimed, and instantly I knew it had to do with the secret.

"It's comin' down the bog road." The boy raced across the field and scrambled up on the dyke. "Can't ye hear it?"

"Yes I can hear it." I got up alongside and peered out over the empty landscape.

"Can you see it?" Mother hurried over to where we were. "Are you sure it's a lorry?"

"No, I can't see it," I replied.

"But it's a lorry alright, Mrs Mateer," the boy reassured her. "It's comin' up te the corner now … slowin' down … if it turns left …" he paused then went on, "no, it's turned right. It's comin' our way." He jumped down and headed for the front of the cottage with me behind him and mother bringing up the rear. A lorry on a road where we rarely encountered a horse and cart was a novelty, but a lorry that had to do with *a secret* …!

"Has this got anything to do with the surprise?" I asked mother as she joined us by the roadside.

"I hope so. But where is it? I can't see anything."

"It's in behind those trees." The boy was sitting on top of an iron gate. "Ye'll see it in a minute. *There* it is. And it's towin' somethin'."

"What?" mother demanded. "What is it towing?"

"A van."

"A van?" I moved out into the middle of the road. I was keeping well away from iron gates.

"*A caravan!*" The boy could hardly believe his eyes.

"*It's come!*" mother clenched her fists and shook them in triumph. "*He's got it.*"

"Is it for us?" I asked in amazement.

"It's for us, it's for us," she waved vigorously at the oncoming lorry.

"To live in?" This was beyond anything I could have imagined.

"To live in," mother repeated and then shouted, "*No!*" Eileen had run out of the house to see what was going on. "Stay where you are Eileen." My sister stopped dead but cried out excitedly,

"Is daddy back, is daddy back?"

"Yes he's back." Mother took hold of her hand, at the same time shouting to me, "Come in off the road, Jim, you'll get run over. Get into the side … the both of you."

We lined up alongside mother and Eileen, all heads turned, all eyes fixed on the oncoming convoy which slowed down and came to an abrupt halt in front of the cottage. Both cab doors opened simultaneously and the driver fell out on his side while father and Uncle Joe tumbled out on the other. They were all flushed, cheerful, unsteady on their feet and had obviously been celebrating.

"Your new home, Jimmy." Uncle Joe put a foot on the towing bar and a hand on the side of the caravan.

"Is it really ours?" I asked in disbelief.

"Yes, it's ours … ours …" father waved his arms in the air, "*all ours.*" The entire audience, which now included the landlady and her husband who had just returned from work roared with laughter.

"And are we going to live in it, daddy?" Eileen let go mother's hand.

"Yes, we're going to live in it, smiler," he lifted her up and turned so she could look in through the window. The rest of us crowded round the back as Uncle Joe opened the door and explained,

"Of course, it has to be fitted up." We put our heads together and looked inside the caravan door. Piled up was a bed spring, a mattress, a cupboard, folding chairs, bits of wood and some small cardboard boxes and brown paper bags. "But we've got all the materials."

"Everything we need." Father, with Eileen in his arms, joined us at the door. "There's the spring for the double bed, a collapsible table and chairs, a food-cupboard and what we need to make a bunk for Wee Jim. It'll be very good when it's finished."

"It'll be marvellous," mother was enraptured, "just marvellous. No more tramping the streets in the dark looking for lodgings. No more putting up with grumpy old landlords and landladies …" she turned in the direction of our hosts and added, "they're not all as nice as the ones standing over there. No more worrying about the kids making a noise. Our own home, our own furniture, *our own bed.*"

The caravan was about twelve feet long, seven feet wide and an average man could stand up inside with room to spare. It had a flat roof, a small window on each side, a towbar at one end and a door at the other. It wasn't a very stylish affair, not quaint or colourful like the gypsy caravans I had seen. Indeed, looking back I realise it was rather plain, just a rectangular box sitting on two wheels and sheeted over with a blue-grey material that I think must have been tin. But it was my first real home. I was thrilled, and the idea of my own bed at last was beyond words. But, as Uncle Joe said, it had to be fitted up first. Though that didn't take long because early on the morning after the arrival of the van, which was parked in the garden alongside the cottage (which was why the landlord had been let into the secret), work got going with a vengeance. Although there were hitches.

Father, as I've already mentioned, was strictly a hammer and nail man. Uncle Joe on the other hand had done woodwork at the tech. and knew something about carpentry. While the landlord, who supplied tools and enthusiastically joined in when he'd finished work on Saturday afternoon (the van arrived on Friday) was a practical man and had knocked up a few sheds and henhouses in his time. There was, therefore, some skill in the workforce and the operation should have gone very smoothly indeed only father, naturally, was in charge. He was also, as usual, in a hurry. The van had to be ready to move on Monday morning. So we were all banned from the area, there was a great deal of shouting and hammering, the three men worked like Trojans and by Sunday evening father declared the work complete and gave us a tour of inspection. That is, he stood inside the caravan while the rest of us stood on the ground outside the open door. Father didn't like being crowded.

"Now the double bed (a spring enclosed in a wooden frame) is hinged and folds up against the back wall, as you can see, during the day. Then at night," father lowered the spring and the mattress down onto two supports fitted to the walls about a foot from the floor, "it comes down like this."

"*Wonderful!*" mother was suitably impressed. Father was very sensitive about his work, all his work, and the slightest criticism or hint that his efforts were not being fully appreciated could provoke a sudden explosion and an instant walk-off.

"So this is where we sleep." He meant mother, Eileen and himself. The sleeping order from the wall out being Eileen, mother and then him. "Then above the double bed," father turned and took hold of what looked like a stretcher (a length of canvas nailed between two poles) "and into the four brackets you see fitted on the walls we slot the hooks at the end of the poles." The stretcher was put in position. "The result ... our Jim's bunk!"

"Great, marvellous." I followed mother's example and responded with vigour, though I was genuinely pleased. It was a bed, a hard bed but my own.

"That's a very clever idea," mother came in again, "brilliant. And so economic." Our praise, as it turned out, was a little premature because on our first night in the van, when the rest of the family were asleep below, I heaved round rather vigorously, one of the brackets gave way and I fell heavily on top of father's head. He swore at me, raged as though

I had done it on purpose. But during the demonstration everything looked perfect and father finished like a conjuror concluding his act.

"And so to bring down the curtain, or to be more precise, to bring *across* the curtain," he stood to one side, "when all those who are in bed and should be asleep ..."

"Me," Eileen said excitedly, "*me!*"

"Yes, when Eileen is in bed and fast asleep, we pull this curtain across and ... Hey Presto! The sleeping chamber disappears and the living room comes into view."

We all cheered, clapped and were then invited in to inspect the rest of the facilities. Over the wheel on one side there was a drop-down table-top with a tip-up chair fitted to the wall at each end. Over the other wheel there was a small cupboard. An oil lamp had been fitted to one wall to provide lighting, though it could be removed and set on the table when father wanted to read. Cooking would be done on the primus and a small oilstove ... the latter also provided heating. Dishes would be washed in a basin (there was no sink unit or anything like that), and a second bowl was set aside for our ablutions. Water we would get from a well or the village pump. Bedding and crockery we would have to acquire although the landlady and several members of the audience who came to inspect our new home brought whatever they could spare from their own homes, so we had enough to begin with. The only other requirement absolutely necessary was a lavatory. And father said we would have to use the one in the hall, but in the event of there not being one in the hall he had procured (in fact it was thrown in with the caravan as a luckpenny) a small canvas wigwam which could be positioned over a hole dug in a field. Grandad would have loved the idea. It would have reminded him of the First World War.

On Monday morning the lorry returned, we loaded up, said our farewells and moved off to the next venue well-pleased with our new home and arrangements. Of course nothing is perfect and we were very cramped in our living quarters. We also got several punctures because the tyres were old. And on one trip the towbar broke, the van careered backwards down a hill and finished up on its end with everything that was loose inside piled up behind the door. I had to be lifted up and squeezed through the window, a caper I enjoyed, so that I could remove the obstacles and let father in. Uncle Joe too had trouble with his living arrangements, his tent. One night a cow lay down on top of it while he was sleeping. And another night the candle he'd left burning while he walked across to the hedge set fire to one wall and he had to sleep on the floor of the van with his feet at the door and his head under the bed. But despite those little incidents we were happy about the new arrangements. As well as providing a home the caravan was an added attraction, an advertisement as we moved away from the lakes and across North Monaghan in the Free State to play in Clones and Ballybay. Then into South Armagh stopping at Darkley, Forkhill and Tandragee. South Down (not for the first time) playing at Newry, Warrenpoint and Kilkeel. Then on through the heartland of County Down – Katesbridge, Ballynahinch and Ballygowan were marked on father's map – until finally in South Antrim we arrived in Carrickfergus. A fine town, a historic town but one that was to be a milestone, you could almost say a headstone as far as The Popular Players were concerned.

Mother took ill. Right at the beginning of the week she developed a terrible fever, a raging throat and couldn't get out of her bed. She was so bad that father had to pay for the doctor to visit her in the van. There he examined her, took swabs, packed up his little black bag and announced,

"Diphtheria."

"*No,*" said father.

"Yes!" The doctor was irritated as well as surprised. "You'll have to get her into the hospital." Mother, lying on her back in the bed shook her head, and the doctor, thinking maybe she didn't like the idea of going into hospital, or perhaps that she was afraid we'd have to pay, laid a hand on her shoulder and said quietly, "But you're ill, Mrs Mateer, it's diphtheria, it has all the symptoms. Don't worry, they'll look after you in hospital and it won't cost you a penny."

"Now doctor," father was calm and very reasonable, "I know nothing about medicine so I'm not in any position to dispute your diagnosis, but I doubt very much if my wife has diphtheria." He then went on to tell the doctor about mother's experience in Dungannon, ending up with, "So if the swabs you've taken prove positive then she'll go into hospital if I have to carry her there myself."

"Alright then," the doctor was reluctant, "on your own heads be it. But diphtheria is serious."

"I know," agreed father.

"It's also infectious."

"We'll be the only ones in contact with her till we hear from you."

"And if we have an epidemic we'll *all* be in trouble."

"I don't think for one minute that will happen," father was very reassuring.

"I hope not, but if she gets worse call me out."

"I will."

"Get these pills from the chemist," the doctor handed father a prescription, "they'll help with the fever. And come round to my surgery in three days' time, I should have the results by then." Father did and they were negative.

In the meantime mother was too ill to work, and though audiences were sparse we needed the money so father got together all the songs, sketches and monologues he could muster and for two nights he, Uncle Joe and I put on a show. Then on the Friday we closed and pulled down the scenery … the town had more attractive entertainment to offer its citizens on payday. And I learnt that Uncle Joe was going to leave. He and father had talked the matter over, they just couldn't go on, so my uncle had got himself a job as a door-to-door salesman in Belfast, with Kleeneze brushes, and was due to start on Monday. Eileen was to go with him to Belfast where she would be collected and looked after by Aunty

Annie who was well-off and lived in a big new bungalow half-way down the Ards Peninsula, about twenty miles from the city. Father and I accompanied the pair to the station, waved goodbye to them on the train and then made our way back home. Nothing was said for most of the return journey and then, right out of the blue, father asked me,

"Would you like to go to the pictures this afternoon?"

"The *pictures*!"

"Yes. There's a cinema in the town and they're bound to have an afternoon performance on a Friday. Would you like to go?"

"Oh, I'd love to go. I've never been to the pictures, not the real pictures."

"Right then, we'll have a cup of tea and see what we can do." I was thrilled. I had once seen a short silent film starring Charlie Chaplin somewhere, but it wasn't in a cinema. I had never been in a cinema, as far as I could remember, never experienced The Talkies in my life. Mother was very envious when she heard where we were going, and as I demolished a couple of slices of bread and jam she related an experience she had once had in a cinema.

"I once saw Lillian Gish and her sister in a picture called *Orphans of the Storm.* It was a wonderful performance and an experience I'll never forget for another reason that had nothing to do with the picture. I was only in my teens at the time and living with my grandma while mother was on tour. I wasn't acting and got myself a job in a jeweller's shop. I don't think I worked a full week but when I got paid grandma said that as these were my first real wages I could keep them providing I didn't spend them all at once. I agreed and worked out I could save two shillings and the rest would take me to the pictures and buy chocolates as a treat. Off I went, saw the picture, wept all the way through it, then when I came out and was walking down the dark stairway that led from the balcony, suddenly, right at my feet I saw a two shilling piece. Immediately I put my foot on it, bent down and pretended to be fixing my shoe, then when there was no-one behind me I picked it up and put it in my pocket. What luck! What a find! It'll just go with the two shilling piece I have … or rather thought I had, because when I got out into the street and looked in my handbag which had fallen open during all the weeping, my savings had gone. I'd found my own two shilling piece! Oh, I *was* disappointed."

"Are you ready then, young Jim?" Father picked up his hat but left his overcoat hanging behind the door as the weather was warm though the sun wasn't shining.

"Yes, I'm ready." I intended to go just as I was … short trousers, jersey and sandals. I wore sandals most of the time because that was the cheapest form of footwear and you never had to pay to get them fixed.

"Let's get off to the pictures then." Father climbed down the steps of the caravan.

"We'll tell you all about it when we get back," I promised mother who stood forlornly in the doorway.

"Enjoy yourselves," she said, and then called after father, "Bring back some fish and chips for our tea."

"I'll see." That could mean anything. Father wouldn't be tied down. And buying food came out of mother's housekeeping money.

The caravan was parked right alongside the hall, a very small hall which stood on some rough ground at the edge of the town. In fact I think we were quite some way outside Carrickfergus because I don't remember any houses or shops. But what I do remember was a huge grey stone building that rose up on the other side of a small river (the Woodburn river I've since learnt) and this we were told was a factory that had to do with the linen trade. Whether it was weaving or spinning I don't know but County Antrim was noted for its textiles, an industry which had been developed and expanded by Huguenot families who had fled the terror and massacres in France. And whether it was still working during The Depression I doubt as we didn't notice a lot of activity.

Out on the main road we walked in leisurely fashion towards the town, and though father was in good humour he was silent, while I was excited but at the same time worried in case there might not be a performance that afternoon, or that father might find the tickets too expensive. Though as he went into a small shop and bought some tobacco en route I didn't think he could be that hard up for money. The cinema, probably a small concrete building like most of the cinemas I'd seen in the province, wasn't difficult to find, and as we approached the doorway father stopped and instructed me,

"Stay out here till I go in and have a word with the manager."

"Alright." I moved out to the edge of the footpath and turned my back on the building. He was gone for quite a long time but eventually he reappeared in the doorway and beckoned.

"Is it alright?" I asked, though it was obvious from father's face there were no problems.

"It's alright. I had a chat with the manager and he said there was no-one in yet but he'd put on a performance."

"Good." I was relieved. Then as father walked right past the paybox without stopping, heading for the foot of the stairs that led up to the balcony, I whispered, "But shouldn't we pay?"

"It's alright." He didn't answer my question. "We go up here." I followed him up the narrow stairway and out onto the dimly-lit balcony where, being the only customers present, we selected seats in the middle of a row not far from the front. Down below I could hear voices but it may have been the manager and the girl from the box. Father sat down, removed his hat, set his pipe on the ashtray fitted to the seat in front and produced a bag of sweets from his pocket.

"Some sweets," he said, removing a few and handing the bag to me.

"Oh, thank you. It's treats all round today."

"I think it's supposed to be a comedy judging by the poster outside, but I don't know."

"It doesn't matter." The prospect of the picture and having father to myself was more than enough for me.

"We'll just have to see." As he spoke lights went up on the platform, loud music crackled and echoed round the empty auditorium, the curtains opened and the titles and credits came up on the screen.

"It's started!" I whispered, then asked the question that had troubled me since we entered the building. "But didn't we pay to get in?"

"No," father replied in a low voice. "I told the manager we were professionals and we got in for nothing."

"Oh ... good." I settled down and prepared to watch my very first Talkie. And it *was* a comedy, in black and white of course, with most of the action taking place on board a ship of His Majesty's (George the Fifth) Navy. The title, of little importance (I don't even know what it means) but stored up in my memory for all time, was *Alf's Button Afloat*; and only recently while poking around trying to find answers to many unanswerable questions I discovered that the artists who provided the mad humour in that film were Nervo and Knox of The Crazy Gang. I expect it was a terrible picture but I enjoyed it, and father chewed his sweets, puffed his pipe and seemed at peace with the world, his own world. Because outside, the monster that had relentlessly stalked and driven a generation, three generations counting me, out of the cities, towns and villages onto remote islands and into desolate places, luring away audiences, destroying a way of life and threatening our very existence, had caught up with us at last. Open-eyed and with that resignation and acceptance that inevitably comes when the end is near, we had chosen to walk into the animal's lair. But we weren't dead yet. We *enjoyed* the performance. And what's more ... *we got in free!*

18

Waterloo

We crossed the River Lagan, collected Eileen, drifted across North Down avoiding the larger towns and villages where we had played with a full company more than once in the past, and sought out sheltered townlands like Conlig, The Six Road Ends, Calhame … and it was somewhere around there that father played his last card, came up with his final surprise.

"Clear the table," he ordered, standing at the foot of the caravan steps, his hands and arms full of mysterious parcels and bundles.

"Right away, right away." Novelties or pleasant surprises, and father was clearly in a pleasant mood, always found mother cheerful and accommodating.

"What is it daddy, what is it?" Eileen got to the head of the queue inside the caravan door.

"You'll see, you'll see, but don't touch that," he held out a warning hand, "it's dangerous." He indicated the "wet" battery he used for his amplifier which he'd set down on the floor. Obviously he'd been to the garage to get it charged. "And you and Jim sit on the bed out of the way." Mother had piled clothes and other things on the bed so that it couldn't be pinned back against the wall.

"What on earth is it?" I was just as curious as Eileen and couldn't imagine what father had been up to.

"Be patient, be patient." Father set an object wrapped in an old cloth on the table, also a cardboard box with a long piece of wire poking out of the top, then gave further instructions. "Close your eyes." We did as instructed.

"I'll close mine too." Mother joined us sitting on the bed. "But I wonder what it could be."

"You'll see, you'll see. Now keep them closed." Eileen screwed her face up into a horrible grimace. There was a rustling of paper, some fumbling, a few moments passed and then father said, "Right. Open your eyes."

"*A wireless*," we chorused, "*a wireless*." There on the middle of the table with batteries and other equipment sitting alongside it stood a small wooden cabinet about fifteen inches high and ten inches across, with knobs, a small dial, and a cut-out covered with gauze to let out the sound.

"A two-valve wireless," father said with pride. "I bought it from the man in the garage."

"And does it work?" Mother didn't sound too certain.

"I certainly hope so. If it doesn't I'll take it back. But I think it'll work alright when I get it all connected up." Eileen got off the bed and cautiously approached the table.

"Will it play music daddy?"

"Play music, tell stories … all sorts of things. Now you get back on the bed out of the way till I put it together. First we fit this large battery in at the back and connect it … right. Then this small one (I think he called it a grid bias) goes in here … that's it. Next we take these leads and connect them to our 'wet' battery …" he turned to us and added, "and you must never, ever touch a 'wet' battery. You know why?"

"Because there's acid." I'd taken the battery to the garage many times before.

"That's right … acid … and acid burns. So never go near it. Now what we have to do next" he pulled the wire out of the cardboard box, "is poke this aerial out and jam it in the window … I'll fit it up properly when I see if everything works. Then we plug it in here at the back and that's it. Now stand back and hold your breath." We stood back and Eileen took a very deep breath. Father switched on and immediately there was a high-pitched oscillating whine, some crackling, and then away in the distance we heard a voice.

"It works," mother said excitedly, "it works."

"*It lives*," father quoted a line from *Frankenstein*, "*it lives*. Let's see if we can tune it in a bit closer." He got down on his knees, twiddled the knob, turned up the volume and the voice of a man, clear and with a beautifully modulated English accent announced that he was going to tell us a story, but …

"Before I start you must all sit down. And you must all be very, very … *Now Eileen do stop fidgeting*." Eileen's eyes, and her mouth, opened wide. We all looked at her, amused by her expression and intrigued by the remarkable coincidence.

"How did he know my name?" she asked in amazement.

"He must be able to see you," father said.

"But where is he?" Eileen got closer to the mysterious voice.

"Oh, he's away somewhere in England I expect. Now you just sit down on the chair and we'll see if we can get you some music." The fiddling started again, and went on until mother got quite indignant. Every time we seemed to have a chance of a good programme father insisted on trying to find a better one. Eventually he settled for one which came through loud and clear and pleased everyone … singing. Popular songs of the day, songs like *Little Man You've Had a Busy Day* (sung by Kitty Masters); *Red Sails in the Sunset* (written, I discovered years later, by an Ulsterman called Jackie Kennedy); *Miss Otis Regrets*; *The Great Big Wheel Came Nearer and Nearer*, and all the cowboy numbers I'd already learnt from Uncle Joe. As well as singing we had dance music, announced by the leader of the band who always declared, "And this *is* Henry Hall speaking." Finally, especially for father – and heaven help anybody who dared to even cough while it was on – we had *The Six O'Clock News*. The outside world was coming right inside our little van.

There were no more surprises after that, no more novelties or excitement, just the slow, steady, inevitable descent to the end of the road. We turned south down the Ards Peninsula with the Irish Sea on our left and Strangford Lough on our right (sometimes you could see both at once), along winding roads, among green hills, stopping but not always playing (there were no audiences) at Carrowdore, Ballywalter, Ballyhalbert, Greyabbey, Kircubbin, until finally, ahead of us lay the tip of the peninsula. And there was nowhere else to go.

I accepted at the time that where we made our last stand, a small hall in the middle of a field a mile away from the nearest farm, was sheer chance. We had simply moved from one place to the next and there we were. But now I know this wasn't the case, far from it. Father had instinctively, if not consciously, chosen the route and the direction in much the same way as an animal that senses the end is near heads for a predetermined spot. For him this *was* the spot because twelve miles to the north, near Belfast, the remains of his father and mother lay at rest; five miles to our rear, not far from the shadowy ruins of the great Cistercian monastery the Normans had founded at Greyabbey, stood the tiny school where his mother had taught; and within walking distance of the school lay the land that his grandparents had farmed. All around us there were country roads, secluded lanes and fields he must have walked and explored as a boy. And on a more practical note, not half an hour's walk from where we were standing at that moment, in its own grounds, behind a neat lawn and surrounded by a well-kept garden, stood the new bungalow that belonged to my aunt. Father had been heading home.

"Well … that's it."

"Yes." Mother got up and slowly made her way to the dressing room to collect the few things she intended to take back with her. She didn't have to remove her greasepaint because she hadn't put any on, none of us had. And as she disappeared into the little back room father climbed up onto the platform, raised the Actdrop revealing the all-too-familiar backscene, made the rope fast, and had a last look round. Nothing would be going on in front of that shabby brown drawing room scene tonight; nothing would *ever* be going on in front of … and yet! He lifted his hat off the small table that was part of the set, got down onto the hall floor and came out to where I was standing.

Moments later mother emerged, made her entrance, her *exit*, wearing a summer frock coloured deep pink and covered all over with large white oval-shaped spots. There were no sleeves on the dress but it had a broad white collar that ended up in a point low on her breast. She also wore a hat, a beautiful broad-brimmed summer hat that had a hatband and was made of a waxy, lace-like material. She was dressed as though she was going to a wedding or a garden party. She looked nice, very nice. Mother got her dress-sense from my grandma and her wardrobe, second-hand, from what she referred to as The Actors' Guild. You wrote to this organisation giving a list of requirements and sizes, together with an address, and they sent on what they could. They catered for actresses (maybe actors too though father never sent for anything as far as I know) who were touring and couldn't afford new clothes.

"Yes ... that's it." Father closed the door behind her and turned the key. Then as he stepped back he caught sight of an inscription cut into the plaster or cement above the doorway which read:

Built to commemorate the famous battle and victory
in 1815
WATERLOO HALL

"Very apt," he remarked dryly, "very apt. Elba the next port of call."

"Where?" Mother hadn't the faintest idea what he was talking about but he didn't enlighten her, he just moved out onto the roadway and began the long walk, at least two miles, back to where Eileen was asleep in the van.

A strange picture we must have presented to anyone looking along the lonely country road that evening. Mother in all her finery sauntering up the middle of the road. Father in an old brown jacket, and shabby trousers that belonged to another suit but looked neat because he'd pressed them under the mattress the night before, strolling along with his hat in his hand as though he wasn't going anywhere in particular. And me following on behind, the only one taking any notice of where we were going. I always looked about me in new places, it was my habit, and later on I would, as I did on that occasion, seek out someone who could tell me what I had seen and where I had been.

So ... the hall we had just left behind stood in a townland they called Blackstaff. The road we had turned into after noting a small group of council houses some distance away near the main road, was the Rubane Road ... a quiet, tree-lined, beautiful road, one I would walk many times in the years to come, just for the joy of it. On each side of us there were stone walls and watery ditches where harts-tongue ferns grew in profusion. Or high hawthorn hedges that opened up occasionally to reveal a hidden gate or the beginning of a lane that curved round to some sheltered farmstead out of sight. On the crest of the only hill we were to encounter we eventually came to the great pillars, and behind them the derelict driveway (now a watercourse) that had once led up to Rubane House. The big grey stone mansion with its trees, lawns, walled garden and outbuildings was still occupied ... by a solicitor and his wife who one day gave me elderberry wine and cake when, along with the rest of the choir, I sang carols outside their front door. And just beyond the estate, past the entrance that had been used by staff, servants and those who worked on the farm in days gone by, I discovered a clump of wild apple trees which would one day provide fruit for mother's first crab-apple jelly. But of all this my parents saw nothing. They walked in silence and took no notice of their surroundings, or of each other. Perhaps they were wondering what we would do next! Or were they, each in their own private world, looking back at all their hopes, dreams and unfulfilled ambitions with sadness … regrets?

Well, father had told me something about his early life, that is before he was married. And from fragments of programmes, cuttings and letters, which I carefully gathered together when his only remaining sister died and the house where the family had lived for nearly eighty years was sold, perhaps I can imagine what was going through his mind. If he had been looking back it would probably have been to those early play productions of his (a brother and several sisters press-ganged into taking part) up in the attic of No. 26. Or to the amateur dramatics he engaged in with The East Belfast Dramatic Club or The Belfast Dramatic and Comedy Company (booked into the Frederick Street Co-Operative Hall on one occasion). Certainly etched on his memory for all time would be the evening when, after an amateur production (the expense account reads: "Cartage to the Ulster Hall 3/-", so it must have been in Belfast), that great old man of the Ulster theatre, Bob McCandless, sought him out and told him he had genuine talent, thus deciding him on a professional career at the age of nineteen.

First it was a repertory company in Dublin where, in a small part and for a very limited period, he trod the boards of the famous Abbey Theatre. Then there was a run at The Queens and The Gate. After that he returned to Belfast during The Troubles (1921, when he said the tram he was travelling in got machine-gunned down the Short Strand) where he met another actor called Johnston, and the pair of them formed a company of their own.

THE JOHNSTON AND MATEER REPERTOIRE COMPANY

presents

The Atheist, Her Rosary, Homeless, A Gay Life, A Woman's Love …

and other better-known plays. What *The Atheist* was like and how it went down in Belfast I couldn't possibly imagine; though somewhere in the suburbs when father went on stage to warm up the audience with a comedy number and began, "The last place I did this I got thrown out", there was a roar and a yell, "An' ye'll bloody-well get thrown out of here too", followed by an onslaught on the stage. He, and presumably Mr Johnston too, left by the rear exit while the audience dismantled the set. After the city the company moved off on what they called an "open tour" (probably booking from one place to the next) and played in Larne, Victoria Hall; Coleraine, Town Hall; a protestant hall in Antrim; and the Town Hall at Portrush. Sometime after that the company broke up and father went to England to work in a Shakespearean company and eventually a rep. where he met mother (who told me she wasn't acting at the time, only visiting her parents, and she had toothache, a swollen face and looked awful. But that didn't deter father).

Back to Dublin and the south again, this time with an English wife, to work in a rep. from which, after only a week, they both got the sack because father represented the entire cast and demanded better wages. They got work in Scotland with another rep. which eventually collapsed leaving everybody stranded. Father dealt with that problem by forming his own company, using any artists or scenery that remained from the wreck. Then, leaving the lowlands to the cinema and the Sassenachs, he headed up into the Highlands and onto the islands of Iona, Mull, Skye and the Outer Hebrides where he met the famous author H.V. Morton who said if he would stay put for a week he'd write an article about the company. But father had to move on. Finally with a baby girl, a small boy and their own Fit-up company they returned to Northern Ireland and began the tour which you have been following up to now. And so, if father had been looking back at his past life, was he disappointed? Did he have regrets? I don't know. He never said.

About mother I'm on much firmer ground. The lure of the footlights or the burning desire to be a famous actress, if they ever existed, didn't occupy her attention for long. She had been born into the business (just like me), nobody asked her what she wanted to do, so she just got on with what was presented. The fact that she was a "natural" and acted-out roles all her life is another matter. But as far as success in the theatre was concerned I don't think she had any regrets, I don't think she gave a fig for failed ambitions and what had happened in the past, although …! There were events that had altered her life! There were things she wouldn't be likely to forget; a whirlwind romance with a wild, handsome young actor from the Emerald Isle for instance. And of course the birth of her first child.

They were both working together in a rep. when I was scheduled to make an appearance, and it was winter. Snow covered the small Scottish town where the company was playing, and to an effete southerner like herself, marooned not far from the north-east coast and in the same latitude as Moscow, it must have seemed like the end of the world. High ground and the Cairngorms lay to the south, while to the west range after range of white craggy heights stretched as far as the eye could see. Mother's time was perhaps another two weeks away, though one can never be too precise about such matters, and she had no relatives near her (my grandparents were playing somewhere in the south of England), no friend in whom she could confide or from whom she might seek reassurance, and the company, including my father, would have to move on. They didn't know where she could go (but it couldn't be far), or where I might be born. The matter was earnestly discussed among the company and in the digs but nobody came up with a solution. Then on the Friday afternoon, or it may have been Saturday, the landlady's boy James, who was thirteen and had fallen madly in love with the beautiful young English actress (mother was 20 at the time) came up to our room when father had gone off to the theatre, and enquired,

"Mrs Mateer, where will you have your baby?"

"Well I don't know James, it all depends."

"Have you got anywhere to go?"

"No, not really."

"So where will you have it?"

"I don't know."

"Have it here."

"*Here?*"

"Yes, have it here. I've talked it over with my mother and she says you can have the baby in our house." And that is what mother did. Father moved on with the company and the boy's family made provision, a home … even took the heavily pregnant girl to the pictures one day, ensuring she had an end seat in case of a rapid retreat. Young James was thrilled and strutted about the place giving orders, showing concern, and then a couple of days before my arrival he came to mother's room and enquired,

"How are you today, Mrs Mateer?"

"Oh, I'm alright James, I'm alright, but I wish the baby would come soon."

"So do I," the boy earnestly responded, then went on, "Is there anything you want at the moment, Mrs Mateer, anything you need … anything at all?" He wanted to do something for the beautiful actress.

"Well you know James," mother got up slowly from her chair, walked across to the window and looked out at the snow-covered town and the leaden sky full of more snow to come, "there *is* something."

"What?" The boy's face lit up.

"Right at this minute, and I know it's crazy but mothers-to-be can be a little crazy at times, right at this minute what I would really like …"

"Yes, yes?"

"What I have a terrible craving for …"

"What?"

"*A great big bowl of icecream!*"

The boy didn't laugh, and he might well have because ordinary people didn't have refrigerators in those days. He just looked down at the floor, gave the matter serious consideration then said, "Alright, I'll see what I can do." With that he left the room and returned in about half an hour with a large bowl of icecream.

"Good heavens!" Mother was flabbergasted. "Good heavens!"

"You said you wanted it." Her admirer looked crestfallen.

"Oh yes, yes I do want it but … The Highlands of Scotland in the middle of winter! Where on earth did you get such a thing?"

"I went to the Royal Hotel." James had thought about and pursued the project with great thoroughness. "I told them we had an English actress staying in our house and she was expecting a baby and she must have a bowl of icecream."

"And they said you could have one?"

"Yes, and I stayed in the kitchen until it was ready."

"James you're a genius." Mother put her hand at the back of his head. "And you're also a dear." The boy blushed and then glowed.

"I'm glad you're pleased, Mrs Mateer, and if there is anything else, anything at all …"

"I'll tell you. I'll let you know. And this icecream is just delicious."

James retired to spread his joy among the rest of the family, and a few days later the doctor was called in, the nurse stood by with a mask (an anaesthetic?) in case of trouble, but mother was strong and at 8.30 on the morning of February 4th (according to the telegram sent to my father), I was born. James was greatly relieved, and when he heard it was a boy and the boy was to be called James …!

"But that's *my* name!" He was allowed a peep at the baby.

"That's right," mother agreed, "and it's also the name of Mr Mateer's father."

"You've named the baby after *me*!" He told everybody. And after the christening, when the head man of the town (was he the provost?) gave the baby a half-crown because that was the tradition in those parts, young James went out on his own initiative, and with his own pocket money bought the most atrocious-looking bonnet mother had ever seen, insisting that *I* wear it and that *he* be allowed to push me round the town. My own father, when he paid a flying visit, must also have been pleased, although his first words when he saw me wrapped up in my swaddling clothes were,

"He's got very short legs!"

"You don't expect them to come down to the bottom of the cot?" mother laughed. "He's got perfectly good legs," she displayed my feet. "He's a perfectly healthy baby." Father was convinced and went back to work.

A week later we too, mother and I, said farewell to James and his family, caught the train and joined the rest of the company who were heading for the Orkneys. Some time after that the company collapsed, father formed his own Fit-up and we set off on a long tour of Scotland. For over three years we travelled the Highlands and Islands until one day at the height of summer we found ourselves on the west coast in a small fishing village called Mallaig, with the company contemplating a tour on Skye, and mother expecting her second child. On this occasion, however, things were a lot less comfortable than they had been during my arrival, despite the kindness of people and the fact that our landlady was also a district nurse. (Before the birth of my sister she left mother a small bottle of a colourless liquid that smelt of ether or chloroform so that she could have "a wee sniff" if the pains got too bad.) There was no trouble with the actual birth as far as I know, but the midwife (a lady dressed from head to foot in dark clothes, only her face and hands visible), had to direct quite a bit of her attention to *me*, because while mother was in the throes I threw a brick which bounced off a fence, hit me on the head and caused quite a bloody diversion. While after the event mother was so weak that she had to stay in bed for a few days, and as the nurse was out on her daily rounds and father was at work she was left alone for a lot of the time. Of course, she still had me for company, but a three-and-a-half year old has limitations, and one evening there was an incident in the lodgings which would have been more appropriate had it been enacted on the stage.

It was several days after Eileen's arrival and father had presented the nurse and her husband with a couple of complimentary tickets. Up until then the thoughtful lady wouldn't leave the house in the evenings, although she dearly wanted to see our show. On that occasion, however, mother insisted and the landlady tore round the house leaving everything in order, then about five minutes to eight poked her head in through our doorway and asked,

"Now you're sure you'll be alright, Mrs Mateer?"

"Perfectly sure," mother replied from her bed.

"I don't like leaving you on your own at night."

"But I won't be alone," mother looked across to where I was amusing myself at the table, "Jim will be here."

"Aye, and just as it happens Mrs Johnston (another lodger who had the room next to ours) says she'll be staying in so if you want anything send wee Jamie to rap on her door."

"That's very nice of her."

"She'll likely look in before she goes to bed."

"Fine, fine, now off you go, it's nearly eight o'clock."

"Ach we'll miss half the show." The landlord who had been following his wife from room to room bitterly complained.

"No, we'll be there on time Andy," his wife reassured him. "We'll *run!*" The door shut, then opened again. "And we'll get you a wee bite of supper when we get back."

"Go, go, and I hope you enjoy the play."

"Bound to … everybody's talking about it. Cheerio!"

The landlady, her husband and most of the population of the area packed into the village hall that evening; all except us and Mrs Johnston who we could hear moving about in her room. Now what Mrs Johnston was doing in that place at that time I don't know. There was no *Mr* Johnston and the lady wasn't overnighting in order to catch the boat to Skye, nor was she on holiday, so I can only imagine she had something to do with the fishing. Everybody, including us (where there was fish there was money), and everything in that place had something to do with the fishing … the boat, the train, the shops, the lodgings, the very air we breathed reeked of fish. So it was quite probable that this solitary woman – I don't know what age she was but she was certainly a working woman – had a job cleaning and gutting fish with the rest down on the quay. Anyhow, whatever the reason for her presence she was a resident and the only other person in the house that night. Which was unfortunate because mother, in her eagerness to get the landlady off on her outing, had forgotten to mention that she needed a little hot water in order to rinse through some nappies for the baby. Also in the last-minute rush nobody had noticed that our fire needed more coal, and although it was the month of July, summers in the Highlands can be wet and cool, and besides, if you wash nappies you have to get them dry. So mother had no hot water, no clean nappies, and she needed help.

"You'll just have to go and ask Mrs Johnston," she finally decided.

"Ask her what?"

"For a kettle of hot water ... there's always one on the landlady's hob. And a shovel or two of coal for the fire. You can tell her I'm very sorry but Mrs McDougall's out and I need clean nappies for the baby. Now off you go and remember: A kettle of hot water and some coal from downstairs."

I did as instructed and within a couple of minutes reported back.

"She doesn't answer. I knocked and there's no reply and no noise. She's not in."

"Of course she's in, we heard her moving about. And Mrs McDougall said she'd be in. You probably didn't knock hard enough."

"I did, I did, I knocked very hard."

"Well do it again, use your fist this time. And wait till you get a reply."

Again I did as instructed, and hammered until I hurt my hand but still got no reply. "She doesn't answer, she's not in." At that point Eileen began to cry and mother became agitated.

"She *is* in, she *is* in, don't be so stupid. Now I can't go all the way downstairs myself, and we've got to have clean nappies for the baby. Knock again ... *hard*."

"But I did knock hard, very hard," I protested.

"Then maybe she's a bit hard of hearing. Try again and this time if she doesn't reply open the door a little."

"Oh, I don't like to open her door."

"Do as you're told," mother shouted. "The baby's wet, she'll catch pneumonia and die if she doesn't get a clean nappy."

I dashed off, knocked, opened the door a few inches and there, fast asleep on a chair by the fireside (though her fire wasn't lit), was Mrs Johnston.

"Mrs Johnston," I said quietly, "Mrs Johnston." She didn't answer, so cautiously I stole up behind the sleeping figure, shook her gently by the arm and breathed in her ear, "Mrs Johnston!" In response I got a groan, a moan and a powerful whiff of alcohol. I flew back to mother.

"She's there, she's in, I saw her, but she's drunk."

"*Drunk?*"

"Yes there's a big bottle on the table and the place smells and she won't wake up. She's drunk."

"Oh, that's all I need," mother moaned and made an attempt to get up, "that's all I need." She sat on the edge of the bed, tears in her eyes and misery on her face, for a few moments, then she got back under the blankets. "I can't go downstairs, I'm too tired, I'm just *too* tired." I stood in the middle of the room not knowing whether to try and comfort Eileen who was still crying in her cot, or mother who lay motionless, her eyes closed, on the bed. Eventually, as I didn't know what to do for the best, I got down on my knees and carefully positioned the last of the coal in order to get the most out of the fire. Mother lay still for a while and then suddenly she sat up and said defiantly, "Alright then, if we can't have hot water we'll have to make do with cold." She looked across the room in the direction of the washstand. "We'll have to get that jug over by the bed."

"Alright." I jumped up, hurried across to where the large delft water jug stood on the floor and got my arms round its neck.

"Mind, it's heavy … it's full of water."

"I can do it." I moved the jug a couple of inches.

"Don't try to lift it … drag it … and don't spill the water."

Inch by inch I lugged the heavy jug and its contents across the floor until I got it alongside the bed.

"Good, good. Now we need the wash basin."

I went back to the washstand, reached up, got my hands and arms underneath the bowl and pulled it towards my chest.

"Don't drop it, for heaven's sake don't drop it."

"I won't drop it." I staggered across the room and dumped it on the bed.

"Right!" Mother sat up with the bowl on her lap and we both got to work. The nappies were rinsed through, wrung out and passed over to me. I carried them to the fireplace, held them in front of the fire I had revived, brought them back again and then mother – re-enacting and no doubt savouring to the full a sequence from *Orphans of the Storm*, her favourite melodrama – *aired them on her chest!*

The landlady was furious when she returned and found our fire out and her lodger dead drunk. I was fast asleep but I believe dire threats were hurled through the open doorway at the half-conscious woman, and the following morning she was faced with eviction. However, mother interceded, and father, as business was good and the hall available, booked in for another week thus giving mother time to get back on her feet. At the end of the second week we gathered up our belongings and joined father and the rest of the company who were down on the quay waiting to board the ferry to Skye. Some of the villagers had turned out to see us off, and at the gangway a fisherman came across, had a look at Eileen, congratulated mother and laid a coin on the baby's chest.

"Oh, that's very kind of you," mother warmly responded.

"No, no."

"And times are hard. I appreciate your good wishes but you don't have to give her money you know."

"Nonsense woman," the fisherman said. "A new bairn and ah dinnae gie her a wee present! There'd be nae fish aboard the boat tenicht and that's for certain."

"Oh well, I wouldn't want to spoil your fishing." Mother laughed and put the money in her pocket.

"Guid luck te the pair o' ye." The fisherman walked back to his nets.

"And to you. And the fishing."

We went aboard and wandered about on deck until the gangplank was pulled in and the mooring rope cast off, then just as the ferry started to ease away we saw a man running like mad down the quay.

"If he's hoping to catch the boat I'm afraid he's had it," mother remarked. But that wasn't his intention. When he got to the water's edge he took a piece of cloth out of his pocket, tied it round a small object and called out father's name.

"Mr Mateer! Mr Mateer!"

"Hello?" Father raised his arm.

"Hold on, hold on ..." The man drew back his arm and hurled the package which landed with a thud on the deck at our feet. Father picked it up and immediately recognised the contents.

"Oh! Thank you very much!" It was five shillings in coppers (old pennies of course and they weighed quite a lot) which father in his hurry had left on a table in the hall. The hallkeeper had found them and was making sure we got what was ours.

"Safe journey!" our benefactor called out as we all waved to him.

"And come ye back again." Other voices on the quay joined in.

"*We will!*" But although we must have passed through Mallaig after our tour of Skye I don't think we played there again. We pressed on until somewhere on the west coast – Stranraer to Larne would have been the best route – we took another, larger ship and began our tour of Northern Ireland, a tour that ended at Waterloo Hall.

*

The past was behind us and now we had to face up to the present, and the future which lay somewhere along the narrow road ahead. Though in fact there were three roads in front of us as we passed the clump of wild apple trees and emerged from the Rubane Road to find ourselves confronting a low, whitewashed smithy and a cluster of grey houses, one of which had been converted into a post office and sweet shop combined. We ignored the road on our left which led to Kircubbin, a village that would see a lot more of us in the years to come. Opposite was an even more secluded byway, not signposted, but one I discovered led past the Glastry Bog and onto the fishing village of Ballyhalbert where we had played some weeks before. The route we had to follow lay on our right along a highway that headed off towards the village of Cloughey and the sea. An empty, open, treeless road with nothing but fields and little hills on either side until we turned a corner, passed another grey house with a pump outside its front gate (our drinking supply from now on), walked along the edge of a small plantation for a hundred yards or so, and then stopped outside two tiny cottages, two tiny semi-detached cottages, that lay low and a little way back off the road. One cottage, like its neighbour built of stone and whitewashed, was bustling and bursting with life; small children played in front of the half-door, larger children romped in the field nearby, and inside, through the window, we could see grown-ups. The other end of the building lay silent and deserted. And alongside it our caravan was parked.

"Home!" father remarked dryly.

"Yes. Oh! And here's our neighbour, Mrs Murphy!" Mother raised the tone and put on a more cheerful countenance as a big peasant woman with a smiling face and two bare brawny arms came out of the other cottage, picked her way through the children and chickens and came alongside her hedge to greet us.

"Hello, Mrs McAteer!" The woman, dressed in a black shirt and long heavy voluminous skirts, pronounced our name after the Irish fashion (father himself had completed the anglicisation of his name to Mateer for professional reasons). "Yer home early."

"No customers tonight," father explained, "no show, no more shows, we've shut up shop."

"Oh dear, ah'm sorry te hear that. But then the weather's good, the nights are clear and all the young uns will be away at the hurlin'. Or maybe there's a dance in Portaferry."

"Of course," mother agreed, "we didn't really expect anybody, we just thought we'd have a final try. However, as my husband says, we're finished, it's the end of the trail, and we're just like nearly everyone else in the country now … unemployed."

"For the present, for the present." Father didn't care for chat and still less did he care for discussing his private affairs with strangers. "I've got ideas but …" he looked in the direction of the caravan, "I think I'd better look in and see how our little girl is."

"Oh, she's fast asleep," the big woman shouted, though father had only moved a couple of yards away. "Ah luked in earlier on an' she was dead te the world."

"Good." Father climbed the steps, quietly opened the caravan door and went in.

"A lovely wee thing she is," our neighbour turned back to mother, "a lovely wee girl."

"Ah yes, she's her daddy's little girl, while this," mother laid a hand on my head, "is his mammy's *big* boy." Gently I moved from under her hand and would have followed father into the van but I didn't think he wanted me to do that just at that moment.

"Aye, and Jimmy's a nice-lukin' polite wee boy as well." Mrs Murphy smiled in my direction (we had all been introduced earlier on). "But have ye just got the two o' them Mrs McAteer?"

"Just the two," mother replied, "and that's quite enough."

Mrs Murphy smiled. "Och well, yer young and ye'll maybe hae a wheen [few] more before yer finished."

"Not if *I* have anything to do with it," mother promptly replied and Mrs Murphy laughed.

"But ye cannae always tell, Mrs McAteer."

"Oh yes you can. Any nonsense like that and one of us will sleep under the van at night." Mrs Murphy doubled up. Mother had hit it off with the big woman (I call her big but it was across and not up) right from the start. Everything she said got a laugh from our neighbour. She also got a great deal of practical help and assistance which was sorely needed at that time.

"But to get down to more serious matters," mother continued, "what's the position about the cottage, Mrs Murphy?"

"Och here's the key." The big woman reached down into the wide pocket of her apron and triumphantly held it aloft.

"So the place is ready? Can we go in?"

"Well now it's ready but oul Barney, who put some slates back on the roof and fixed the chimney, says he's left a pile o' bricks and cement in the kitchen but he'll be up first thing in the mornin' te redd [clear] it out."

"Oh, that's wonderful."

"So ye can move in when ye like. What about yer furniture?"

"We haven't any."

"Oh!" Our neighbour was taken aback.

"But we hope to get some," mother added quickly. "You see my husband's sister who lives not far away in a big bungalow – the posh side of the family you know, bathroom and all that!" Mrs Murphy smiled knowingly. "Well, her husband died and she's just married again, a widower, and he's leaving his house and moving in with her. So there'll be furniture they don't want and we're bound to get some of it."

"Och well there ye are then, yer landed."

"We won't need a lot, just a bed … the one in the van has no legs."

"Oh well, ye'd need te have legs on the bed certainly."

"And if we had a table and chairs it would be a start."

"It would, and ye cud build up after that. In the meantime ye have the van."

"Well no, you see we're going to sell the caravan, we need the money to see us through till my husband gets a job."

"Oh, has he no work?" Our neighbour showed concern again.

"Well no, the theatre was our work, our living, and now it's finished we're broke." I edged away towards the cottage. Mother always talked openly about our private affairs and I disliked that as much as father did. "But the van should give us a few pounds and keep things going until Mr Mateer gets a job."

"Och aye, an' he's likely to get somethin'." Mrs Murphy was trying to be optimistic though she knew as well as we did that the situation was hopeless. "A clever man like him will ay [always] find somethin'. Anyhow he'll have the dole for a while."

"No, I'm afraid he won't. You see we're self-employed and my husband's stamps don't cover him for dole money."

"Oh, that's terrible. So how … I mean what …?"

"Ah we'll manage. And anyhow my husband's sister …" At that point the caravan door opened and mother quickly changed the subject. "So what I need to think about at the minute is getting the family something to eat."

"An' how are ye fixed for groceries an' the like? There's no shops, nothin' round here but the post office an' all they sell is cigarettes an' sweets."

"Well I got a brown loaf and some corned beef when we came through Kircubbin … Corned beef is a great stand-by."

"But have ye any sweetmilk, sugar or tay?"

"I've a packet of tea and a tin of condensed milk, that'll do for tonight."

"That'll not fill much of a hole."

"It'll do and I'll go into the matter of groceries tomorrow."

"I cud let ye have some buttermilk and flour and maybe ye cud bake a few wheaten farls. But of course ye've no fire."

"No, and I'm not much of a baker. With all the travelling I never really got round to baking."

"Well then, I cud give ye three or four eggs … my hens are layin' well just at the minute … and ye cud add them te the corned beef!"

This was the essence of our neighbour who lived with her husband, a farm labourer, and seven children in a cottage that had only two rooms, the largest of which was about twelve foot by nine. Mind you they'd knocked a hole through the gable so they could build a small extension which was fitted up with five bunks to accommodate the boys. The girls slept up in the roof space – it was too small to be called a loft – while Mr and Mrs Murphy and the baby occupied the bedroom where there was just enough space for a double bed, a cot and a chest of drawers; anything else and you couldn't open or shut the door. They were a poor family and we'd met plenty in our travels (though not quite as poor as we were at that moment), but ready to share anything they had.

Mother didn't accept the eggs, said we'd manage, and then turned her attention to father who came round from the back of the van and approached us, I thought with the intention of getting mother away from Mrs Murphy. But that wasn't the case.

"Yes, she's fast asleep." He walked up the slight incline and out onto the road to where mother was standing.

"Oh, she's never moved," Mrs Murphy shouted over the fuchsia hedge ("Bleedin' Hearts" she called it).

"And you know," father addressed this to mother, "I've just looked at my bicycle and I've got a puncture in the front wheel."

"Oh dear," mother instinctively knew he wanted assistance and followed up with, "And you've got to go into Kircubbin first thing in the morning."

"Yes, I've got to see Annie," he turned and drew our neighbour into the conversation, "that's my sister, the one who told us about the cottage."

"Oh aye."

"So I need my bike and I'm right out of patches."

"Oh well," Mrs Murphy turned her head and let out a yell, "Devlin! Devlin!" A twelve or thirteen-year-old boy came running round from the back of the cottage.

"Aye?"

"Away in an' get Mr McAteer some patches and solution, he's got a puncture."

"Ah!" The boy looked at father. "Right." Then he crashed through the children and chickens and disappeared into the cottage.

"He'll get ye some."

"That's very kind of you."

"Not at all. We've three oul bikes in the house an' there's always punctures."

"You see I've got business with my sister tomorrow." (Obviously father intended to tell Mrs Murphy what she would eventually find out for herself.) "Annie owns a small drapery shop in the main street, you may know it."

"An' there's a wee sweet shop as well?"

"That's right … Pattersons."

"I know it, though I'm not often in Kircubbin."

"Well my sister was a Buyer up in Belfast before she married her first husband, and she's going to supply me with drapery, wholesale, and I'm going to retail it round the country."

"Ach well there ye are," Mrs Murphy was delighted, "so ye'll have a job after all. Ye'll work fer yerself!"

"Till something better turns up."

"An' ye'll do alright for nobody comes round the doors these days. And folk want the odd wee thing. I'll need some things meself."

"Then you can be my first customer."

"Certainly, certainly, you bring yer stuff in when you get it an' we'll see if we can do business."

"And of course as my very first customer there'll be a discount."

"Better still, better still. But how will ye get yer drapery round the country, Mr McAteer? Can ye get a wee van?"

"Oh no," mother said, "I'm afraid a van is out of the question."

"Couldn't afford it," added father, "and I'd have to learn to drive. No, what I'm going to do is take two empty suitcases to my sister's shop, fill them up with drapery, small items, tie one case on the back of my bicycle, lay the other across the handlebars, and then pedal my way around the world."

"Good fer you!" Mrs Murphy laughed and slapped her thigh. "Good fer you! That's the way te do it." At that point young Devlin joined his mother alongside the hedge, as did several other members of the family who were keen to get in on the act.

"Here's the patches and solution, Mr McAteer," the lad said.

"Oh, thank you," father reached over. "I'll return them when I get supplies in Kircubbin."

"Aw there's no need, we've plenty more in the house." Devlin reassured him.

"Thanks. And now," father prepared to make his exit, "I'll get my bike in going-order so I can start cycling."

"That's it," Mrs Murphy encouraged him, "good for the legs."

"And you know," father addressed this to no-one in particular, "when you think about it, I don't suppose in the long run there's a great deal of difference between peddling plays and *peddling ladies' underwear.*"

Howls of natural and shrieks of unnatural mirth rose up behind the fuchsia hedge as father disappeared round the side of the cottage. Before it got completely out of hand, however, (a couple of the youngsters had started thumping each other in their excitement, or craving for excitement), Mrs Murphy pointed towards the cottage and bawled,

"Right, that's enough. *In ye go!*" The noise subsided and the audience quickly dispersed. Mrs Murphy could make use of her arms and fists as well as her lungs when it was necessary.

"Oh, there's one other question I wanted to ask." Mother took advantage of the lull in activities.

"And what's that, Mrs McAteer?"

"School. Eileen's still a bit young but Jim will have to go." I pricked up my ears. "Where's the nearest school?"

"Ah well ..." Mrs Murphy hesitated. She was in no doubt as to where the schools were and how you would get to them, but without being told she knew we were protestants, just as we knew that she was a catholic, so it wasn't quite clear to her what information was required. Mother helped her out.

"Where do *your* children go?"

"Ah well," the big woman swung round and pointed up to what seemed to me to be the sky, "you see the chapel up there?"

"Oh yes." It wasn't difficult to see the chapel; it was a huge building, had a great spire, and was built on top of a hill so that it could be seen for miles in any direction.

"Well our school's up there. But if ye want a protestant school I suppose Kircubbin ... or in the opposite direction Portavogie ... though they're both a couple of miles each way by road. It's a long walk for youngsters every day, summer and winter."

"So how far would you say your school was?"

"Och my weans go across the fields so it's less than a mile."

"Then Jim will go to your school. He doesn't mind whether it's catholic or protestant, do you, Jim?"

"No," I replied. It was all the same to me though I quite liked catholic schools because I got special treatment, and time off: "Would the wee protestant boy like to go out to the playground during prayers?"

"Religion makes no difference to us, Mrs Murphy, as long as people are decent we think their religion's their own affair."

"And that's the right way te luk at it. That's how I see it meself."

"So Jim will go with your children if that's alright."

"Certainly it's alright. The big boys leave early … they don't want youngsters hangin' roun' their heels, but there's a girl lives up at the Three Trees an' she luks after my young ones. Jimmy can go wi' her."

"Fine, and he can start … let's see … Monday." That gave me another day or two's freedom. "Oh, and there's one more thing I have to ask you: what about the rent?"

"Same as mine, one and eleven pence a week." (Ten new pennies.)

"And rates?"

"Oh, no rates. What wud we pay rates for? Sure we've no drains and no water te the house. No, just the rent an' ye pay on a Friday up at the farm. Ye can get yer sweetmilk while yer there, an' when they churn there's buttermilk and country butter."

"And as far as groceries are concerned, you said there were vans?"

"A grocery van, a butcher's, a fish-merchant, the bread-server and the coal man."

"Everything the heart could desire. All we have to worry about is the money."

"An' ye can let them wait fer that. Get it on tick."

"And what do the traders think about that?"

"They can think what they like, it's that or nothin', they can take their pick."

"I don't think my husband would approve of that, he won't take anything he can't pay for."

"Och but sure ye can't always have ready money. An' it does the traders no harm as long as they get it sometime. You take it on tick when ye can, Mrs McAteer – they won't all let you have it. And don't ever give them what they ask for (mother's education had started), bate them own."

Mother looked, dwelt deliberately, on Mrs Murphy's powerful forearms and remarked, "I don't think I'd be as good at that as you are."

"Ye'll learn," the big woman said, "ye'll learn."

"I'll have to, I'll have to. But now," she placed a hand on our garden gate, what was left of it, "I must go and see to himself."

"Right, an' if there's anythin' else ye want just ask."

"I will."

"Blatter at the door."

"Very well. Goodnight."

"Goodnight." Mrs Murphy turned, raised both her arms and shouted at the small gathering outside her door. "In ye go! Wash time fer some o' ye. In ye go!" She scooped up the youngest in her arms and without pausing in her stride disappeared inside the cottage.

"What do you think of our new home, Jim?" I had come round from exploring the back of the cottage and joined mother standing at the door.

"Oh, it'll be alright." I was cheerful and confident; a permanent home of any kind was alright by me. "At least it won't fall over or move about."

"I hope not. Though it's a pretty ancient building. What's it like inside?" She tried to peer in through the small grimy window. "Can't see a thing. Shall we have a quick look?"

"Oh yes." I eagerly took the key she offered, inserted it in the lock and turned it with ease. Old Barney must have oiled it.

"Mrs Murphy says an old fellow lived here on his own for years, and after that it was empty."

"For a few more years by the look of the garden." I pushed open the half-door, bent down and from the inside undid the bolt that held the top half in position. Mother followed me into the cold, dimly-lit interior and looked round at what was to be our living room, kitchen, bathroom, scullery, everything except a bedroom.

"It smells damp," she screwed up her nose. "And Old Barney must have smoked Warhorse [a powerful plug tobacco of the day]."

"There's no back door to the place," I pointed out.

"Oh. So there's no way of avoiding the tick men when they come for their money!"

"You certainly couldn't get out of the bedroom window, it's even smaller than the one at the front."

"Yes, there's not much room in the bedroom, barely enough room for a bed. And the living room's not much bigger. What about up in the roof?"

"I'll have a look up there." I went over to the wooden staircase (a short ladder with flat treads and no handrail) that stood close to the end wall and disappeared through a trapdoor in the wooden ceiling.

"Mind how you go," mother warned. "You don't know what you might find up there."

"It's very dark!" Of course there was no electricity and we would use the oil lamp out of the van.

"Is there much space?"

"I could stand up in the middle but nowhere else. And you can see daylight through some of the slates."

"Oh dear, I thought Old Barney had fixed the roof."

"Maybe he has, maybe that's the way it is. They're only narrow slits."

"Oh well, we'll find out when it rains. Come down."

"There's just rafters up there, no floor." I came down backwards which was the safest, the only way. "But you could lay something across and put in a bed … I could sleep up there."

"I suppose you could."

"The Murphys do." This was a wonderful idea because not only would I have a bed but my own room, my own space. "I could use Uncle Joe's camp-bed."

"True, and there's no room in the bedroom. Eileen's cot would have to go in there with us."

"I'd be very comfortable up in the roof, and warm from the fire."

"Yes, alright. But we'd better get back to the van before your father starts shouting for something to eat." She walked out into the open again and waited while I closed and locked the door.

"I like the half-door," I remarked.

"Yes, it's alright," she replied without much enthusiasm. "It'll have to do. What's round the back? I can't be bothered to go round there at the moment. And you never know what you might put your feet in."

"Well, there's a dry lavatory ... pretty smelly. And an ashpit which is also pretty smelly. I think maybe they empty the lavatory bucket there."

"Wouldn't surprise me in the slightest."

"There's not much space, but on the other side of the caravan there's the garden. The Murphys grow potatoes there ... and they have goats."

"Oh yes?" Mother had lost interest.

"And further over behind that big thorn tree and all those scruffy bushes there's a deep dyke with water in it." In fact, this deep, rat-infested dyke turned out to be a tributary of the Blackstaff River, which I'd discovered earlier on quite close to the hall. Well, it was designated a river on the ordnance map but mother said it was a stream, I called it a burn, while Mrs Murphy in that basic, earthy manner of hers referred to it as The Main Drain. Certainly it carried off waters from the flat farmland around us and eventually eased them over mudflats and out into Strangford Lough.

"Yes, it'll do." Mother sighed heavily and had a last look in at the gloomy interior of the cottage through the front window ... the stone flags, the dead fireplace, the grey stone walls that hadn't been painted or even washed in years. "It'll do, but it's absolutely filthy ... it's *black!*"

For a moment or two she looked despondent, then the light of battle came into her eyes. "*It needs a damn good scrub.*" She turned away and headed for the van.